# China Market

# China Market

## America's Quest for Informal Empire
### 1893–1901

BY

## THOMAS J. McCORMICK

CHICAGO

*Quadrangle Books*

1967

*Library of Congress Catalog Card Number: 67–21637*

DESIGNED BY VINCENT TORRE

FOR

*My Mother and Father*

# *Preface*

This is a book about the dynamics of American expansion in that turn-of-the-century epoch often referred to as "America's Rise to World Power." My research began with its focus on Grover Cleveland and the anti-imperialists, and with a working hypothesis that such elements, for all their ideological and practical objections to *political* colonialism, were actually "free-trade imperialists" seeking the economic fruits of expansion without the burdens and risks of governmental force and a formal empire; that, moreover, after the brief fling at the "large policy" of war and colonialism in 1898, the anti-imperialist ideology ultimately triumphed and thereafter channeled American expansion into economic rather than political-military pursuits.

This simplistic approach, however, could not stand the gaff of complex and contrary data, though it did provide, I believe, a valid understanding of Cleveland's initial beliefs and behavior. What it did not anticipate was the effect of domestic and world reality upon the expansionist approach of the anti-imperialists in the second Cleveland administration, for they had to bear the burdens of power and concrete decisions. Nor did my hypothesis foresee that the McKinley presidency was anything but a bland sponge fought over by anti-imperialists and imperialists alike. On the contrary, utilitarian expansionists like McKinley were amazingly consistent and conscious in their efforts to create a workable, tactical blend of informal empire and insular imperialism, of marketplace expansion and political protection, of private initiative and governmental responsibility. Viewed from this perspective, the expansionist policies of the McKinley administration—from the Spanish-American War to the Boxer Rebellion—acquired an inner logic and thrust quite at odds with our images of irrationality or innocence.

My delineations of time and geography also grew out of inquiry rather than predetermination. Originally, I centered my research in the 1880's and the first Cleveland administration in an effort to investigate the elements of continuity and change between a "trough" decade and an "explosive" one—that is, I was searching for a continuing, substructural reality rather than a sporadic, superficial one. I still regard this as a valid and vital quest, as witnessed by the recent and important contributions of David M. Pletcher, Walter LaFeber, and Richard W. Van Alstyne. Nevertheless, both personal interest and conviction led to an eventual focus on the 1890's. My own empiricism persuaded me that American historians had not yet fully appreciated and understood the catalytic role of the Panic of 1893 in bridging the very real gap between expansionist tendencies and expansionist fulfillment.

As for the decision to limit my investigation to the Pacific generally and to China specifically, this reflected several considerations. The more practical ones involved my personal predilection at the time for Asian affairs, as well as the fact that my good friend, Professor LaFeber, had already dealt with the Latin American sphere in a way that defied substantial improvement. The more intellectual considerations reflected my belief that the late 1890's witnessed, in a relative way, an emphasis on the Pacific area; and that, moreover, the complex interaction of great-power rivalries and the diversified nature of events in that sphere—partitioning, war, insular imperialism, the open door, rebellion, and pacification—would yield information that might be both more comprehensive and more susceptible to sophisticated analysis.

One might well characterize this book as an economic interpretation—a fact that requires no apologies but does necessitate a few qualifications. In the first place, it is generally not a narrow economic interpretation—a "pocketbook" determinism—that centers on special interest groups and efforts to shape policy according to their special needs. This is not to deny that such interplay existed or to say that it was unimportant, but simply to suggest that its ultimate impact on policy was more modest than one might usually assume; that, indeed, at times policy formulation proved curiously immune to interests' pressures. Partly this reflects the obvious: that special interest groups were not monolithic, that they had different functions, different needs, and sometimes favored different policies. Thus the government could not, by the definition of things, react in any one-to-one fashion. But this also reflects the reality that policy-makers and a great many business leaders as well sometimes operated from a more sophisticated and cosmopolitan position than many functional spokesmen; they were more precisely cognizant of the larger relationship between foreign policy and the ongoing effort to save the status quo from its own stresses and strains. And because they analyzed the causes of social instability as economic, their attempts at social rationalization were necessarily economic as well. It is that fact, and my perception of it, that has largely determined the materialist bent of my presentation.

Of course, it is axiomatic that ideas and ideology were not simply afterthoughts in the process of expansion. They played their role in the 1890's just as they had earlier. Indeed, it strikes me as inconceivable that any society would undertake a dramatic course that did gross violence to its ideology—at least not without a psychological wrench far more traumatic than America experienced at century's end. Still, a national ideology is an amorphous thing, and all elements—imperialists, anti-imperialists, and utilitarians—dipped into it. And popular assumptions notwithstanding, it would appear that the doctrinaire imperialists (if there were any of significance) did so with the least success of all; there was a striking disparity between the grandiose rhetoric of Manifest Destiny and the simpler reality of a consciously self-limited imperialism. In fact, far from justifying the heady acceptance of some White Man's Burden, American ideology generally sought to impose limits that would lighten the burdens and responsibilities of expansionism. Putting it more succinctly, pragmatism—not Social Darwinism—was the primary component of the expansionist outlook.

The central actor in this book is the "power elite" of late nineteenth-century America. By that rather loose term (and other synonyms) I mean those social elements with the most *direct power* to influence national decisions and alter events, and/or those who controlled *property* and affected the social relationships that flowed from that control—in short, the business community (exclusive of small and local enterprises) and its political and intellectual allies. I acknowledge the weakness of this approach, for it fails to show in any adequate way how such non-elite groups as farmers and industrial workers limited the freedom of choice and action available to those closer to the centers of power; or, more importantly, it fails to examine in detail the parallel expansionist sentiments of such elements—especially the agrarians. Nevertheless, I feel justified in my emphasis. Just as some contemporary historians, such as Gabriel Kolko, have seen the business-oriented community as the prime dynamic for progressive reform at home, so it seems to me wholly demonstrable that the same elements acted as the chief shapers of expansionism in the 1890's—and for many of the same ends: stability, predictability, and prosperity in the political economy.

T. J. McC.

*Pittsburgh, 1967*

# ACKNOWLEDGMENTS

My first debts are financial ones: to the University of Wisconsin Graduate School for a research fellowship that launched this study, and to the American Philosophical Society for a summer research grant that enabled me to finish it. My thanks also to the editors of the *Pacific Historical Review* for allowing me to use material from the two articles I have published there. And, of course, my great gratitude to the staffs of all the research libraries where most of the information for this book was found, especially to the Wisconsin State Historical Society, the Manuscripts Division of the Library of Congress, and the Foreign Affairs branch of the National Archives.

Many people helped me with their insights and encouraged me with their confidence, notably Burton J. Beers of North Carolina College; Samuel P. Hays and David Montgomery of the University of Pittsburgh; and William L. Neumann of Goucher College. And a special word of thanks on both scores to my editor, Ivan Dee.

Finally, I happily acknowledge my largest and most unpayable debts: to President Fred Harvey Harrington of the University of Wisconsin, who guided this book at the dissertation stage and who imparted to me an interest in Asian affairs, an understanding of the internal dynamics of foreign policy, and a smattering of his unparalleled knowledge of historical materials; to Professor William Appleman Williams of the University of Wisconsin, who has inspired me with his teaching, provoked me with his intellect, and sustained me with his friendship; to Professors Lloyd C. Gardner of Rutgers University and Walter La-Feber of Cornell University, with whom intellectual dialogue and personal communion have become wonderfully inseparable; and to my wife Jeri, for her material help as literary critic, proofreader, and typist—and because . . .

# Contents

# China Market

# ◎ Prologue: *Paths to Empire*

In the beginning of the republic, the founding fathers debated the ways of making a society that would be both viable and good—one that would avoid the European morass of economic crises, factionalism, and authoritarianism. They concluded, among many things, that America would need an expanding economic and political marketplace. Such expansion, they agreed, would provide the underpinning for material prosperity; it would sublimate particularism in a great common effort and offer satisfactory (if not equal) rewards to all classes and sections; it would preserve republicanism by making the nation-state too large and diffuse for any single element to dominate.

Acting on this premise, nineteenth-century Americans put many of their eggs in the expansionist basket. They might (and did) debate whether Colbert or Adam Smith was the more proper guide to the good society, but none could sustain a vision of an affluent, tranquil, representative America without constant recourse to an expanding empire. So the builders of the empire— by negotiation, subversion, intimidation, and war—secured the Floridas, gathered in the great Mississippi heartland, conquered the northern provinces of Mexico, and acquired the western seaboard. That finished, America fought a Civil War over the spoils of empire, subdued the Indians, and filled in the last frontier with free-soilers and corporations. Perceiving all this, Frederick Jackson Turner declared at the end of the nation's first century that the open door at home had closed.

Still, other doors remained open in the 1890's, for continentalism was not (and never had been) the sole avenue of expansion. Since the formative days of the nation, many Americans had defined overseas mercantile expansion as a significant source for capital accumulation and economic modernization. In conception, this American commercialism strongly resembled England's mercantilistic expansion in the early seventeenth century. The latter de-emphasized mass population migrations and large land acquisitions; instead it stressed the development of commerce through the vehicle of small trading posts. In a similar way, America's mercantile expansion emphasized the carrying-trade and market penetration, rejected the possibility of colonialization in heavily populated areas, and restricted its territorial acquisitions to islands and enclaves that might be useful as strategic stepping-stones to major areas. In the beginning this commercialism stressed outlets for farm surpluses, but the "take-off" stage of industrialization in the 1840's and its post–Civil War maturation added a new concern for manufactured exports as well. In the beginning, also, sectionalism strongly colored the forms and directions of commercialism, but by the late nineteenth century the nationalization of business and the crescendo of American nationalism helped to blunt past differences and make economic expansion abroad a national undertaking.

Like the frontier, the course of commercialism was often westward. Indeed, of all the world's mercantile lures, none was more long-lived, more persistent, or more mesmeric than the fabled Far Eastern markets; of all the expansionist developments, none more epic and fateful than the conversion of the Pacific basin into an American lake. On the eastern shores of that vast ocean, the United States acquired California and Oregon—"the windows to the orient"—and tied them to the heartland and the eastern metropolis through the great transcontinental railroads. Farther south, in Central America, American diplomats and entrepreneurs worked for the day when an isthmian canal would give the industrial East and later the New South a short cut to

Cathay. In the Pacific basin, Americans fished, traded, explored, proselytized, and prepared the way for the coming of their government. And it came—along the pincer route William H. Seward envisioned: first securing the northern flank of the basin by purchasing the Aleutians, then strengthening its position on the southern flank by taking Midway Island and by pulling Hawaii into the American cultural and economic orbit under the protective umbrella of an enlarged Monroe Doctrine. Finally, in northeast Asia itself, the United States established commercial ties with China on an open door, most-favored-nation basis; opened Japan to the outside world and helped keep her open through both force and accommodation; and, with the help of China, became the first Western nation to secure diplomatic and economic intercourse with the Hermit Kingdom of Korea.

Finally, in the 1890's, this trans-Pacific commercialism reached a climacteric marked more by a startling acceleration than by any change in form—a quickening that catapulted America to "great power" status in the western Pacific. That is: under the stimulus of a narrowing marketplace at home and the widening market opportunity of an awakening China, America's leadership made a conscious, purposeful, integrated effort to solve the economic-social crisis at home by promoting the national interest abroad; by securing, at long last, the southern flank of the northern Pacific basin; by using America's most potent weapon, economic supremacy, to begin the open door conquest of the China market; by employing the traditional tactics of *realpolitik* to safeguard that economic stake.

# 🎜 Chapter I: *Exporting the Social Question*

"We shall begin to compete with European countries in all the markets of the world . . . The economic pressure exerted upon Europe by the United States will soon become very great indeed."
—*John W. Fiske, 1880*

" 'Overproduction' compels a quest for 'ultimate supremacy' in 'the markets of the world' . . . The United States is to be 'the mighty workshop of the world,' and our people 'the hands of mankind.' "
—*Josiah Strong, 1885*

"Whether they will or no, Americans must begin to look outward. The growing production of the country demands it."
—*Alfred T. Mahan, 1890*[1]

The two and a half decades between the Panic of 1873 and the War with Spain encompassed one of the most profound social crises in American history—the inability of laissez-faire capitalism to function either rationally or equitably in a period of rapid industrial maturation. Hence the Janus-faced image of the economic terrain: skyrocketing production which made America an industrial giant second to none, but at the same time plummeting prices, falling rates of profit, and enervating depressions—the crisis of overdevelopment.

One source of the crisis was the industrial machine's penchant for overproduction. To be sure, the economic system itself was not solely responsible for this tendency. The closing of traditional areas of investment, such as railroads and western lands, flooded capital into more narrowly productive channels, while the technological revolution produced more goods per dollar invested.[2] But to a perhaps greater degree, surplus production reflected an endemic quality of laissez-faire capitalism: over-competition— excessive, wasteful, duplicative, self-destructive competition which made the industrial order into a dog-eat-dog, Social Darwinistic arena where both the thirst for profit and the instinct for survival made "production, production, production, faster, greater" (as Samuel Gompers put it) "the impulse, the thought and the motive of the capitalist class."[3] The result was an economy that was chaotic, unstable, unplanned, and unpredictable, one that could not rationally resolve its own dilemmas.

The fruits of such irrationality might have proved more digestible had they coincided with some equitable change in the pattern of income distribution and *effective* consumer demand, but no such radical changes occurred. Even accepting the most optimistic projections of living costs and income (items still open to debate), neither *real* wages of urban workers nor real *income* of agrarian producers enjoyed more than a modest increase in the late nineteenth century. In fact, other variables seemed to worsen the plight of such consumers. For one thing, the nature of economic organization and the abrupt fluctuations of the business cycle made income gains intolerably uneven and unpredictable. The average wheat or cotton grower took little solace in long-term price trends when occasional shifts in the world commodity market could—and sometimes did—cut the bottom out of his existence; and the common steelworker or textile mill hand derived small satisfaction from real wage statistics when depression could—and sometimes did—mean unemployment and no wages at all. Beyond that, the absolute rise in real incomes seemed, in the relative sense, inadequate to the farmer's and laborer's personal level of expectations. Agrarian magazines of the time are filled with the farmer's acute sense of growing contrast between urban wealth and agriculture's declining share of the nation's economy; and union periodicals repeated the theme that the gap between workers' wages and the conspicuously consumed profits of the entrepreneurial class was growing wider and wider.

Finally, the very nature of social change inherent in industrialization—compounded by the irresponsibility of those who led it—diminished the social status and economic security of such non-elite groups and depersonalized and dehumanized their very existence. The farmer, no longer the sturdy, semi-mythical yeoman, found himself caught in the unfamiliar world of commercial farming: working larger, more mechanized, more fertilized farms; growing specialized cash crops to sell via complex mercantile and financial arteries in the distant markets of urban America and the world at large. The resulting problems of personal business expertise, collective organization, and capital accumulation were awesome. They grew to overwhelming proportions when the farmer had to work them out within the inhibiting context of an urban-industrial imperialism which reduced the agricultural sections to the status of internal colonies (i.e., suppliers of food and raw materials and consumers of finished products) and subordinated them to the unpredictable, market-dictated demands of merchants, bankers, processors, and railroads. In like fashion, the worker gradually awoke to the shocking realization that he had lost his lengthy battle to avoid the permanency of "wage slavery" and to keep open the roads to self-employment and entrepreneurship; that he had been reduced to selling his personal wares in a labor market over which he exercised little control. Again, his problems of analysis and response were complicated by a capitalistic class-consciousness which produced overt hostility to unionism and an increasing tendency to move away from the piecework wage theories of the artisan stage to the "real wage" theories (i.e., subsistence wages) of the heavy industrialization stage.[4]

The narrow result of this irrationality, this unevenness, this revolutionary change was an economic crisis, mirrored most grotesquely in the frequent, severe, and prolonged depressions of the age—the Panic of 1873 and its extended aftermath, the economic downturn of the mid-1880's, and the cataclysmic Panic of 1893, capstone to twenty years of bust inside boom. Therein were the hard reflectors of unemployment, farm foreclosures, business bankruptcies, railroad receiverships, bank closings, and under-capacity production.

The broader result, less tangible but more fearfully felt, was the social crisis—ugly afterbirth of the seemingly senseless and endless economic disasters. In shock, alienation, and anger, countless Americans, in not-so-quiet desperation, lashed out at the existing social order of the Gilded Age—sometimes violently and blindly, sometimes deliberately and profoundly. Most perhaps sought simply to chastise; some sought to change—back to some agrarian utopia, forward to some workers' paradise. Whatever, the consequent social upheaval was a frightful spectre to the political-economic elite of the day, and in the eyes of such anxious beholders, agrarian and industrial unrest sometimes grew into harbingers of "revolution"—"an internecine war" in which "fire and sword will devastate the country."

Such un-American thoughts were not new. The railroad strikes and urban riots of 1877 (*The Year of Violence,* as historian Robert Bruce has described it) first posed the possibility of revolutionary confrontation, and the "great upheaval" of 1886 revivified it in the southwestern rail tie-up and in the post–May Day hysteria that has been labeled the Haymarket Affair. But it was not until the Panic of 1893 that the fear of the elite became intense, unreasoning, and widespread. Confronted by the rising force of Populism among western and southern farmers, the growing strength of socialism inside the labor movement, the traumatic Pullman boycott, strikes by textile workers and coal miners, and the bonus armies of Coxey, Fry, Kelley, Hogan, Sanders, Cantwell, and Randall, the conservative power structure could easily imagine radical, "mobocratic" threats to the very fabric of the "good society" of property and propriety. Walter Q. Gresham, the judicious and respected Secretary of State, said the situation "seemed . . . to portend revolution"; A. D. Noyes, influential financial analyst, felt that "industrial unrest seemed to assume proportions of anarchy"; Urieh H. Crocker, popular pamphleteer on economic matters, concluded that "the laboring classes . . . are every year showing themselves to be more and more ready to resort to violence" and predicted that "socialism, with its promise of relief . . . may well gain in the future"; and newspapers, such as the *New York Tribune,* editorialized that "social restlessness" was "arraying class against class and filling the land with a nondescript Socialism as dangerous and revolutionary as it is imbecile and grotesque." For them, the period became (as Harry Thurston Peck described it) one in which "those elements of dynamic discontent which had long been gathering strength, half unperceived, now loomed upon the political horizon with the black and sullen menace of a swelling thunder-cloud, within whose womb are pent the forces of destruction."[5] The characterization was extreme, but it differed from that of most conservatives more in style than in substance.

The social question, then, that was the rub. How to stabilize the economy and tranquilize the society? It was a question that could not be begged, for the drama of depression in the midst of plenty demanded solutions—and increasingly so with each reenactment of the tragedy. It particularly demanded them from those dominant social elements that had the most power to manipulate society and alter events: the business community and its political-intellectual allies.

Effective solutions, of course, required an accurate consensus as to the causes of America's recurrent economic ills—no easy thing to come by. Before 1873 "business crises . . . in America [had] been interpreted chiefly" in terms of the monetary system. Entrepreneurial debtors, both rural and urban, generally blamed hard times on a scarcity of money and proclaimed greenbacks and free-silver coinage as the only avenue of salvation. But the more dominant creditor elements insisted that the gold-backed currency system was more than adequate to meet the nation's needs; that if money grew scarce, from time to time, it was because the "widespread fear" generated by agitation for easy-money inflation led domestic investors to hoard their gold and foreign investors to withdraw it, thus curtailing needed capital investment and business expansion.

Even after 1873 it seems clear that monetary theories remained the dominant analytical tools for explaining the fluctuations of the business cycle. As late as the 1890's the desperate effort of the Cleveland administration to repeal the Sherman Silver Purchase Act and halt its consequent gold drain, as well as the ill-placed optimism that accompanied fulfillment of the repeal, made it clear that a great many Americans continued to define economic recovery in monetary terms. And certainly the pivotal election of 1896, with its campaign rhetoric about the virtues and vices of "free silver" and the gold standard, offered stark evidence that the money question remained one of the chief political battlegrounds in American society.

Nevertheless, in the two decades that separated the panics of 1873 and 1893 there "came into vogue" a new "explanation for commercial and industrial depression"—the theory of generalized overproduction (characterized by classical economists as, "in the nature of things, an absolute impossibility").[6] It did so for the simplest of reasons: overproduction seemed demonstrably obvious. Most American manufacturers periodically suffered from growing stocks and stagnant demand, and it was only a matter of time, communication, and traditional American empiricism before they broadened their individual experiences into a general truth. So what began in the 1870's in a crude, intuitive, particularistic way ultimately evolved into an articulate and comprehensive theory that American industry, as a whole, produced more than could be consumed; that market stagnation accounted for the intermittent "long depression." If the analysis was heresy, so be it! American businessmen had always given more weight to concrete reality than abstract theory anyway.

Before 1893 the economic heretics espousing ideas about stagnation were a decided minority in the business, political, and academic worlds; but their personal and collective reputations insured rigorous attention to their views. After all, one did not lightly dismiss the ideas of Charles H. Cramp, America's leading shipbuilder; or Jeremiah W. Jenks, famed Cornell economist and later president of the American Economic Association; or W. Elroy Curtis, one of President Benjamin Harrison's confidants and early chief of the Bureau of American Republics.[7] Most of all, one gave more than passing thought to the widely publicized pronouncements of David A. Wells and Andrew Carnegie—the two men, above all others, who were most persistent and persuasive in their intellectual groundbreaking; in preparing a viable alternative to money theories where no other alternative existed; in speeding the metamorphosis in economic thinking that was to reach its climax during the Panic of 1893.

Wells was one of Grover Cleveland's chief financial advisers and (by one account) "the representative economist of the United States." His views on cyclical theory first appeared in a series of nine magazine articles in 1887 and 1888 and in book form a year later: *Recent Economic Changes and Their Effects on the Production and Distribution of Wealth and the Well-Being of Society*. They immediately sparked an intense controversy, with Professor Jenks lending Wells his most effective support, while the brilliant Simon N. Patten led the majority of the economics profession in critically dissecting Wells's argument. The chief point of contention was Wells's insistence that the monetary question was utterly irrelevant in explaining both the falling "rate of profit on even the most promising kinds of capital" and the

"unprecedented" decline in "the prices of nearly all the great
staple commodities." (Patten, for example, saw an almost one-
to-one relationship between price levels and the supply of gold,
and he assumed that any marked and continuing fall in commodity prices had to reflect a scarcity of gold.) Instead, Wells
saw the key correlation in the enormous increase in production
that coincided with the fall in prices. Initially attracted by production statistics in the iron and steel industry (output rose 40
per cent in one year alone, 1885–1886), he soon discovered that
despite frequent depression "the volume of trade" in all industries "has all the time continually increased." From all this he
concluded that "capital . . . has accumulated faster than it can
be profitably invested," and he warned that resultant "industrial
over-production—manifesting itself in excessive competition . . .
and a reduction of prices below the cost of production—may soon
become chronic."[8] Interestingly, Wells's suggested solutions were
not unlike those ultimately followed a decade later: business
consolidation at home and market penetration abroad.

Carnegie, as a more conspicuous public figure, had perhaps
greater impact than Wells. As early as 1889, if not before, the
steel magnate began to take public issue with the classical theory
that when supply exceeds demand, "goods will not be produced
at less than cost," thus restoring the equilibrium of the marketplace. "This was true when Adam Smith wrote," he commented,
"but it is not quite true today" when "manufacturing is carried
on . . . in enormous establishments." Under such conditions, he
insisted, "it cost the manufacturer much less to run at a loss for
ton or yard than to check his production"; that "stoppage would
be serious indeed." Thus emerged what Charles Schwab called,
a decade later, Carnegie's Law of Surplus: (1) "the condition
of cheap manufacture is running full"; (2) foreign markets, even
"at low foreign prices," were the only feasible way to dispose of
the resulting surplus—"in order to keep running" in hard times,
and "in order to hold the market" in good times. "The result of
all this is that we will be able to sell our surplus abroad, run

our works full all the time, and get the best practice and costs in this way."[9]

@

Despite such celebrated advocates as Wells and Carnegie, the overproduction thesis neither replaced nor subsumed the conventional wisdom before the final decade of the nineteenth century. The initial inclination in 1893 was to blame the panic chiefly on the overt threat to the sound, creditor, gold standard, and to sound the clarion call for immediate and unconditional repeal of that arch offender, the Sherman Silver Purchase Act. Political advisers, business friends, trade journals, financial chronicles, and conservative dailies supported President Cleveland's frenetic but successful efforts to do precisely that.[10] Like *Iron Age* and the *American Wool and Cotton Reporter*, they donned anew the "goldbug's" mental straitjacket, admonished that "there is no commercial panic," and observed that "the restoration of values appears to be a simple matter" of repealing "the Sherman law, the one obstacle in the way of restoring confidence." Unfortunately, such simple faith proved grossly misplaced, for repeal failed to break the downward trend or to fulfill the widespread expectations of rapid recovery. "Hopes are not always facts," the *New York Tribune* pointed out, "as those learned who predicted that the Silver bill would make everything prosperous."[11]

Nevertheless, most conservatives continued to define monetary problems as the panic's prime catalyst, and the more sophisticated (including President Cleveland) urged that repeal of the Sherman Act be followed by more positive and fundamental reforms geared to creating greater flexibility in the monetary system. But as panic produced depression, and as the offspring grew more persistent, more brutal, and more traumatic, there came both gradual awareness and sudden shocks of recognition that this was no simple financial crisis, that monetary palliatives alone would not suffice. This was a real commercial depression whose complex causes were rooted in the industrial order itself.

By almost any standard of measurement—prices, profits, unemployment, wages, business failures—the depression of the
1890's created "a greater loss and more suffering than ever before
in the history of the country." This fact was compounded by concern over the "tremendous loss of business"—30.2 per cent—
"whose ratings in the business world were good or even of the
highest character." (Apparently even the fittest did not survive
this catastrophe.) It was compounded by the enervating awareness that the panic followed eight years of a somewhat sluggish
economy instead of the "great wave of prosperity" that normally
preceded a crash; that the old cyclical pattern of boom-panic-
depression-recovery-boom seemed to be giving way to downward
stagnation broken only by partial and short-lived upsurges.
Finally, it was compounded, of course, by the shrill-pitched
voice of social anger and despair which came with such startling
swiftness and severity in the "Année Terrible" of 1894; that led
A. D. Noyes (who lived through every panic from 1873 to 1933)
to conclude that "talk of 'the country being done for,' of American prosperity being gone forever, of a future which would
bring only economic decadence . . . came much sooner after the
panic of 1893" than "on any similar occasion of our time."[12]

It was this consciousness of the economic and social crisis
that precipitated—perhaps psychologically compelled—a concerted search for more meaningful explanations of the national
disaster—a search that led almost inevitably down the corridor
marked "overproduction." It did so in part, as I have already suggested, because the theory of stagnation seemed to jibe with
perceived reality, and because that theory already benefited from
able and influential advocacy. But the turn to an overproduction
analysis also resulted from two additional phenomena that were
crucial in making it more acceptable and more credible.

In the first place, the stagnation theory offered an umbrella
broad enough to include the continuing debate of the monetary
theorists. Or, put another way, overproduction analysis was so
amorphous that it could subsume monetary arguments without

necessarily destroying them. More significantly, not only did the new orthodoxy leave room for the old to survive, it actually revived it—*but* in a substantially altered and redefined way. Thus, while "goldbugs" and bimetallists continued to argue the merits of their respective beliefs in the mid-1890's, they increasingly did so within the body of the assumptions of stagnation: which monetary standard was the best international exchange vehicle to foster the export of American goods into foreign markets?

The crux of the bimetallist position was the insistence that a combined gold and silver standard would give America a definite competitive edge in penetrating the markets of key silver-standard countries in Latin America and Asia. Not only was this a cardinal article with agrarian silverites but with an enlarging group of conservative eastern mavericks, including Brooks Adams, Henry Cabot Lodge, Thomas B. Reed, and William C. Whitney. Many of the latter were members of or sympathetic with the aims of the famous Boston Bimetallic Club which, by 1895 (two years after its founding), was stressing the international trade advantages of bimetallism perhaps more than any other theme.[13]

Underlying this approach was the belief that the future of America's trade expansion lay not with Europe but with the underdeveloped areas. Europe's diversified, industrialized economies would compete with and ultimately discriminate against American exports, but the more simplistic, extractive economies of underdeveloped regions were complementary—they would offer cheap raw materials for the American industrial complex and markets for its surplus products. Working from this first premise, conservative bimetallists pointed out that key market areas in Asia (China, Japan, India) and Latin America (Mexico and Brazil) employed the silver standard, and that a bimetallic America would have an important currency exchange edge over the European gold standard in those areas. "Trade between gold and silver standard countries," they pointed out, "is always hazardous on account of the danger of a change in the value of one or both of these metals in the interval between the making of a contract of sale and its execution." Hence, "tying together of the two metals . . . would eliminate this risk, since it would prevent any change in the ratio between gold and silver." The anticipated result: a competitive advantage for American market expansion.

Significantly, most "goldbugs" did not dispute the need for increased foreign commerce but accepted it and used it as another valuable weapon in their intellectual arsenal. Noting that adoption of the gold standard historically coincided with foreign trade expansion (Great Britain in 1821, Germany and France in the 1870's), most conservatives concluded that any surplus-absorbing thrust by the United States required (as one economist put it) "a monetary system that is definite, rational, and unchangeable," one which would insure that "all nations will have the same faith in the dollar that they have in the pound sterling." Thus David Wells's minor-key variation of the 1880's now became established dogma for the money-changers themselves, canonized by Secretary of the Treasury John G. Carlisle's lumbering remark that "this country could not long maintain its present position as one of the most conspicuous and important members of the great community of commercial nations which now controls the trade of the world, unless we preserve a monetary system substantially, at least, in accord with the monetary systems of the other principle nations."[14]

If breadth and flexibility made the overproduction analysis more easily digestible, the export trade revival of 1897–1898 and its psychological impact made the theory more believable. What happened initially was relatively simple and not unlike the events of twenty years earlier: nascent economic recovery coincided with a dynamic upsurge in exports, leading many Americans to deduce that markets (not simply money) *must* have been the problem all along. Or, carried one step futher, this circumstance led many to define foreign markets as the key *marginal*

difference between stagnation on the one hand and prosperity on the other; to concur with Michael G. Mulhall's remark (in his oft-quoted "Thirty Years of American Trade," 1897) that "an enormous export trade" was blazing the path to "industrial recovery." Symptomatic of such thinking was the remarkable emphasis placed upon the export trade in the *Consular Reports* in the spring of 1897, as well as the subsequent across-the-board instructions to all American consuls (August 10) "to give special attention to the question of extending the sales of American manufacturers."

What happened thereafter was a good deal more complex and quite unlike the events of the late 1870's. Put most simply, the business community began to shed its uneasy feeling that it could compete in world markets *only* during depression periods of low wages and low prices; that with full recovery (and higher costs), American goods would be forced back within the confines of the home market. Instead, American corporate leaders—resplendent in their retooled, refinanced, reorganized armor—now seemed prepared to make good on an earlier British prophecy that the United States "will meet us in all the neutral markets of the world, or even extinguish the furnaces of Cleveland and Cumberland, of Scotland and Wales."[15] In short, stagnation theories now could be more than alleged; they and their implications could be acted upon—a fact that made them infinitely more attractive in 1898 than in 1878.

What chiefly accounted for this change from self-doubt to self-confidence was a hardheaded appreciation of newly won technological, cost-production advantages over European rivals (higher American wages notwithstanding). But one can legitimately speculate that another factor, more intangible yet real, was involved: America came to believe foreign press clippings about its overwhelming power—and not power in the abstract, as some contemporary scholars indicate, but *economic* power.[16] The nation began to take perverse pride in Europe's fears of "the American invasion"; in the admonition (sounded in the French Cham-

ber of Deputies) that "recognition of the much more serious
American Peril" took precedence over all else; in the Austrian
Foreign Minister's declaration that "the destructive competition
which transoceanic countries are carrying on . . . require prompt
and thorough counteracting measures if the vital interest of the
peoples of Europe are not to be gravely compromised"; in the
German Emperor's anxious proposal that the Russian Czar help
block the American trade threat with cooperative economic action;
in the warning of British economist Mulhall that "the world is only
beginning to have evidence of the enormous productive power
of the United States." In short, in a curious fashion, Europe's
image of America became America's image of itself. It was an
image that the brilliant Henry Adams captured well when he
declared, "It is we who are now strong and Europe whose markets
will be destroyed. . . . If I live and keep my mind a few years
more and the world moves at the same rate as since '93, I shall
live to see Germany and England wrecked."[17]

For all these reasons, the years between panic and war, between 1893 and 1898, produced a full and swift current of support for an overproduction analysis. If the world of rhetoric
has any meaning, then it is clear that by the Spanish-American
War a consensus already existed among conservative businessmen, politicians, and journalists on the reality of an industrial
glut and the pressing need for a new frontier in world markets
to relieve it. Indeed, one must say—both for the sake of accuracy
and impact—that it is nearly impossible to find *any* prominent
members of the power structure who did not, by 1898, think
and act within such a conceptual framework.

The prime illustration is the business community. Normally
fragmented by a host of divisive forces, American capitalists
spoke out with nearly monolithic agreement on the causes of
the depression and the measures for its cure. For example, overproduction views were held not only by those who produced

(i.e., industrialists). Merchant capitalists, with their endemic interest in an enlarged foreign trade, quickly picked up the theme and argued (as did Charles R. Flint of the Pacific Clipper Ship Line) that "our output of manufactures far exceeds the demand for home consumption," and the "only way out of our straits is through commerce with the world. Thus will be brought about an industrial revival that will end the present popular discontent."[18] Likewise, finance capitalists, with their own stepped-up activities in the industrial sphere, modified their preoccupation with the monetary crisis and evidenced a sharp concern for the problems of the marketplace. Thus, as Ernest R. May recently noted, even the "staid and respectable" *Commercial and Financial Chronicle* trumpeted the Marxist-like line "that American industry produced too much and had to find foreign markets if the country were to escape economic collapse." Moreover, so did the *Bankers' Magazine* and *Bradstreet's* and the American Banking Association *Proceedings*. (The latter, for example, produced in 1898 the classic and oft-quoted declaration of ABA President Joseph C. Hendrix that, as the result of overproduction and labor discontent, "we have the Anglo-Saxon thirst for wide markets growing upon us. We have long been the granary of the world, we now aspire to be its workshop, then we want to be its clearing house.")

As for the manufacturers, one is struck by the lack of disagreement along the usual lines of function, geographical location, and corporate size. Thus, while a heavy-industry journal like *Iron Age* could propagate Carnegie's Law of Surplus and advise (in 1897 and 1898) that "conditions now appear more favorable than ever for extending the export trade," so could a consumer-industry periodical like the *American Wool and Cotton Reporter* concede in 1897 (in a total reversal of form) that "supply exceeds domestic demand" and the only "possible alternative . . . is the utilizing of a foreign outlet for the goods."[19] The stagnation rhetoric of the heavily depressed southern textile industry was a bit more frenetic than most, but it did not differ in substance from that of the eastern industrialists who dominated the Philadelphia Commercial Museum or the midwestern manufacturers who played such a powerful role in the National Association of Manufacturers.

The only difference in approach concerned not the overproduction theory itself but the tactical responses to it. Generally, large-scale economic units (such as Carnegie Steel or Standard Oil) utilized their own organizations to push surplus sales abroad. But small-to-medium-sized corporations, with their higher costs and more limited resources, often pooled their efforts in broad-based trade associations. Of these, none was more significant than the National Association of Manufacturers and the Philadelphia Commercial Museum.

Organized in 1895 by representatives of some three hundred companies (few of them king-sized), the NAM's major *raison d'être* was the assumption that "our manufacturers have outgrown or are outgrowing the home market," and the "expansion of our foreign trade is [the] only promise of relief." Acting on this premise, the association collectively did two things. First, it began establishing sample warehouses abroad (chiefly in underdeveloped countries like China and Venezuela), where NAM members could attractively, permanently, and economically display their wares for interested foreign buyers. Second, in the role of lobbyist and propagandist, it zealously pushed its own brand of neo-mercantilism among fellow businessmen and national political leaders. Reciprocal trade, shipping subsidies, a Board of Trade (i.e., a Department of Commerce), consular service reform, the gold standard, the metric system, an isthmian canal— all became cardinal tenents in the NAM's liturgy.

The Philadelphia Commercial Museum was organized in 1897 by Philadelphia business leaders—but, significantly, with endorsement and encouragement from dozens of trade groups throughout the land: from the Maine Board of Trade to the Southern Manufacturers Club, from the Newport News Business Man's Club to the San Francisco Chamber of Commerce. Like the NAM, its sponsors were heterogeneous and generally second-echelon in size.

Like the NAM, it predicated its existence upon the reality of cyclical excesses and the permanent need for an export safety valve. (Consider its official slogan: "When orders are brisk and the Home Market good, LOOK AFTER YOUR EXPORT TRADE. Then, when business falls off at home, your foreign markets will keep you busy.") Like the NAM, it acted essentially as a clearing house to gather trade information on world markets and to exhibit American industrial products for foreign purchasers. The museum's first major undertaking—a "national exposition" for the "encouragement of the export trade"—received (in early 1898) a $350,000 federal subsidy to aid construction of exhibition halls and the collection of sample American products. Interestingly, Congress justified this expenditure (as Representative Oscar W. Underwood put it) on the grounds that "we, as a rule, have outgrown the home market" and "must reach out in foreign countries to sell our surplus products."[20]

Business support for an overproduction thesis and the commitment to marketplace expansion was highly significant. But economic expansion, as America was shortly to discover, inevitably met external obstacles (for example, xenophobia, rival expansion, social instability) which could be surmounted only with governmental aid. Thus it is crucial to realize that principal foreign policy decision-makers shared the businessman's version of cyclical theory and (as we shall see later) ultimately accepted the responsibility of promoting and protecting the export trade. Both Presidents between 1893 and 1898 embraced the new economic orthodoxy and its corollary prescription. Grover Cleveland, as early as 1893, frequently stressed the narrowness of "the home market" and the need to "find markets in every part of the habitable globe"; and William McKinley, after 1895, indicated a primary concern for the problem of "surplus products" (production "beyond consumption") and a firm conviction that "it should be our settled purpose to open trade wherever we can."

Similarly, Secretaries of State, between panic and war, expressed like-minded views. Walter Q. Gresham found the prime danger of social "catastrophe" in the fact that "our mills and factories can supply the home demand by running six or seven months in the year," and he saw his solution in a freer tariff "to enable our people to compete in foreign markets." Richard Olney believed that "the present crying need of our commercial interest is more markets and larger markets for the consumption of the products of industry"—anticipating his later pronouncement that "the home market fallacy disappears with the proved inadequacy of the home markets." And William R. Day, the *de facto* Secretary of State under John Sherman (and later Secretary in his own right), counseled Congress "that the output of the United States manufacturers . . . has reached the point of large excess above the demands of home consumption." Day urged a vigorous "commercial expansion" into "the southern half of the Western Hemisphere" and the "vast undeveloped fields in Africa and the Far East."[21]

Finally, for sake of completeness, one must say a word about the conservative press in America and its place in the growing intellectual consensus—not as a shaper of popular opinion (though this no doubt was important) but as a reflector of the elite community. After all, perhaps no functional group had its feet so firmly planted in both the political and economic camps of the influential. Certainly, the Fourth Estate in heavily populated metropolitan areas was *big business*. It held significant assets of its own and was tied intimately to other business through advertising. Powerful editors and publishers were often prominent political figures in the councils of the established parties (Whitelaw Reid, of the *New York Tribune*, a case in point).

Thus it is not unimportant that conservative newspapers— irrespective of political identification, business ties, or geography —embraced a stagnation theory with near unanimity. From the ocean-bound East to the heartland West to the New South came the same perception of reality: "our manufacturers have so increased that their output now exceeds the demand of the home market"; "the home market no longer [is] sufficient to absorb their manufacturers and products"; "the producing force is now sufficient in many branches of industry to meet all the needs of this country and a considerable foreign demand also." From the *New York Tribune* to the *Chicago Inter-Ocean* to the *New Orleans Times-Picayune* came the same shared solution: "This part of the New World has grown old at last," and the "United States can no longer afford to neglect even the most distant markets."[22] In general, the free-trade rhetoric of low-tariff papers, like the *New York Times,* eased them into the overproduction camp as early as 1893, while the protectionist mentality of others, such as the *New York Tribune,* delayed the metamorphosis until 1897 or early 1898. The end result, however, was the same.

What I have reconstructed thus far may be criticized as little more than a *papier-mâché* model, a paste creation of abstracted pieces of rhetoric that may as easily mislead as enlighten. But in fact one can demonstrably relate such rhetoric to relevant, definable issues and to subsequent behavior. Moreover, one can establish such causal relationships not only in the traditional realm of foreign policy (where this book will largely focus) but in the large twilight zone that inextricably ties foreign and domestic considerations together—a zone where one issue has always been the most important and usually the most vexatious: the tariff.

In post–Civil War America no issue remained (as Winfield S. Hancock put it) such a "local issue," such a collage, such a peculiar product of "logrolling" sectional and economic interests. No issue so defied change (save for minor modifications that grew more from pragmatic concern for an unwieldy treasury than from abstract commitment to free trade), and it would not be surprising to find the tariff question untouched by the implications of stagnation theory. Yet even the tariff could not escape the practical impact of the overproduction consensus. In the case of the depression tariffs of 1894 and 1897, the more things stayed the same, the more they changed. The nature and intent of administration proposals (both Democratic and Republican), the shifting orientation of debate in committee hearings and floor dialogue, the significant (albeit nascent) changes in the final legislation itself—all reflected a new emphasis upon the tariff as a lever to open foreign outlets abroad and thereby solve the marketplace crisis at home.

It is now clear that the tariff of 1894 was, in its intent, much more than a typical Democratic effort at revision downward or another hackneyed attempt at "tariff-for-revenue-only." This tariff session brought into being a full-blown theoretical basis for freer trade and produced a substantive effort to translate that theory into fact.

In analytical terms, Cleveland and his supporters simply echoed the mid-century tenets of Great Britain's "free-trade imperialism"; indeed, their rhetoric reminds one more than a little of John Cobden's speeches. Briefly, they made two points. On the one hand, America had a pressing *need* for foreign market expansion. As Henry L. Wilson, House engineer for the bill, put it: "There is not one of our leading industries that can find free and healthful play within the limits of our home markets . . ."—an opinion shared by Populist spokesman Jerry Simpson, who blamed the economic congestion upon the fact that "there is no more new country to be thus opened, and the great tide of population is turned back again upon the East." On the other hand, America had the consummate *capacity* for penetrating economically "the very countries we are seeking to capture." Again, as Wilson proclaimed: "We could throw down to-day our tariff walls and defy the world's competition." Or as Simpson once more echoed: we were "ready to tear down the customhouses and challenge the world for competition in its markets." In short, America's "manufacturing supremacy of the world" was both the source of the economic problem (i.e., overproduction) and the means for its solution (i.e., the ability to produce more, make it as well, and sell it for less than any other advanced, industrialized nation). Given a freer and more open world marketplace, America's economic superiority would necessarily reap a bountiful harvest. Had Grover Cleveland been a reader of Friedrich Engels, he undoubtedly would have seconded the latter's 1893 prophecy that "The introduction of at least relative free-trade policy in America is sure to complete the ruin of England's industrial position and to destroy, at the same time, the industrial export trade of Germany and France"; that "America bids fair to drive them all out of the world's markets."

Reflecting practical politics, the Wilson tariff bill sought not free trade but only the halfway house of free raw materials— that is, the inclusion (or retention) of most key, imported raw materials on the duty-free list. Hopefully, this maneuver would benefit American industrial exports in two ways. First, it would lower the cost of certain raw materials widely used by American manufacturers (such as coal, iron ore, lumber, copper, and wool), ultimately putting the subsequent finished products in a better price-competitive position in world markets. Second, on the premise that one buys from whom one sells to, the larger importation of specialty raw materials (such as wool, raw sugar, raw silk) from underdeveloped nations would automatically produce a warmer reciprocal climate for American manufactured products in those same countries.

As it turned out, even a halfway house was not feasible, and the administration's tariff bill suffered the same senatorial emasculation that normally befell such legislation. The final result, passed into law unsigned by Cleveland, was a hodgepodge affair which, while cutting the average tariff duty to about 40 per cent, also reduced the once-lengthy free list to a puny three (wool, lumber, and copper).[23] Nevertheless, congressional grappling with the tariff issue was not meaningless. It verified that overproduction sentiment was already strong early (1893–1894) in the depression; it occasioned the formulation of a free(r) trade philosophy geared to the enlargement of foreign markets for industrial exports; and it produced a successful low tariff bill in the House of Representatives. All were important straws in the wind. Viewed in historical perspective, the tariff of 1894 was not *that* far removed—either in time or conceptualization—from the Underwood tariff of 1913.

Comparatively, the Dingley tariff of 1897 was in many ways more significant than its Democratic predecessor. For one thing, it came at a time when overproduction views were considerably more comprehensive and cohesive than they had been in 1894— a fact that facilitated a more rigorous debate on tactical responses: that is, free trade versus reciprocity. Moreover, for all its gross protectionism (57 per cent average duty compared to the earlier 40 per cent), it offered more substantive incentives and stimuli for the industrial export trade than had the Wilson-Gorman tariff. And finally, its primary emphasis, *reciprocity,* proved to be a far more important antecedent for twentieth-century tariffs than the free-trade theorems of Grover Cleveland, William L. Wilson, and Roger Q. Mills.

The specific roots of reciprocity went well back into the nineteenth century—the Canadian trade treaty of 1854 and the Hawaiian agreement of 1875 being obvious cases in point. But as a generalized stratagem it did not emerge full-blown until the McKinley tariff of 1890 designated it as the vehicle "most likely to succeed" for Pan-American economic penetration to the south (for example, in Cuba and Brazil).[24] Temporarily put on the shelf by the tariff of 1894, it reappeared in the election of 1896 when the Republican party platform committed itself to both "protection and reciprocity" as "twin measures of American policy" going "hand in hand." Similarly, the party's victorious presidential candidate, William McKinley, devoted considerable space to the tariff issue in his first inaugural address—space de-

voted to one thing, and one thing only: reciprocity. "In the revision of the tariff," he remarked, "especial attention should be
given to the re-enactment and extension of the reciprocity
principle. . . ."[25]

Reciprocity was (as William Diebold put it decades later) a
sort of "adjusted protectionism," an "eat-your-cake-and-have-it-too"
commercial tactic. On the one hand, it retained the high protective barrier against the competitive exports of industrialized
Europe, thus "build[ing] up domestic manufacturing and trade
and secur[ing] our market for ourselves"—or so said the GOP
1896 platform. On the other hand, it instituted reciprocal trade
agreements with the underdeveloped countries of Latin America
and Asia—agreements that effected the relatively free exchange
of the full range of American finished products for the one or two
or three raw materials or agricultural specialties that character-
istically dominated pre-industrial, extractive economies. In the
exchange, the value increment of finished products clearly gave
most of the advantages to the more advanced nation ("conquering
by . . . commerce," as one merchant defined it.) In short, as
McKinley phrased it, protection plus reciprocity equaled a great
"stimulus . . . to our foreign trade in new and advantageous markets for our surplus agricultural and manufactured products,"
and without "involv[ing] any loss of labor to our own people."

Reflecting his convictions, McKinley in his inaugural called
for "a further experiment and additional discretionary power in
the making of commercial treaties." Shortly thereafter he called
Congress into special session and on March 18, 1897, Congressman
Nelson Dingley, Jr., of Maine introduced the proposed Republican
tariff into the House of Representatives. One day later the Ways
and Means Committee reported the bill out—without the benefit
of any hearings whatsoever. Section 3 on reciprocity, however,
had already received its day in court a year earlier, and a memor-
able day it was. On June 8, 1896, following extensive investigation, the House Subcommittee on Reciprocity reported a near
"unanimity of opinion among the commercial and industrial

associations of the United States" in favor of reciprocal trade. Among these supporters were the National Association of Manufacturers, the National Board of Flour Millers, the National Live Stock Exchange, the National Association of Wool Manufacturers, and numerous boards of trade and chambers of commerce. Particularly forceful was the NAM, whose convention a year later was to damn the tariff of 1894 for having "destroyed for a time much of our export business" and call for a "revival of all our reciprocity treaties and the making of new ones with every country of the globe."[26]

But the House version of reciprocity was hardly the extensive experiment the President had urged. Section 3B simply reenacted the reciprocity segment of the 1890 tariff, in which the retention of certain articles on the free list (in this instance, coffee, tea, and raw hides) was contingent on reciprocal concessions from the countries exporting those commodities. Section 3A avoided such coercion, but the products covered were rigidly limited and—save sugar—largely insignificant (for example, tartar, brandies, champagnes, wines, silk laces, mineral waters, molasses, paintings, and statues). Essentially, the Dingley proposal created an optional and lower schedule for these items, which the President could invoke in return for favorable concessions on "the products and manufactures of the United States."

The subsequent two-week House debate was striking for its *oneness*. Vituperation notwithstanding, both defenders and critics of Section 3 showed a common commitment to use the tariff as an aid to foreign market expansion. Representative Dingley and his cohorts stoutly insisted that their "scientific protection" (as they defined reciprocity) would help solve the nation's dual-edged economic crisis. First, it would ease the problem of overproduction by "extend[ing] the markets for the products of our mills and factories." Second, it would ameliorate the related problem of domestic underconsumption by "opening up employment to the masses of our people at good wages," thus restoring their "purchasing power."

Section 3's critics sharply objected to such analyses on two grounds. Representatives from heavily agricultural states in the deep South and Border regions pointed out that Republican reciprocity aimed for an increased exchange of American manufactured products for foreign raw materials but made no meaningful provision for the sale of American farm surpluses. As Missouri Democrat Charles F. Cochran noted, reciprocity was *not* geared to deal "with the great states of Europe, that consume the surplus of agricultural products of this country, but with some of the Spanish-American countries and with some of the small islands adjacent to our coast." Agrarian spokesmen picked up the related theme that Dingley protectionism was as irrelevant as Dingley reciprocity in promoting agricultural interests—because there was no foreign competition to protect against at home. Thus the whole idea of equal protection for farm goods and for manufactured goods seemed wholly fallacious to these critics. For such men, only free trade or export bounties could aid the farmer. Reciprocity—at least as structured in the Dingley bill—clearly could not.[27]

These same critics went beyond a narrow agrarian dissent to meet reciprocity proponents on their own terms: to insist that halfway measures were not enough to meet the pressing need for even *industrial* market expansionism; to demand that the manufacturing sector cut the protectionist knot completely and go the whole, logical route to free trade. This is not surprising, for these same agrarian spokesmen were often industrial advocates as well. After all, save for certain prairie regions, no area of America was any longer exempt from the inroads of local manufacturing; nor in an age of agro-industry—where wheat and flour milling, livestock and meat-packing, cotton and textiles were inextricably tied together—was it possible to make hard-and-fast distinctions between an agrarian and an industrial interest.

As a consequence, southern and border Democrats did not quarrel with the reality of *industrial* overproduction and the need for foreign market outlets. For example, Joseph Wheeler of Alabama, a chief representative of southern textiles, compared America's mammoth share of the world's production with its diminutive "4% [share] of the population," and concluded that "it will be impossible for us to continue a great progress and development unless we can open the markets of the world to become the purchasers of the products of American toil." Similarly, Edward W. Carmack of Tennessee insisted "that in nearly all the great branches of industry in this country there is a capacity to produce in six months more than the American people can consume in twelve months." And so the expressions came in nearly torrential fashion: "ample markets for our surplus products"; "large surplus products" of our "manufactories"; "the home-market" idea—a "fake" and "hoary-headed pretense"; "overproduction"; "raising more products than can be consumed."

The disagreement was largely over tactics. To its Democratic critics, reciprocity (beyond its anti-agrarian bias) was insufficiently bold and comprehensive to carve out adequate markets for manufacturing surpluses. To the powerful Champ Clark of Missouri, reciprocity was a "deceptive scheme"—"nothing but free trade in spots or 'protection with free trade on the side.'" Arguing in the same metaphors, Clark rhetorically inquired "if free trade in spots or on the side is good, why is not free trade everywhere better?" Again, the sentiment was an oft-repeated one: *only* pure free trade could avoid surrendering "the great highways of ocean commerce to England"; "every restraint upon the importation of foreign goods is a restraint upon the exportation of American goods"; "nothing but 'free-trade,' pure and simple," could get "the foreign markets we are after for our exports." "Simply turn [the United States] loose in the great arena of nations, and she will take care of herself."[28]

Nearly lost amidst such contentiousness was perhaps the most significant fact of all: two of the Republican party's most ardent reciprocity men in the House—William Alden Smith of Michigan and Winfield S. Kerr of Ohio—examined Section 3 of the Dingley bill and found its means "insufficient" to fulfill its ends. They suggested an expanded and more flexible reciprocity section, and the idea was picked up by the administration's chief spokesmen in the Senate. There the Committee on Finance produced a remarkable report that took sharp exception to the Dingley bill, chiefly for its inadequacy in looking after the export trade. (Clearly, what had sufficed in 1890 did so no longer.)

The core of the committee's critique was that America not only needed foreign markets but that "improvements in methods and economies in production" had given her the competitive capacity to fulfill that need. Thus Nelson W. Aldrich—the committee's chairman and preeminent spokesman for the eastern business community—publicly predicted that the nation's "manufacturers will be able to go out into the neutral markets of the world and compete with great industrial nations of Europe." Speaking specifically of one great neutral market, "the countries of the East" (which he defined as "the Philippine Islands, Java, and China"), the Rhode Island Senator urged that some oriental exports, such as tea and tea plants, be placed on the free list to facilitate their exchange for American "cotton cloth, petroleum, and other manufactured products."

The Finance Committee's report produced a mixed bag of results. It did not generate senatorial approval for revised rates "considerably below those imposed by the House bill, and in most instances below those contained in the act of 1890." (In that sense, the Senate's protectionist stripes remained unchanged from 1894 and 1890.) Yet, more interestingly and more importantly, the report did touch a startlingly receptive nerve in its call for a drastically new reciprocity section "looking to an extension of our foreign trade." Junking the House bill's Section 3 altogether ("not . . . effective" was the judgment), the committee structured a new and expanded section that in substance gave the President a two-year period during which he could exercise great discretionary power in making bilateral, reciprocal trade treaties of one to five years duration. Specifically, the President could negotiate such treaties on any or all of three bases: (1) a reduction, up to 20 per cent, on *any* article in the tariff schedules; (2) a transfer from the duty list to the *free list* of any article which the President designated as the "natural" product of the treaty country (but not of the United States); (3) the *retention* on the *free list* for a "specified period" of any product already on that list.[29] Overall, it was a section that could not fail to please President McKinley.

A seemingly sterile and redundant debate followed in the Senate. Republicans, sticking to the practical problems of log-rolling, spoke for reciprocity chiefly with their votes. Predictably, several Democrats, echoing their House brethren, denounced the committee's bill and preached the free-trade gospel. To wit: "Take down the barriers, lower the wall, and our ships will plow the seas, and the proceeds of our manufactures will be in every market of the world." *Ad infinitum,* or so it seemed.

Yet two factors made the Senate debate more than an abbreviated version of what had gone before in the House. For one, it produced several deserters from the anti-reciprocity posture of the Democratic party. Most prominent and influential were John T. Morgan of Alabama (enthusiast for open doors, Pan-Americanism, a battleship navy, and a Nicaraguan canal) and George Grey of Delaware (anti-imperialist, marketplace expansionist, and later chief dissenter on Philippine policy in McKinley's Peace Commission of 1898). To be sure, both couched their support of Section 3 in free-trade terms: "free trade is disguise" and "a little bit of free trade and free sunshine." Yet both proclaimed reciprocity a potentially effective device. Morgan, for example, after explaining at length what he meant by his remark that "We desire markets for our surplus products," concluded that "This amendment [Section 3] fosters that idea." Indeed, he saw reciprocal trade treaties as "a very great advantage to the commerce of the United States, particularly with the Orient and with South America and Central America"—areas of long-standing interest to that Bourbon spokesman of the "New South."[30]

What was still more distinctive about the Senate debate was

the vocal presence of a small, bipartisan group of primarily far western Representatives who, in this sea of consensus, made the only explicit criticism of the whole expansionist rationale. In the last analysis, they were so caught by their own contradictory attitudes and interests that they could not square the circle. Spokesman for this group was Frank J. Cannon, a Silver Republican from Utah, but about a half-dozen colleagues implicitly accepted all or part of his views.[31] In essence, Cannon began with the premise that the search for industrial markets would lead to wars of such magnitude that the social stability of much of the world would be threatened. "I believe," said Cannon, "there are coming movements which will shatter thrones and destroy republics, and that the policy of non-commercialism is the policy for us in America . . . so that we may not share in the sins of the world nor partake of its plagues."

*Except* that Cannon's economic isolationism embraced only industrial exports, not agricultural ones. On the contrary, Cannon, like most agrarians, had long argued that large foreign markets were indispensable if the farmers' own problem of overproduction (the eternal surplus) was to be solved. In trying to resolve this apparent contradiction, the Utah Senator fell back upon the analysis of his intellectual mentor, David Lublin, a California merchant (dealing in agricultural exports) and chief publicist for the western granges. Lublin's "out" was his insistence that agricultural exports did not demand any forceful tampering with the market area and a foreign surplus market was therefore consistent with isolationism. More specifically, farm surpluses were "sold at international prices at the world's . . . exchanges" and thus offered "less temptation for commercial or political entanglements with other nations." "Manufactures," however, were "sold at local prices and at fluctuating profits," and in a "world . . . market" situation, this virtually "invite[d] local energy to be directed in foreign quarters . . . in its endeavors to set aside foreign obstructionism." End result: "foreign alliances, treaties, and political entanglements"; or, worst of all, "conquest."

In practical terms, the Cannon-Lublin analysis produced a twofold recommendation: (1) protectionism (without reciprocity) for the manufacturer, in order to focus his attention on the home market; (2) government-subsidized export bounties for the farmer. But the recommendation avoided any meaningful confrontation with the industrial sector's problem of overproduction. If an external solution was to be prohibited, what was the viable, internal alternative? Cannon recognized that any policy of "non-commercialism" had to be "a just policy." "If not, then the elements within the wall of the tariff, incited by injustice and indignation, will turn and tear the fabric of our own social order."[32] But neither Cannon nor other non-commercialists defined "just"—beyond perhaps the warmed-over vehicle of free silver. None appeared to recognize and cope with the implicit dichotomy between means and ends; with the real possibility that their "non-commercialism" might necessitate a substantive, even radical restructuring of the political economy if a self-contained America was to remain (or perhaps become) "just" and democratic. Their critique was perceptive: industrial, marketplace expansionism would involve inevitable (and perhaps undesirable) political burdens and military risks. But their own self-interested concern for the export trade and their inability to provide a solution for the economy's industrial surplus reduced them nearly to the posture of narrow, parochial agrarians—a position of gross irrelevance in an urban, industrialized, capitalist society.

On July 7, 1897, amending stopped, debate ceased, and the Senate passed the Dingley tariff—the expanded Section 3 intact —by a 3 to 2 margin. Had it ended there, Cordell Hull might have had to build his career upon something other than tariff revision. But it did not. Instead, the intricate maneuvers of the House-Senate Conference Committee produced a final reciprocity section very much different from that of either house. In one sense the final bill broadened reciprocity by incorporating *both* the House and Senate versions—the former as Section 3, the latter as Section 4. But having done so, the conference bill seriously undercut the potential effectiveness of Section 4 by requiring that trade agreements made under it be submitted back to the Congress for approval of both the House and Senate.[33] Motivation for this emasculation lay, most probably, with the House's jealous guardianship of its tax-making powers and its concern over undue executive power. Whatever, it deprived the President of the flexible, discretionary means necessary to the effective utilization of trade reciprocity—a fact reflected by McKinley's inability to produce concrete trade agreements acceptable to Congress. Nevertheless, the near-victory reflected in the Senate's bill, the administration's real efforts at implementation, and McKinley's renewed and eloquent plea for more expansive reciprocity in 1901 —all made the tariff of 1897, both in time and conceptualization, not so far removed from the Reciprocal Trade Agreements Program of the New Deal.

In sum, the committee reports, the floor debates, and the tariff legislation of both 1894 and 1897 all demonstrate that even so immovable an object as the protective tariff had to give—even if just a little bit—in the face of so irresistible a force as the conservative consensus on industrial overproduction. All bolster the prior assertion that by early 1898 a new cyclical orthodoxy had subsumed (though not replaced) the old, and that the primary consequence was concerted agreement on the necessity of a militant, broad-gauged expansion into the surplus-absorbing markets of the world. Of course, several labor spokesmen and some agrarian rebels occasionally suggested that the nation's fundamental problem was underconsumption and implied that any lasting solution would have to be an internal one. But such sentiments were conspicuously absent among business Republicans and Bourbon Democrats, both in and out of government. Indeed, no figure of national prominence and respectability spoke openly of internal social reconstruction—"to open doors at home, to substitute an intensive cultivation of [America's] own garden for a wasteful and ineffectual extension of interests" abroad. Some posed it privately but concluded that any worthwhile effort to raise purchasing power at home involved basic and radical changes which would threaten their conception of the good society and their own vested interests in it. As Elihu Root put it: "If you once begin to limit [wealth], you can never stop short of a general division."

With this perspective, it is clear that the real "great debate" on expansion ended *before* "America's Colonial Experiment" began. It centered on the nature of the social and economic crisis, and its resolution defined, as a major component of the national interest, the goal of a new frontier in the market outlets of the world. In this sense the subsequent debate over imperialism versus anti-imperialism was in part a debate over means rather than ends: specifically, whether or not economic expansion required the accoutrement of a colonial empire for its successful fulfillment; whether closed markets or open doors would be most effective. On this and related questions, significant differences did exist, and only time, fortune, and tradition would resolve them. Still, such differences, while relevant and meaningful, were secondary and less important than the common ground shared by most influential and powerful American leaders. Like Brooks Adams, they agreed that "all the energetic races have been plunged into a contest for the possession of the only markets left open capable of absorbing surplus manufactures, since all are forced to encourage exports to maintain themselves. . . . A good illustration is the case of the United States."[34]

# Chapter II: *The Frustration of Laissez Faire*

"This country will expect equal and liberal trading advantages . . . as the result of the war, and all your efforts, so far as they may properly be put forth, should be expected to secure expanded privileges of intercourse, trade and residence in which our citizens may share."
—*Edwin Uhl*, Acting Secretary of State, to Charles Denby, Minister to China, 1895

Time is one of the most fascinating elements in the historian's grab bag, for it multiplies chance variations many times over. Witness the crisis of the American marketplace: had it happened at any other time than the 1890's, it might have taken very different directions, shapes, and dimensions. But coming when it did, the crisis in the marketplace coincided with yet another crisis—that in China, occasioned by the Sino-Japanese War of 1894–1895. And it was the intersection of these two crises, reinforced by the traditional Asian orientation of American commercialism, that led many Americans to define the China market as the solution to the closed frontier and the industrial glut at home.

The myth of the China market did not originate with the Sino-Japanese War. Its obscure beginnings certainly predate the Renaissance, and its early influence upon men does much to explain the expansion of Europe and the continual, quixotic search for the Northwest Passage. In America the founding fathers made the myth an integral part of their concept of mercantile empire; the clipper ship heyday of merchant capitalism nourished it; the blandishments of missionaries kept it alive; and the writings of Anglo-American "old China hands" gave it renewed vitality in the late nineteenth century. Still, it remained for the Sino-Japanese War to redefine the myth of the China market in terms of nascent reality, to give it both the credibility and immediacy necessary to provoke a broad-gauged, intensive effort to translate fancy to fact.

The Sino-Japanese War of 1894–1895 was the great rehearsal for the Russo-Japanese conflict a decade later. Differences between China and Japan over the administration of Korea provoked the war, but Japan quickly converted it into a larger effort to block future Russian expansion. As the British Minister to Japan correctly noted: "Whatever the ostensible reason for going to war with China may have been, there can be little doubt that the main object was to anticipate the completion of the Siberian Railway and to prevent Russia from gaining free access to the Pacific Ocean."

Such motivation was scarcely apparent in the beginning, however, and if apparent was rarely regarded seriously—at least not by American observers. China, in American eyes, was an impenetrable, somnolent giant; Japan might sting her with quick naval victories, but when aroused she would smother the Japanese war effort in Korea beneath a mass of Chinese soldiers. Acting on just this analysis, the United States government greeted the war with detachment, certain that it threatened no disruption of the Far Eastern equilibrium. Neither President Grover Cleveland nor his Secretary of State, Walter Q. Gresham, could unearth any American interest or policy that "the deplorable war" might endanger; and the Assistant Secretary of the Navy confessed to the press that no one in the government had even considered supplementing the American naval force (then one cruiser) in Korean waters.[1]

Japan's staggering triumphs (on land as well as sea) and her extension of the war into Manchuria and China proper soon demonstrated the bankruptcy of American assumptions and the indifference they bred. Thus, by the autumn of 1894, a confused Cleveland administration faced some unexpected facts of life. First, barring new obstacles, Japan would soon be in a military position to dictate a peace that would give her an important foothold on the Asian mainland. Second, the anticipated Chinese capitulation posed the imminent possibility of a Russian-led intervention to deprive Japan of victory's spoils and thus keep open Russia's potential avenue to the sea.

New realities, once revealed, demanded new responses, but the Cleveland administration was not initially up to the task. Gradually, indifference did give way to growing concern. Cleveland, for instance, finally discovered that the war "deserves our gravest consideration by reason of its disturbance of our growing commercial interests." And the Navy Department soon found compelling reasons to reinforce the Asiatic Squadron. Consequently, by the end of 1894 five additional ships had joined the *Baltimore* in or near Korean waters, and two more cruisers were on their way via Suez. By spring the entire squadron (save one) was concentrated at Chefoo, site of Sino-Japanese peace negotiations.[2] Yet, for all this evident interest, the American government found it difficult to confront three obvious and pressing questions. First, and most important, did the United States consider the mainland expansion of Japan consistent with American national interests and traditional policies? Then, did the situation demand any specific American actions, either to preserve or deny Japanese war gains? Finally, if measures were required, should they be taken alone or in conjunction with other powers?

Events soon caught up with the stalled American policy machine and ultimately forced these issues. In October 1894 the British government posed the key question: would the United States "join England, Germany, Russia and France in an intervention" to deprive Japan of any mainland acquisitions and thus limit her plums to a monetary indemnity from China? The request marked a major turning point in Far Eastern international relations, for heretofore British policy (by action) and American policy (by "hitchhiking" acquiescence) had each sought to work directly through China to preserve open door commercial entrée and to prevent the fragmentation of the Chinese Empire. The British inquiry was the final expression of that policy. But America refused and thus by implication first suggested a very different technique to safeguard the open door and Chinese integrity.

Many factors produced the American declination, among them the traditional American desire to preserve its own freedom of action. But there is also speculative evidence to suggest the influence of a vague belief that China, without some provocation, would remain (as Gresham said) "a vast inert mass of humanity," unable to protect itself against foreign spoilation and unwilling to modernize and accept the inflowing currents of foreign commerce.[3] Clearly, the circumstances demanded some new ingredient, some external catalyst which would provide China with a model for her own stabilization and modernization, safeguard the open door, and thwart the expansionist ventures of anti–open door powers, such as Russia. The order was a tall one, but no nation fit the bill so well as Japan.[4] The island empire was an Asian nation, yet one that had profitably absorbed Western technology and commerce. It was, so most believed, thoroughly committed to the commercial, non-discriminatory open door in China (even the American Minister in Peking, Charles Denby, who had no great affection for Japan, conceded "that the Japanese will in [no] wise interfere with foreign commerce, or with the foreign residents at Taku or Tientsin"). Finally, Japan, in her conflict with China, had amply demonstrated her capacity to fight a complex, mechanized war on a par with most European nations.

(Indeed, when war between Japan and Russia was narrowly averted in 1895, H. S. Sternburg confided to Theodore Roosevelt that he would "have put my money on [the Jap]. There's not a navy afloat that is in better fighting trim than the Japanese.") It was perhaps this analysis that led Secretary of State Gresham to pronounce in January 1895 that "Japan has stepped out into the light of a better day, and she regards the United States as her best friend." And the awareness of this attitude led the *New York Times* to report in April 1895 that America stood "at Japan's back."[5] Thus began the long and ill-fated American effort to cast Japan in the role of stalking-horse and protector-of-the-open-door extraordinary.

Having implicitly cast its lot with Japanese ambitions (provided they remained reasonable), the Cleveland administration now looked for some shortcut to head off the threatened European intervention—an intervention that might nullify Japanese influence in China and possibly precipitate the general disintegration of the Celestial Empire. Short of an unthinkable military commitment, only one course seemed promising: effect a quick peace settlement before the interventionist threat became fact. Acting on this line of thought, the administration, in November 1894, pressed upon Japan repeated offers of American mediation. In each instance Secretary Gresham stressed American "friendship toward Japan" and the corollary conviction that the Japanese war effort "endangered . . . no [American] policy in Asia." On the contrary, he emphasized "that the only contingency which the United States fears is that Japan's victorious progress may provoke the forcible intervention of other nations."

Japan refused at once, indicating it could not accept an arrangement that implied any Japanese need to initiate peace overtures or to use the offices of a third party. But in closing the front door Japan left open the back, for it intimated that it would welcome peace negotiations—if China requested them, and if they were direct rather than mediated. Disappointed in the Japanese refusal of American intercession (that chance would be reserved to Theodore Roosevelt a decade later), Cleveland nevertheless determined to make the most of the positive aspects of Japan's response. Finding China willing (even anxious) to make peace, he suggested that preliminary negotiations begin at once, and that they be facilitated by using the American diplomatic representatives in Peking and Tokyo as go-betweens—not as mediators but as messenger boys.[6] This more modest proposal met with acceptance from both China and Japan. Though it gave the United States no chance to shape the final peace terms, it hopefully offered an opportunity to speed the process of peace settlement—and in view of the proposed European intervention, speed was of the essence.

Despite the minor task involved, the Cleveland administration nearly bungled the opportunity, thanks to the misadventures of two "old China hands," Charles Denby and John W. Foster. Denby, the American Minister to China, could not tolerate the idea of Japan as "a continental power" and apparently made his views known to the Chinese government. Foster, a former Secretary of State, went even further, accepting a post as adviser to the Chinese peace commission and then warning against territorial indemnification (perhaps because a syndicate he reputedly represented wanted a larger monetary indemnity to heighten its own chances for loan concessions from China.)[7] Together, the actions of both men raised serious Japanese suspicions about the nature of the American efforts and threatened to disrupt the attempt to initiate early peace talks. Aware of all this, the Cleveland administration moved firmly to allay Japanese doubts. In the case of "Foster's mission," Gresham privately and publicly assured the Japanese that it "is entirely without the sanction of the United States Government." Denby's indiscretions brought him a pointed admonition that he had gone "too far in aiding China" and a reminder that he was not "conducting the peace negotiations" for the Chinese. In each instance Japan seemed assuaged.

In the meantime, Sino-Japanese negotiations produced, by April 1895, a peace treaty of staggering proportions—one that granted

Japanese demands for territorial holdings in southern Manchuria, Formosa, and the Pescadores, a monetary indemnity, trade concessions, and recognition of Korean independence. Of all the provisions, none was more significant than the Japanese acquisition in Manchuria, for it constituted a clear roadblock to the extension of the Russian railway system (and with it, Russian political and economic influence). For Russia it was a moment of truth. Either she moved to block final ratification of the treaty, perhaps at the risk of war, or she acquiesced in the final outcome, thus sacrificing a whole range of vital interests and traditional objectives in the Far East. Actually, the choice was easy, for Russia had already anticipated the situation and prepared the machinery for possible intervention. By the spring of 1895 she could count on the support of both France (Russia's entente partner) and Germany (who hoped for a *point d'appui* in China as a reward for saving the Celestial Empire). Thus bolstered, Russia did what the United States feared: she demanded that Japan give up the southern Manchuria cession in exchange for a greater monetary indemnity.[8]

England, in a startling about-face, refused to join the efforts of France, Germany, and Russia—the *Dreibund*—to "save" China. Instead she encouraged Japan to resist the coalition demands to abandon claim "to appropriate territory on the mainland of China." This amazing reversal capped six months of policy reexamination and reflected the new English view (perhaps already held by the United States) that China was no longer strong enough to guarantee "a wide opening for [foreign] commerce and capital" or to act as "a political prop, and even a military one, if necessary, against the Empire of the Tsar." Suddenly, Japan loomed large in the English mind as a far more effective "bolt to fasten the door against the ambitions of Russian expansion." Consequently, the British government encouraged Japan to establish herself "in Korea and on the northern coast of the Gulf of Pe-chili," while advising the Chinese government to reestablish itself "nearer the centre of the Empire" where the English, already supreme in the Yangtze Valley, could continue to dominate it politically and exploit it economically.

Japan needed more than words to withstand the *Driebund's* insistence, but words were all England could offer. In the overall scheme of British imperial interests, the open door did not seem worth a fight, especially one that might be transformed into the much-dreaded world war. Nor could Japan expect more from the United States, for the open door was to America a technique of avoiding military-political responsibilities, not creating them. If force was necessary (and it was) to make the open door work, it would have to be someone else's force. So the island empire faced a most unhappy choice. She could fight alone against the coalition to preserve her own national interests (while pulling the Anglo-American chestnuts out of the fire), or she could give up southern Manchuria. A decade later a more confident Japan, backed more vigorously by England and America, would make the former choice. Now she acquiesced and chose to bide her time.[9]

🕮

The conclusion of the Sino-Japanese War left Pandora's Box wide open, but many Americans mistook it for the Horn of Plenty. The threatening implications of the tripartite intervention were, for the moment, only vaguely felt. Instead America chose to see China's defeat as the start of the long-awaited commercial awakening of the colossus—the translation of the China market from myth into reality.

Two lines of thought led to this single conclusion. One stressed the immediate material benefits of the peace treaty itself: the opening of seven new Chinese ports and three new rivers; the abolition of some internal taxes; the permission to establish warehouses in the interior; the right to create foreign-owned industrial enterprises; and the removal of the Woosung bar obstructing the entrance to Shanghai. All these concessions would presumably step up foreign trade with China, an advance in which the

United States would share through the unconditional most-favored-nation arrangement, an earlier treaty stipulation that automatically gave the United States any trade concession garnered by another foreign power.

The other path of reasoning was less tangible but more compelling. It stressed the belief (or the wishful thought, overstated) that China's ignominious defeat had "taught the folly of [her] exclusive and conservative policy"; that China, to survive as a national entity in a modern world, would have to emulate the Westernizing ways of her Japanese conqueror.[10] In the short run this meant, hopefully, the importation of foreign capital, equipment, and technicians to create a modern military force (strong enough—though just barely—to defend Chinese integrity), an integrated railroad network (to tap unexploited interior markets), and a more productive agricultural system (which could produce a surplus for foreign exchange purposes). In the (not-so) long run, it meant, hopefully, vastly accelerated Chinese purchases of foreign manufactured goods to fulfill the wants of a growing Chinese middle class.

Americans on both sides of the Pacific projected such analyses. In China the American Consul General in Shanghai thought the missiles of war had made "a decided opening . . . in the opposing wall of Chinese conservatism, and that a widening market may be expected for western production." Thus, with obvious relish, Thomas R. Jernigan foresaw revolutionary "new developments" in China's status as "the great undeveloped country of the world" —developments "attended with profit" for American merchants, manufacturers, and financiers. In Peking the veteran American Minister Charles Denby generated less optimism, for the international complexities and hurdles were all too apparent to permit an overindulged imagination. Still, even he held out hope that the Cleveland "administration could get the glory of greatly increasing and spreading American interests in China."

In depression-racked America many others grabbed the same brass ring. In governmental circles the influential Frederic Emory

best caught the gist of things and their implication for "our foreign policy." From the commanding heights of the State Department's Bureau of Statistics, he pointed out "a great field for the
nascent commerce of the United States in the countries and the
islands of the Pacific," and he predicted that "the recent war
between China and Japan will probably have the effect of opening
vast markets to us." And if the daily press was any barometer,
Emory cast his seed upon ready ground, for those makers and
takers of public opinion were already singing a similar refrain.
Typical was the *Chicago Inter-Ocean*, which found that "The
time is propitious . . . to an opening of the vast area of China
to the commerce and civilization of the Aryan race." Working
from this premise, the paper's editors warned European powers
that Asia was a "field of American influence" and called at home
for "protection to American ships and construction of the great
American canal" to help penetrate "the natural foreign markets
of the United States." For a more select and interested clientele,
the *Commercial and Financial Chronicle* concluded that "the
opening of new Chinese ports and the great stirring up which
the war has caused must in the end result in considerable expansion of the foreign trade with the East." Nor did it find any reason
to alter an earlier prophecy that "We, more than any other Power,
are to have the Pacific trade . . . in our hands."[11]

⬛

The Panic of 1893 and the "awakening of China"—economic
need and apparent opportunity—these were the propellants for
America's expansion across the Pacific. These were the material
ingredients that lent a certain air of inevitability to American
imperialism. Yet choices did remain, for there was nothing preordained as to *how* America was to expand. Therein entered
ideology.

In 1895 the ultimate choice as to means rested with Grover
Cleveland and his like-thinking associates. The President was one
of America's most articulate spokesmen for the old and dying

order of laissez-faire liberalism. He aimed for a society of free
men and assumed it could be reached, a la Adam Smith, through
a free and expanding marketplace; and this assumption shaped
his view of government's role at home and abroad. On the domestic scene the national government was to eliminate state
favoritism (for example, pensions, railroad subsidies, protective
tariffs), permitting the toil of free men and free competition to
expand the marketplace. Similarly, in the world it was to lower
the American tariff while securing equal and liberal access to
desirable foreign markets, leaving the competitive zeal and economic efficiency of American corporations to do the rest. Colonies
and military force were undesirable accoutrements to economic
expansion, for both involved a bureaucracy and military establishment which might threaten freedom at home or entail the
ultimate hypocrisy of free men ruling unfree men abroad. But
such handmaidens were not necessary anyway, for given "a fair
field and no favor" it was confidently assumed that "American
economic supremacy" (to borrow from Brooks Adams) could
win its share of expanded markets *without* political and military
burdens.[12] In short, the Cleveland administration's answer to
the question of how to expand was the Open Door Policy, but
one with a laissez-faire twist; one without the insular imperialism
and governmental involvement that was to mark the Open Door
Policy of William McKinley and John Hay; one that merely up-
dated the mid-century British system of "free-trade imperialism"
and decked it out in an Uncle Sam suit.[13] Denby's State Department instruction of June 8, 1895, said it briefly but well: "This
country will expect equal and liberal trading advantages—certainly in Korea and presumably in China—as the result of the
war."[14]

In China, the open door (laissez-faire style) placed the burden
of market expansionism upon the Yankee entrepreneur. The administration's role was limited to preservation of the existing

commercial system (the unconditional most-favored-nation) and protection of the lives and property of American nationals. It was chiefly in this latter sphere that Adam Smith's "hidden hand" most often showed itself, with an eye cocked for market possibilities and a keen sense of what makes an image profitable.

In the summer and fall of 1895, the "awakening of China" took an unpleasant turn. Anti-foreign, anti-missionary riots and massacres broke out in various interior areas—first in Kutien district, then in Szechwan province. None of this especially surprised the Cleveland administration, for Denby had warned that such outbreaks were inevitable, given imperial impotence and the anti-foreign feeling stimulated by China's defeat. The administration, taking him at his word, had alerted the Navy for possible action, either to carry out victims or carry in investigators.

Despite this forewarning, the storm found the Cleveland administration unsteady on its feet. For one thing, the Kutien uprisings produced no clear-cut American public reaction which the administration could use as a guideline. Some howled for the heads of the Chinese rioters; others demanded that meddling (and unwanted) missionaries come home. One New York daily thought the lesson clear: "the commercial nations" must assume "a virtual protectorate over all that part of China which is opened to commerce or to Christianity." Another seemed to think that China ought to be left alone to determine her own course. To make matters worse, no one stood at the helm of the State Department amidst this babble of voices. Walter Q. Gresham was dead, and his successor, Richard Olney, had temporarily taken leave of Washington's heat, dust, and mosquitoes.[15]

Given such confusion, Acting Secretary Alvey A. Adee determinded to play it safe. He did what America had done so often in China throughout the nineteenth century: he latched onto the tail of the British kite. Declining unilateral action, the State Department simply sanctioned cooperation with a British investigating team in Kutien. Yet, curiously, the safe line proved unsafe, for China, already beset by Europe's postwar machinations, professed

to see sinister, political motives in the Anglo-American cooperation. This was no mean embarrassment for the Cleveland administration, for it bent a bit the carefully cultivated image of the
American Innocent, untainted by European imperialism and chi-
canery seeking only amity and trade—an image geared to heighten
diplomatic influence and sell more goods. Clearly, the situation
demanded some backpedaling. Adee began it with verbal assurances to the Chinese that "the co-operation had come about simply
because Great Britain and ourselves were in this case 'in the
same boat.'" Pressed further by the suspicious Chinese Minister,
the Acting Secretary finally provided "a written acknowledgement"
that "this Government is investigating the Kutien riots concurrently
with Great Britain only so far as is necessary to protect American
interests of person and property and not in conjoint furtherance
of any supposed political object which the latter may have." The
Chinese legation seemed satisfied and the State Department had
learned a lesson. It would not make the same mistake next time.

Next time was not long in coming. In September new riots
erupted in Szechwan province, affecting some American nationals
and their property. Richard Olney, now fully cognizant of the
situation, determined to hold China strictly accountable for vio-
lations of treaty right; but he also determined to go it alone, maintaining American freedom of action and the desired posture of
benevolent firmness toward China. So he quickly ordered the prep-
aration of a solely American commission to Szechwan. (The commission consisted of the American Consul at Tientsin, a missionary,
and a naval officer—the expansionist trinity.) But the imperial
government, always obstructionist in such matters and fearful that
a foreign investigation might provoke new riots, vigorously pro-
tested Olney's decision. Damages to American interests were small,
the Chinese argued, and in any case they would be thoroughly investigated by a Chinese commission. But Olney's commitment was
too firm to reverse, and on Denby's advice the State Department
reiterated its plans for "an American Commission with a Chinese
member to Szechwan." To emphasize the point, it warned that any

Chinese failure to cooperate might force the United States "to send [a commission] with the British as originally contemplated, and this we assumed China would not like."[16] Under the shadow of that club, China discovered merit in Olney's plan and bestowed her official sanction upon the American investigation.

Evident in the American response to these early anti-foreign uprisings was a regard both for the safety of American citizens and for national prestige. But the crescendo of riots in October revealed still another dimension of American concern—alarm that the social chaos might abort efforts to expand trade into the untapped hinterland provinces, thus making the China market much ado about nothing. When the commander of the American Asiatic Fleet suggested "that the government recall the missionaries in the interior to the treaty ports until conditions settled down and they could return," his seemingly harmless and humane recommendation provoked a harsh response from Denby and ultimate rejection by the Cleveland adminstration. "Missionaries are the pioneers of trade and commerce," said Denby. "Civilization, learning, instruction breed new wants which commerce supplies. . . . The missionary, inspired by holy zeal, goes everywhere, and by degrees foreign commerce and trade follow." Thus, he argued, to pull back these pathfinders of God and Mammon now risked possible difficulty in returning them later to their advanced posts in the interior. Given the commercial stakes involved, it was a risk not worth taking. Acting on Denby's advice, Secretary Olney ignored the Navy's suggestion and left the missionaries to fend for themselves, perhaps hopeful that the Minister's prophecy would come true—that "These pioneers of civilization will open up China to . . . the ordinary merchant and professional man."[17] The Secretary's decision offers an illuminating insight into means and ends in the expansionist syndrome of the 1890's.

The laissez-faire conception of market expansionism did not include any direct government role in aiding business ventures abroad. The government's sole concern was with the structure of things, while the actual dynamic was to come from the private sector. American capital and American goods would have to make it on their own merits, without diplomatic, political, or military support. Dollar diplomacy, even in a nascent sense, was almost absent as an element in the expansionist ideology of the Cleveland administration.[18]

Sharply illustrative of this approach was the affair of the first and second Chinese indemnity loans. The large war indemnity due Japan forced China, in 1895, to turn to foreign moneylenders. This in turn precipitated a mad scramble among the powers and their financiers for such concession plums, partly as vehicles to employ surplus capital and partly as levers to secure more liberal trading rights. Anticipating some American runners in the race, Denby pleaded with the State Department to give him liberal leeway to employ on-the-spot diplomatic pressure in behalf of American capitalists. He pointed out that the standing Instructions of 1887 denied him the right to offer any such assistance without prior departmental approval, and that this requirement often involved a fatal delay for American entrepreneurs competing with their less-encumbered European counterparts. Denby's point was well taken, and it underscored the central flaw of laissez-faire expansionism. For in defining market penetration as part of the national interest, the Cleveland administration had embarked upon a course that could not be fulfilled without the very use of governmental force that it wished desperately to avoid.

As with the tango, it takes more than one to play the laissez-faire game, and no one—save the United States—was really interested. While the other great powers rolled out the full arsenal of governmental support, American financiers entered the fray armed only with good will and money—and often too little of either. Angling for the first indemnity loan (even before the final peace and subsequent bond flotation) was a shadowy New York syndicate fronted by John W. Foster. The conflict of interest implicit in his role as adviser to the Chinese Peace Commission did not

bother Foster, and he urged China to reject Japanese territorial
claims in favor of larger monetary indemnification. His syndicate,
in turn, would finance the indemnity through a $400 million loan
to the Chinese government. But the scheme received no support
from the Cleveland administration (though Denby probably approved it), and any glimmer of success flickered out with the
*Dreibund's* diplomatic intervention in Sino-Japanese peace-
making.[19] In that one power thrust, Russia and her French ally-
banker acquired all the leverage necessary to secure the first
Chinese indemnity loan.

Competition for the second indemnity loan produced more
substantive efforts from a new group of Americans dominated by
the American Trading Company of Shanghai and New York. But
the United States government systematically refused any succor for
the group. Denby's initial plea (registered within the framework
of his 1887 Instructions), that the Department grant him special
permission to assist the American syndicate, met with swift rejection. In a telegram personally directed by the President, the
"Home Office" ordered its Minister in Peking "not in any manner
[to] lend your Diplomatic influence to aid the proposal for a
loan and [to] . . . confine your action to a formal presentation of
the parties interested, if in your judgment such action appears
proper." Nothing could shake that position, not even word that
J. Pierpont Morgan was interested in the syndicate's efforts. In
the end, despite Denby's repeated inquiries (or perhaps because
of them), the Cleveland administration simply reaffirmed and
reemphasized the 1887 Instructions, ordering Denby to "abstain
from using your diplomatic position to promote [American] financial or business enterprises. It is only in an extraordinary case—
to be first submitted to this Department with all the facts and reasons pertaining thereto—that any different course should be followed." Clearly, the Department did not view this as an
"extraordinary case," and, predictably, the American Trading
Company lost the loan concession, and with it (so Denby thought)
"a powerful leverage for other enterprises of our countrymen of

great commercial importance."[20] Cleveland had remained true to his principles but at the expense of the very marketplace expansionism he defined as vital to the survival of free men and free enterprise in America.

⚅

Awareness of this dilemma was a long time coming. The administration's approach to economic expansion in China was a fairly simplistic one, almost entirely commercial in its orientation. Like the McKinley administration to follow, it precluded any large-scale investment offensive by American financiers on the ground that it was not yet feasible. American capital in the mid-1890's was in no position to compete on equal terms with European. Moreover, other capital demands took clear precedent over Chinese investment, especially the reorganization of American industry at home and the elimination of America's debtor position vis-à-vis Europe. So the administration put all its eggs in the trade basket— an area in which America could compete with Europe and which, in any case, was more directly relevant to the problem of unemployment at home. European concession-grabbing excited no alarm so long as it did not directly threaten the open door funnel for American surplus products. Thus the State Department reacted indifferently to Denby's cry that the first indemnity loan, "at one bound," made Russia "the dominant country in the Far East" and "correspondingly depreciated . . . the influence of England." And it viewed with similar detachment the combined Anglo-German maneuvers to secure the second loan for the Hong Kong–Shanghai Bank and the Deutsch-Asiatische Bank.[21] So long as the range remained free and unfenced, America did not care who owned the corral.

It remained for the Li-Lobanov Pact of 1896 to reveal the administration's lack of sophistication; to dramatize that political strings were sometimes attached to financial loans; to point up that who owned the corral (i.e., the railroads) might render the commercial range unfree. In May 1896 the Russian policy of peaceful penetration in China (brainchild of Finance Minister Count Witte) bore triumphant fruit. In that month Li Hung Chang and Prince Lobanov signed the Sino-Russian Alliance and Railway Agreement. The alliance obligated Russia to aid China against external aggression; the railway agreement was Russia's reward—and a handsome one it was. It permitted the Russian Siberian Railway Committee (acting through the Russian-Chinese Bank) to build an extension of the Russian transcontinental system across northern Manchuria. Control of this Chinese Eastern Railway (CER) carried with it political authority along the rail route, the free right of public domain, and a one-third tariff reduction on all goods entering China over the CER. In addition, the Russian-Chinese Bank—financed by French capitalists—acquired the right to coin money, collect dues, gain concessions, and pay interest. In one fell swoop Russia had acquired the ingredients for hegemony in part of Manchuria, and with it the capacity to slam closed the commercial door.

Secretary Olney encountered the Li-Lobanov Pact in the *New York Sun* rather than the departmental dispatch bag. There, on April 26, he noticed a letter to the editor from Sir Robert Hart, the renowned British expert on China. Its whole content referred rather ominously to far-reaching political and economic negotiations between Russia and China. Alarmed but uncertain, Olney fired off stern instructions to Denby to supply "any additional information you can . . . on this question at the present time, and to [keep us] posted hereafter on all that appertains to this subject." By June, Olney's worse fears had been realized, as Denby confirmed the signing of the pact and substantiated its major provisions.[22] The dilemma was at last growing apparent.

In the meantime, business pressure also modified the administration's addiction to John Stuart Mill. Since the end of the Asian war, American economic interests in China had enjoyed a steady though unspectacular growth. By April 1896 Denby could report happily that Chinese development was engaging "the attention of American financiers and builders of rolling stock and equipment"—among them "at least two combinations of American capitalists . . . prepared to build and equip from beginning to end any railroad system which China may desire." Moreover, China's military needs claimed the avaricious concern of agents from the Cramp Ship-Building Company, the Union Iron Works, and the Bethlehem Iron Works. And to top it all, the famed American China Development Company ("a wealthy combination of capitalists in New York," as Charles Denby, Jr., described it) completed the organizational-financial structure that hopefully would catapult the United States to the fore in the scramble for Chinese railroad and mining concessions.

Still, American businessmen interested in China labored under two grave handicaps. First, they found it difficult to overcome the inertia of many of their corporate brethren, who, for all their giddy clichés about "China's awakening" and the "markets of Cathay," were reluctant to venture from more traditional fields to less familiar ones in east Asia. Second, of course, they found it hard to operate competitively in China without vigorous assistance from the American government. But in the late summer of 1896, fate—in the shape of Li Hung Chang's visit to America—was to go a long way in surmounting both these obstacles.

Li's visit originated in that haphazard way so common to human events. Word came to America in early 1896 that the Chinese elder statesman was to attend the Russian Czar's coronation and then tour the capitals of Europe. On the basis of an invitation from John W. Foster, Li also declared his intention to return to China by way of the United States. The announcement met with warm response from interested American businessmen, for it was common belief that the Viceroy determined dispensation of economic concessions in China.[23] Nonetheless, the laissez-faire heart of the Cleveland administration skipped no beats. All it managed, by way of response, was a certain casual jocularity, with the President and his Secretary of State debating whether "fir[ing] off

a bunch of fire crackers" or holding "an afternoon tea" would be
a more appropriate greeting for "Esquire Li Hung Chang."[24]

Such governmental apathy rapidly eroded under pressure from
an aggregate respectability that could not be ignored: from business spokesmen outside government (led by John J. McCook, railroad counsel); from businessmen inside government (such as
Daniel Lamont, Secretary of War); from "old China hands" (like
W. W. Rockhill and George Seward). All stressed two related
points: first, "the advantage, from the commercial point of view," of
Li's tour of American cities and industries; second, the need to expand markedly the administration's role in Li's reception in order to
demonstrate clearly that the government shared the business community's interest in the China market. In the end the administration capitulated, abandoning its meager, nominal plans for all the
trappings of a sumptuous, semi-state visit, with the government
in charge of (and paying for) most arrangements. "The North
Atlantic Squadron," it was agreed, would pay Li "naval honors"
as his ship passed in review. President Cleveland would participate
in "the grand scheme" by offering the visitor an almost regal reception, while Secretary Olney would take part in most of Li's
activities in New York City and would confer with him in Washington. The Navy would handle Li's trip to West Point, and the
Department of War would shoulder his expenses at Washington
and Niagara. Between such points of interest, Li's party would
travel gratis—compliments of the Pennsylvania Railroad, McCook's
chief client.[25]

Judged by newspaper accounts, Li's visit was a wild amalgam
of exotica and a comedy of errors. The presidential reception in
William C. Whitney's palatial town house; the grand military pa-
rade down Fifth Avenue with Li and Olney riding in an open carriage; the trip up the Hudson in Cleveland's own boat—all provided enough color to satisfy even the most demanding city editor.
On the other hand, Li's failure to review the White Fleet (a
McCook associate was talking business with him at the time in
a below-deck stateroom); his decision not to go ashore at West

Point because of a steady downpour; his cancellation of a day's events in New York City because of a smashed finger (victim of an errant carriage door); his unintentional omission of the Cramp Shipyards from his agenda because his frightened servants would not arouse him from an afternoon nap—all offered unwanted comic relief.

Notwithstanding excessive formalism and low comedy, Li's visit was a most important event. Not only did it involve the administration in a more dynamic posture, but it helped broaden American business interest in China. The Chinese dignitary had ample opportunity for long and candid talks with leading members of the eastern business community. It appeared to be time well spent. Both by private assurance and public pronouncement, Li showed a keen interest in American economic ventures in China and encouraged large-scale efforts there—especially by American railroaders. Better still, his professions *seemed* more than polite talk, for his return home coincided (perhaps significantly) with important Chinese contract grants to Baldwin Locomotive, Bethlehem Iron, and Cramp and Company. Needless to say, both rhetoric and seeming reality were welcome music in the midst of the 1890's depression, for this was the stuff of which business dreams were made.[26] As the NAM soon put it: "we must make our plans to secure" our "full share of the great trade which is coming out of the new industrial era in the Orient."[27]

Caught between this rising business interest and its own apprehension over the Russian threat in Manchuria, the Cleveland administration finally came to modify its ideology with expediency (as it had already done in Latin America). First it changed the ground rules for governmental participation in economic expansion. Reversing the standing 1887 Instructions, Olney ordered Denby to "use your personal and official influences and lend all proper assistance to secure for reputable representatives of [American] concerns the facilities for . . . contracts as are enjoyed by any other foreign commercial enterprises in the country." In effect, the Secretary gave Denby *carte blanche* to do whatever he felt necessary to aid American business, telling him that it was not "desirable that any instructions which have been given should be too literally followed." Moreover, Olney forcefully instructed the American Minister to keep the Department more intimately informed on American economic activity in China—"this most interesting and important subject." The only qualification in this amazing about-face was the administration's good laissez-faire admonition not to aid "any one firm to the exclusion of others."

Having changed the guidelines, the administration initiated a series of moves quite at odds with its prior hands-off passivity. It first ordered Denby to oppose vigorously the plans of the Shanghai Chamber of Commerce to develop manufacturing industries within China proper. In fact, this action was less significant than the reasoning that prompted it, for it laid bare the fundamental American opposition to industrialization of underdeveloped areas (such as China). Ignoring special American business interests in the manufacturing projects, State Department officials (including Olney and his chief assistants, Rockhill and Adee) viewed the Chamber of Commerce plan as "a cheap labor dodge" in "favor of local manufactures [whether set up by Chinese or foreign capital] for the purpose of competing . . . with foreign importations," and such ran counter to "our interest . . . to keep foreign markets open for our manufactures."[28] This view was to become the conventional (though often unstated) orthodoxy in twentieth-century American diplomacy.

At the same time the administration threw its weight behind the American China Development Company's effort to secure the construction contract for the Peking-Hankow Railroad—one of the main lines in the proposed Chinese system. In late 1896 the company had managed to obtain a preliminary contract from the Chinese government, and an elated Denby predicted that "this almost limitless field of financial and industrial operations will be occupied, dominated and controlled by Americans." At that happy juncture, however, negotiations bogged down (under British pressure, Denby believed), and the final contract appeared lost. But the American Minister, exploiting his newly liberalized powers, strenuously intervened with the Yamen (the Foreign Affairs Committee of the Chinese Ministry) to demand the contract for the American company. In unequivocal, almost threatening terms, he insisted that China owed the United States as much for her part in making peace in 1895 as other nations had "received rewards for their actions"; that "Americans could better than any other people build great railroads"; that "the United States had . . . no ulterior designs on Asiatic territory"; and that loss of the contract "would develop a bad feeling among our people at home." In short, he warned the Chinese government that it "must treat the Americans fairly and make a contract with them to build the Hankow-Peking line or road." Under such pressure the Peking regime agreed to follow through on final negotiations with the American syndicate—perhaps to continue the traditional Chinese chess game of playing foreign powers off against one another; perhaps because it honestly believed (as the Chinese Railroad director said) that "the Americans . . . have shown no covetous spirit toward China."

In the end, nevertheless, the American China Development Company lost this pivotal concession, and for a highly significant reason. Not because of Chinese opposition; indeed, the Chinese seemed anxious that the award go to an American company. Not because of administration indifference; the State Department through Denby, had intervened as vigorously as circumstances permitted. Instead the company lost out because it regarded the Chinese terms as illiberal and rejected them. Just as Denby had feared, the company's desire to "make money out of the specific contract" took precedent over "the broader view" as to "whether Americans shall control the industrial progress of China." The collapse of contract negotiations also indicated that American capital was not yet competitive enough to accept the more marginal terms that European capital would risk.[29] Perhaps the realization of this fact led the incoming McKinley administration to forsake large-scale financial ventures in China and to cast the Open

Door Policy in a strictly commercial mold—an open door for American goods but not necessarily for its capital.

In any case, notwithstanding the ultimate collapse of negotiations, the Cleveland administration's effort to secure the Hankow-Peking concession marked a major turning point in American diplomacy. From this point onward the American government would accept responsibility for the dynamics of expansion as well as its structure; from this point onward American diplomacy and American economic expansion would walk hand in hand.

# ✆ Chapter III: *In the Eye of the Storm*

"Partition would tend to destroy
our markets. The Pacific Ocean is
destined to bear on its bosom a
larger commerce than the Atlantic
. . . . Having such interests, is it
our duty to remain mute should
her autonomy be attacked?"
                    —*Charles Denby*, 1898

The gradual demise of Cleveland's "Cobdenized" policy in China developed in great degree out of a reorientation of American attitudes toward Russia. The nineteenth-century tale of diplomatic romance between the American republic and Russian czardom had by 1896 begun to lose its appeal. Instead many American political and economic leaders, who looked to the markets of Cathay as balm for the Panic of 1893, increasingly found in Russia and its Far Eastern policy not a traditional friend but a new and formidable foe. Nor did contemporary accounts of pogroms and Siberian prison camps help the Russian image.

Russian actions, culminating in the Li-Lobanov pact, had apparently reversed the balance of political power in China. English preeminence for the moment seemed gone. Now, instead, Russian diplomats most often prevailed at the Chinese Imperial Court; Russian corporations reaped the railroad concessions of Manchuria and hurried to complete the Trans-Siberian Railway across Chinese soil; Russian bankers (and their French backers) dominated the financial affairs of Manchuria and fared well in Peking itself in the bitter contest for China's war indemnity loans. As Denby summarized it: "China . . . became the bondman of her most powerful neighbor" (or, as his original draft phrased it, "her most dangerous neighbor").

With this power came a capacity for perniciousness which, if used, might undo the American hope of an open door economic frontier in China—especially in the lucrative hunting grounds of Manchuria. Most Americans feared the worst and saw in Russian actions "a threat . . . against all the commercial nations." Conversely, they acquired newfound affection for England and her championship of the open door. Americans began to define "our own interests" as "the same as those of Great Britain."[1] Thus by the time of McKinley's election American policy had taken on an anti-Russian, pro-British coloration.

But the interregnum between the Democrats' electoral defeat and McKinley's *effective* takeover of decision-making (the post-appointment stage) amply demonstrated that the new anti-Russian vogue was not without its challengers. Of these, none was more formidable than James Harrison Wilson and John James McCook, a pair of second-echelon chieftains as fascinating as any in American history. Wilson was soldier, railroader, adventurer-extraordinary. He had been many places (including China), done many things, and knew many people "of the best sort," as he liked to say. He was almost without peer among that colorful, ebullient, and effective breed of contact men that graced the Gilded Age. McCook was one of America's foremost corporation lawyers—legal counsel for the Pennsylvania Railroad system, the Atchison, Topeka and the Santa Fe, and other related enterprises. A superb behind-the-scenes manipulator in both economic "establishment" and Republican party politics, he was an ideal complement to Wilson. Their friendship, born in the Civil War and fused in later entrepreneurial battles, lent added efficiency to their joint ventures.

Wilson and McCook took heated exception to the new orthodoxy. They did not deny "the thralldom of China and the triumph of Russia in Eastern Asia." But for them a "Russian protectorate in China" spelled opportunity, not danger. China unprodded, they believed, would remain conservative and undeveloped, an embodied frustration of America's commercial dreams. China under Russian dominance might provide a golden chance for joint Russo-American economic undertakings of a vast nature, not only in China but in Russian Siberia as well. The compact could be a perfect one. Russian political power would turn the "concessions key" in "both Russia and China," while American economic power would provide capital and know-how to implement the opportunities. Both nations and their entrepreneurs (including Wilson and McCook) would share in the material rewards. Both men, moreover, were convinced that the prospect would appeal to the realistic Russians who, like Americans, understood that "diplomacy is the management of international business."[2]

Specifically, Wilson and McCook envisioned a worldwide transportation system spreading east and west from the orient. The core of the project would be an integrated network of American railroads in China and Russian railroads in Manchuria. These would tie in directly with the nearly completed Trans-Siberian Railway, and by coordinated steamship lines with the American transcontinentals. Short-term benefits would accrue from construction profits; long-term and more important gains would develop from the system's penetration of untapped markets and resources in China and Russia. The scheme was not unlike that pushed a decade later by Edward Harriman and Willard Straight.

Out of these attitudes and visions, Wilson and McCook evolved a plan—complex, almost intuitive in the beginning, but firmly conspiratorial by the end. Its stages, though overlapping, were nevertheless definable: first, secure tentative approval from Russian and Chinese authorities for the railroad schemes; second, organize an American syndicate with capital sufficient for the task; third, gain control of the key diplomatic levers inside the Republican administration they felt would win power in the election of 1896; and finally, negotiate the necessary economic and political arrangements with the Russian government.

The key to the initial stage of this loosely conceived conspiracy was Li Hung Chang's visit to America in September 1896. McCook, as noted earlier, played a primary role in pressuring the Cleveland administration into modifying its initial hands-off policy toward the Viceroy's journey. Moreover, both McCook and Wilson exploited the situation to arrange extensive talks with Li concerning their railroad schemes for northern Asia. Singly or together, they were at Li's side during the shipboard entrance to New York City, the President's reception, all the public reviews, the leisurely journey to and from West Point, and the evening dinner party given by the New York business community. In terms of Li's apparent interest, it was a most rewarding expenditure of time.

At the same time McCook was active on a closely related subject, for he knew (well before the State Department) that Prince Hilkoff, "Russian Minister of Railways," planned a visit to the United States in late summer which might well coincide with Li's tour. McCook knew the Prince well, both personally and professionally, and there seemed some chance that the Russian Minister might be simultaneously interested in a joint Russo-American railroad project. Accordingly, McCook persuaded Olney to permit Herbert D. Pierce, secretary of the American legation in Russia (and a minor member of McCook's growing in-group), to leave his post temporarily and accompany Hilkoff on his trip to America. McCook argued successfully that this would give the State Department (and presumably McCook himself) "accurate official knowledge" of Hilkoff's findings and feelings on the American scene.

Unfortunately, the vagaries of circumstance and late nineteenth-century travel put a slight crimp in matters. By October 18, when Hilkoff completed his trek across Russia, across the Pacific, across America, the Chinese Viceroy had long since departed. So the hope of joint talks with both the Chinese and Russian representatives never materialized. Still, separate conversations with Hilkoff, however tardy, proved an important part of the Wilson-McCook schemes.

Taking the Prince in tow as he crossed the Hudson, McCook began a whirlwind campaign of public tours and private business talks that was to last four days. He capped his efforts on the final night with a sumptuous banquet for the Russian at the Metropolitan Club. There, Wilson, George Westinghouse, Chauncey Depew, George W. Pullman, Collis P. Huntington, Philip D. Armour, August Belmont, and other business leaders gathered (as one report went) in the fond hope that Hilkoff's visit "forshadow[ed] large developments." The Prince did not disappoint them. His prediction of an integrated, around-the-world system, and his avowal that the Siberian railway would "be laid with American rails upon its roadbed and equipped with American engines and cars," told his listeners what they wanted to hear.[3] More important, the startling similarity of his prospectus to that of McCook and Wilson apparently told those gentlemen what they wanted to hear as well.

Stimulated and encouraged by the talks with Li and Hilkoff, the two adventurers pressed on. Wilson took the lead. In a letter to McCook in late October 1896 the general outlined these three steps to Russo-American economic cooperation in the Far East. First, he suggested the organization of "a Syndicate to secure an interest in Chinese and Russian Railroad business." Second, to assure "the appointment of proper men as Ambassador to Russia and Minister to China." Finally, these preliminary moves accomplished, Wilson advised the sending of "three persons, a businessman, a lawyer and a diplomat to St. Petersburg, to discuss the operations with the Russian Government and the proper Russian officials and Capitalists and to agree upon a plan of operation." McCook concurred, and step one began.

Nothing was too good for Wilson and McCook. Their syndicate required much influence and money. If neither was forthcoming in the quantities desired, it was not from lack of effort. Needing political stature for their inner circle, the two men approached only "the best people—those who will be closest to McKinley's administration." Even Mark Hanna encountered their blandishments.

Requiring great capital as well, Wilson and McCook centered their attentions only upon leading capitalists such as John D. Rockefeller, J. Pierpont Morgan, Andrew Carnegie, Frank Thompson, and John H. Converse. Unfortunately, the response was not all that had been anticipated. Some individuals firmly declined. Carnegie, after a lengthy interview with McCook, concluded that he would stick to "the business of making and selling of steel," leaving more speculative ventures to others. Henry M. Flagler of the Standard Oil Trust declined on the grounds that McCook's proposals would increase Russian influence in China, leading to heightened Russian competition with American petroleum products. But a few apparently cast their lot with the syndicate. Foremost among them were the chief executives of the Pennsylvania Railroad and of Baldwin Locomotive. Most, however, emulated Morgan in expressing interest without commitment, preferring to wait until the plans moved beyond the preliminary stage. Still, despite the mixed results, McCook and Wilson remained optimistic, certain that eventually "a Syndicate including only the best . . . of the various groups" would "make a vigorous systematic and united effort to control the railroad building and kindred business, not only in *China* but in Siberia."[4]

Undaunted, they went forward with the all-important effort to capture key diplomatic levers inside the incoming McKinley adminstration. Wilson, it was decided, would seek the ambassadorship to Russia in order to control the planned Russo-American economic negotiations. McCook was to angle for the Secretary of War position in McKinley's cabinet, a post which presumably carried some weight in foreign matters. In addition, W. W. Rockhill, "old China hand" and author-to-be of the Open Door Notes, was to be pushed as Minister to China. Together the triumvirate was to give the new administration the pro-Russian cast so necessary to the implementation of the Far Eastern railroad scheme.

McCook's candidacy required little direct effort. His place in Republican party politics made a cabinet offer a virtual certainty. Wilson's quest demanded more purposeful pressure, and the general applied it in the monumentally overdone style that was his trademark. The unsuspecting McKinley was barely settled in office when a plethora of Wilson's handpicked supporters descended upon him. There were only chiefs in Wilson's camp: business scions such as Jacob Schiff, Abram S. Hewett, George Pullman, and Marshall Field; political leaders like Theodore Roosevelt, John W. Foster, Cushman K. Davis, William F. Frye, Henry Cabot Lodge, William B. Allison, and William E. Chandler. The lineup in Rockhill's behalf was only slightly less impressive, with Theodore Search, president of the National Association of Manufacturers, Alba B. Johnson of the Baldwin Locomotive Company, Theodore Roosevelt, and John Hay among it.

All was for naught. McCook received a cabinet offer, but not the right one. The political musical chairs of cabinet-making found him as Secretary of the Interior when the music stopped. The job did not fit his training, and it was far removed from the realm of foreign affairs. Thus he declined. Wilson received consideration, but no job. In part he fell victim to the geographic realities of patronage. Overloaded with eastern appointees, McKinley wanted "suitable . . . men from the West" for the remaining key diplomatic posts. In part, as well, the general oversold himself, so that the President finally succumbed to the "annoyance he felt at the 'persistent pressure' of [Wilson's]name." Rockhill, despite his legitimate credentials, never came close to securing the China position. McKinley's preference for a western man, the opposition of church mission boards to Rockhill's heretical views on missionaries, and Grover Cleveland's inexplicable warning to his successor that Rockhill "was not to be trusted," all took their toll.[5]

The Wilson-McCook scheme was dead. Deprived of influence inside the McKinley administration, the two men could not muster sufficient authority and prestige to dicker with the Russians; nor could they attract needed capital to their young syndicate. Their hope of personal fame and fortune was gone.

Also gone was any real chance for Russo-American cooperation in the Far East. John J. McCook and James H. Wilson had advanced the view that American interests in China could best be served by working with Russia—a position contrary to the growing stream of Anglophile sentiment in governmental circles. The frustration of their plans left no one to argue the case for a pro-Russian orientation in American policy, thus strengthening by default the drift toward Anglo-American cooperation. The trend proved irreversible. Russia, as we shall see, soon thereafter abandoned her past policy of peaceful penetration, creating a sphere of interest in southern Manchuria and posing a direct threat to the American textile and petroleum trade. Whatever chance may have existed for joint American-Russian development of Asia vanished. Even Wilson reluctantly concluded that the opportunity he had sensed in early 1897 could not be re-created in the crisis day of 1898: "our interests are with our old antagonist, England, and for the first time against those ancient allies, France and Russia."[6]

Drift had become a course; alternatives had closed. For good or ill, the frame of reference for McKinley's policy in the Far East had been established. It was to remain almost statically anti-Russian thereafter.

Despite such events (or non-events), the incoming McKinley administration found sufficient reason to view Chinese affairs optimistically. Compared to the previous three years of chaos, most of 1897 proved relatively (albeit superficially) calm and stable—so much so that the *New York Times* could find no need between January and July to make a single editorial pronouncement about the eternal "Chinese question." To an administration that equated tranquility with prosperity (whether in Cuba or China), this must have been a welcome development indeed. In fact, evidence and analysis seemed to bear out the equation. Trade statistics, through their diplomatic interpreters, spoke forcefully of one key reality:

the emergence of a favorable American trade balance with the Chinese Empire (the first in history), gained "chiefly in manufactured cotton, Indian yarn, kerosene, woolens and metals." Moreover, so Denby felt, even these statistics shed only a particle of light, for they ignored the immense amounts that China imported indirectly from the United States "*via* England, Hong Kong and other places." In support he unearthed one estimate that "60% of the goods exported and imported at Shanghai are of American origin or destination." Though he admitted the possibility of exaggeration, the American Minister did not "hesitate to predict an enormous development of our trade within the next few years."

In seeking to make good Denby's prophecy, the McKinley administration, in its first 250 days, engaged in a variety of unspectacular activities—but then the circumstances did not seem to demand heroics. Illustrative were the efforts to expand the right of foreign residence in the Chinese interior—on the assumption that so long as China restricted foreign merchants to the treaty ports, the expansion of the China market would proceed at a rather minimal pace. Accordingly, the American government did two things. First, it utilized the "most-favored-nation" clause to demand (and receive) the right of American citizens (including merchants) to reside throughout Hangchow province—a right secured by the Japanese two years earlier in the Treaty of Shiminoseki. Second, it sought to make better use of American missionaries who already held interior residence privileges; missionaries who, in their impact upon the existing social structure, created wants that only commerce could supply. Seeking to evaluate this impact and to exploit it more fully, the State Department ordered all its consuls in China to make a systematic survey of American missionary property and non-religious activities: for example, the operation of small, profit-making businesses, the practice of medicine for fees, or the local sale of goods produced in missionary-run industrial schools. As Denby noted, such a survey would be "of great usefulness" to his legation, the State Department, and American businessmen interested "in the trade and commerce with

China." At the same time the government continued to encourage American missionaries to use their treaty rights to establish residence in new and untried areas of the interior. Thus, in late 1897, when an American missionary finally settled in Hunan province, Denby reported exultantly that "this is the first permanent lodgement made in Hunan by foreigners," and he waxed eloquent on the size, population, and natural resources of the province and their possible significance for American trade. Apparently he saw no religious importance in the event.[7]

Other administration efforts to expand the China market were more nominal. One was the use of official diplomatic channels to urge Chinese participation in American trade fairs, in the hope that such expositions would impress Chinese representatives with the superior quality and price of American goods. Thus the State Department, in mid-1897, persuaded the Chinese government to send an official exhibit to the Trans-Mississippi International Exposition, scheduled for Omaha, Nebraska, in June 1898. Similarly, the American government, both through Denby and the Chinese Minister in Washington, Wu Ting-Fang, secured Chinese participation in the Philadelphia Museum's federally subsidized International Commerce Congress. The diplomatic exchanges in both cases involved the usual earnest declarations about the mutually "advantageous and beneficial" nature of the events and their "importance to the commerce of China."

In like fashion, the administration sought to use Chinese pressure for more tariff revenue as a lever to eliminate inter-provincial assessments which were a formidable barrier to the expansion of trade throughout the Chinese marketplace. Essentially, China wanted to collect her tariff in gold rather than silver. The justification for this, first voiced by Li Hung Chang in his 1896 visit to the United States, rested on the indisputable fact that the twenty-year depreciation in the world price of silver had cut Chinese tariff income drastically—a loss made more critical by the heavy financial burden of the Japanese indemnity of 1895. The State Department accepted the validity of the Chinese position but at the same time revived Richard Olney's prior position that any tariff increases be coupled with "the abolition of all species of internal taxation"; that "Goods having paid import duties should . . . go all over free from taxation." In a note to Chinese Minister Wu, the Secretary of State made it clear that the United States would not readily accept changes in tariff collection unless the American *sine qua non* was met. "I trust," wrote John Sherman, the new Secretary of State, "that in case it shall be decided to carry out the suggestion of the memorandum in the matter of collecting duties, I may be advised that all kinds of internal taxation have been discontinued."[8] Similar qualifications by other trading nations apparently persuaded China to drop the matter, but, as we shall see, subsequent circumstances surrounding the Boxer Rebellion were to resurrect the two related issues rather dramatically.

American efforts in behalf of trade expansion fared better than attempts to foster investments in China, particularly in railroads. Of course the two spheres were hardly distinct, for railroad investments would theoretically aid American commerce: immediately through the corollary sale of American steel rails, locomotives, and rolling stock; ultimately through the creation of a transportation system that would facilitate the distribution and sale of American products. Nevertheless, the initial concern of most would-be American investors was the potential profit to be gained from interest on concession loans. In this sense, American investors faced greater risks than their commercial brethren.

Chief example of the railroad-concession enterprise was still the famous American China Development Company. Having earlier bogged down and apparently failed in its efforts to secure the Peking-Hankow Railroad concession, the company suddenly resurrected the dead beast in early 1897, perhaps in the hope that the McKinley administration would be more helpful than its predecessor in a last-ditch effort to save the contract. But the new quest proved unavailing, and in mid-May 1897 the Chinese government

awarded the contract to a Belgian syndicate. It did so for two
reasons—or so the State Department believed. First was "the
ominous suspicion that European politics" had subverted the influence of the pro-American Director of Railroads, Sheng Taotai, and
intimidated the Chinese government. More specifically, it was
widely assumed that old tandem of Russian diplomacy and French
finance was responsible; that French bankers had gained internal
control of the Belgian group and that Russia had then used its
influence with China to "[aid] the Belgian Syndicate in securing
the Railroad contract."

Second and equally important was the recurring realization that
the American China Development Company, as before, either
could not or would not meet the contractual terms insisted upon
by the Chinese.[9] Denby in fact admitted "that our fellow citizens
failed solely because they were unwilling to accept the terms
offered by China and which have been accepted by the Belgians."
(Actually, the Belgian syndicate accepted terms even *more* strin-
gent than those proffered the American, especially on the key
issues of collateral and procurement procedures.) Nevertheless,
the American Minister tended to excuse the American group on
the grounds that the Chinese stipulations were indeed too harsh:
to wit, "low rate of interest, the absence of government guarantee
and the want of effective foreign control of construction and
management." Given the later Belgian difficulty in securing sufficient capital and gaining adequate control and security in the
company, Denby's point was, at the very least, a plausible one.[10]

The State Department, however, was not so charitable. The
general view in Washington was that railroad concessioneering in
China was an essentially speculative, non-productive venture which
potentially retarded, rather than developed, the much-needed
railroad system for the China market. Given this outlook, the
administration's inclination was to commend support of financial
enterprises in principle, while in practice withholding meaningful
aid. Denby clearly did not share this approach, so it was inevitable
that he find himself out of step with the "Home Office" drummers.

Thus, in early 1897, with McKinley barely settled in the White House, Denby found himself the unhappy recipient of a departmental reprimand for his overzealous "endorsement of the financial standing" of the American China Development Company—particularly his statement to the Chinese government that the company "was composed of men who were worth several hundred millions of taels." Hearing of this, the Secretary of State sent a curt reminder to his subordinate "that the Company is a limited liability company, with a very small capital." "The individual financial standing of the various persons composing the company has consequently, little to do with the matter."[11] Obviously, the McKinley administration, like that of Cleveland, entertained few hopes that wildcatting financial adventures (as the government viewed them) would be either very competitive or very constructive—a fact that helps to explain later reluctance to create an open door for investment as well as trade.

Unfortunately for the open door, commercial or financial, the "quiet time" of 1897 was only ephemeral in the escalating spoilation of the Chinese Empire. Economically inviting but politically unstable, China simply proved too tempting a prey, particularly to those less-advantaged European nations which could not afford an open-market situation on the Asian mainland. Thus, on November 18, 1897, Germany shattered the apparent calm by seizing Kiaochou, "an excellent port situated near the Shantung promontory." A participant in the *Dreibund* intervention of 1895, Germany had "received practically nothing" from China for her efforts, while profitable "favors . . . [had] been showered on Russia and France." Consequently, in 1896 and 1897 Germany "repeatedly demanded the cession of a port to be used as a naval depot." When such was not forthcoming, she acted aggressively and on her own. The transparent excuse offered for the Kiaochou takeover was the murder of two German missionaries, but the subsequent demands for exclusive railroad and mining rights in Shantung province,

plus the insistence on a fifty-year occupation of Kiaochou, proved
—if proof was needed—that the Kingdom of God weighed less
in the balance than the mundane aspirations of Imperial Germany.
China, too weak to resist alone and—ominously—unable to secure
any Russian help, ultimately capitulated and in the first week of
1898 formally consented to the German demands.[12]

The German action and the Shantung agreement forced agon-
izing reappraisals of China policy in almost all the great power
chanceries. Nowhere were the results more dramatic than in Russia,
where the response involved an internal power struggle which
fulfilled the widespread fears that "if Germany retains possession
of Kiaochou Russia will take [Port Arthur]."[13] In fact, Russia
decided quite early that it was in her interest to *permit* (even
encourage) Germany to realize her aims in Shantung. Led by Count
Mouraviev, the Foreign Minister, the territorial expansionists in the
Russian government persuaded the Czar that "the occupation of
Kiao-Chow . . . offered a favourable occasion . . . to seize one
of the Chinese ports, notably Port Arthur or the adjacent Ta-lieng-
wan"—ports of "enormous strategic importance." Count Witte
predictably opposed such overt, territorial absorption and continued to advocate his past policy of peaceful penetration in the
name of Chinese friendship. But Mouraviev carried the day with
his insistence that England would take Port Arthur if Russia did
not. Thus, on March 8, 1898, Denby confirmed that "Russia had
demanded the cession of Port Arthur and Talienwan" on "the same
terms which are accorded Germany." Fearful that this meant war
or partition (with the open door as prime fatality), the American
Minister urged "an energetic protest from our Government against
the dismemberment of China" in an effort to strengthen "the hands
of nations like Japan and Great Britain who are freer to act in
this contingency than we are." In the meantime, China—with little
choice—granted Russian demands for a twenty-five-year lease of
a southern Manchurian zone (twenty-three by fifty-three miles),
including the two desired ports.[14]

These German and Russian moves threatened American commercial interests in several ways. Immediately they threatened existent American trade in northern China (including Manchuria), an area that absorbed two-thirds of all American exports to China. Excepting Tientsin, most of these goods found their way into the treaty ports of Newchwang and Chefoo where they fared well in competition with European products. (In Chefoo, for example, the American Consul reported, in December 1897, that "United States exports are forcing out the English and German goods all along the line"—especially in cotton textiles and kerosene, where American exports jumped 200 to 400 per cent between 1894 and 1897.) Unfortunately, Chefoo and Newchwang fell within the German and Russian spheres respectively. This raised not only the spectre of possible tariff discrimination but the likely eventuality that American goods, moving from the port cities into the provincial market, would have to use German and Russian railroads—and perhaps pay a differential overcharge in the process.

As the *New York Times* noted, however, the more profound "interest imperiled . . . is not yet our *present* trade with all Chinese ports, but the *right* to all that trade with its *future* increase"— increase that would "become a source of great profit in the period of rapid expansion in foreign commerce upon which we are tardily entering" [italics added].[15] The "right," the "future," the permanent open door: these were the substantive things ultimately endangered, particularly if other nations, as was expected, followed the German-Russian lead and entered the partitioning scramble. If that happened the result could well be a China drawn and quartered (like Africa) into colonial bits and pieces. And America, with no natural sphere of its own, with an essentially anti-colonial ideology, with a desire to exercise its economic power in the *whole* China market and not just a slice of it, could not reasonably hope to find relief for her domestic economic problems in the frontier of Asia.

In its evolving response to the renewed Chinese crisis, the McKinley administration had to act within the framework of a number of internal forces. One of these was the pressure of special

business groups with already existing vested interests in China—
pressure which indisputably affected the timing and (perhaps)
the substance of administration policy. The chief expression of
these interests came from the Committee on American Interests
in China (later broadened into the American Asiatic Association).
Formed on the very day that China ratified the Shantung agreement, the committee numbered among its leaders the editor of the
influential *Journal of Commerce,* the chief project engineer for
the American China Development Company, a representative of
Bethlehem Iron, the president of one of the largest export-import
houses in Shanghai, and an executive in the textile-exporting firm
of Deering, Milihen and Company. Overall the committee members were interested mainly in commerce and viewed financial
concessioneering as neither profitable nor feasible. Even Clarence
Cary, who only seven months earlier, as representative of the
American China Development Company, had been trying to save
the Peking-Hankow contract, concluded by January 1898 "that
the undaunted concession-seeker" was "chasing rainbows"; that
"it seem[ed] hardly worthwhile, under existing conditions, for
foreigners to consider Chinese railway projects." Significantly,
Cary remained more optimistic about trade expansion, despite his
conviction that European powers would discriminate against it in
their new spheres. Even in March 1898, at the height of the China
crisis, he believed the situation could be stabilized if the American
government would "abandon its policy of inaction and look to
the care of our existing trade rights." Apparently his fellow committee members shared his views sufficiently to mobilize sixty-
eight business firms in support of a general petition asking for
protection of American trade against the threats of partitioning
and discrimination.[16]

Other business groups acted in similar fashion. The New York
Chamber of Commerce, for example, under prodding from the *New
York Times* and after much debate (weighing the potential profits
of the China trade against the dangers of an alliance with England), sent a petition to the administration asking for "proper

steps" for the "preservation and protection of . . . important commercial interest in [the Chinese] Empire."[17] It, in turn, served as the model for petitions from the chambers of commerce in Boston and San Francisco. Those from Philadelphia, Baltimore, and Seattle differed in wording but conveyed the same sense. The first round of petitions during the Shantung crisis was fairly vague and cautious ("too colorless" said the *New York Times*), expressing only general concern while shying away from any specific policy recommendations. The second wave of petitions, occasioned by Russian actions in Manchuria, was somewhat stronger. For instance, the New York Chamber of Commerce not only reaffirmed its original memorial but seemingly endorsed a resolution passed by the cream of American merchants in Shanghai urging "immediate action necessary to protect American interests against aggression in Northern China."[18] Throughout the crisis, leading commercial and financial journals gave fairly vigorous support. The *United States Investor* even talked of war to prevent "the door" from being "closed" on "equal trading rights." The *Commercial and Financial Chronicle* warned the administration that the possible "absorption of Manchuria in the Russian Customs area" required a "strong representation in favor of keeping open the trade on equal terms to all nations."[19]

To emphasize only business pressures, however, would distort reality by ignoring the larger, quite receptive context in which these pressures took place and which helped to make them effective. For one thing, it would ignore the interesting fact that the conservative, non-jingoistic, big city newspapers—normally regarded as quite cautious on foreign affairs questions—often matched or even surpassed the clamor of business groups in demanding strong governmental support of the open door against the dangers implicit in partitioning. In New York the *Times* denounced the German attempt "at a monopoly" as "an act of hostility . . . to all mankind." It reminded its readers, when speaking of China, that "We need no more territory," but "we must have more markets, or suffer a terrible check to our growth and prosperity";

and it wailed that "We are in a fair way to lose all and get nothing." By mid-March 1898, with the Cuban confrontation visible on the horizon, the *Times* was denouncing "the headless State Department" for its "ignorance and apathy about our commercial interest abroad" (China) and pressuring for the removal of Secretary of State John Sherman. In like fashion, its influential metropolitan competitor, the *New York Tribune*, editorialized that "commercial interests, which are now great and which promise one day to be enormous," compelled America to be "deeply involved in China." It also defined American aims as non-territorial and identified the sole national concern as keeping "Chinese markets . . . open to American traders on equal terms with the rest of the world." But the *Tribune* warned that "Treaties do not, however, automatically enforce themselves"; that "without strenuous insistence by this Government the indisputable treaty rights of the United States are likely to be ignored and violated by the more aggressive European powers." Significantly, the eastern press held no monopoly on such sentiments. The *Chicago Inter-Ocean,* musing on the possible "tenfold" increase in the China trade, advised "that this country" could not "remain quiet if the Chinese coast is to be parceled out among European powers, each with its hinterland, its 'spheres of influence' from which United States trade may be excluded." The *New Orleans Times-Picayune*, working from the premise that "A large foreign trade can be maintained only by a vigorous foreign policy," concluded that "The United States trade interests in China are immense, and they should not be allowed to slip away from us without an effort to preserve them."

Business interests also benefited from the analysis and advice offered the administration by its own "man in Peking," Charles Denby. From early December 1897 onward, his reports stressed the conviction that general partitioning would make "prohibitive duties" a certainty and "war . . . among the European powers" a possibility. His dispatch of January 31, 1898, syllogistically summarized his views most thoroughly with the major premise that "The Pacific Ocean is destined to bear on its bosom a larger commerce than the Atlantic"; the minor premise that "Partition would tend to destroy our markets"; and the conclusion that "We should not hesitate . . . to announce our disapproval of acts of brazen wrong, and spoilation, perpetrated by other nations toward China —should any such occur." Meanwhile, Charles Denby, Jr., just returned to America after a stint as First Secretary in Peking, echoed his father's reports in an article for the *North American Review*. Declaring the China market a necessity because "the productiveness of American industry has outstripped the demands of the American market," he urged that "the powers of Europe should be assured that whatever disposition they made of the land, the trade must be open to all; that no future tariffs . . . shall be allowed to discriminate against the United States."[20]

Just how much these opinions affected the substance of American policy and how much they simply reinforced the administration's own inner anxieties about the Chinese situation must remain conjectural. Certainly it is plausible to argue that business petitions, press criticism (such as the *New York Times* broadside that "none of Mr. Sherman's utterances have given the country confidence that he will protect our Chinese commerce"), and Denby's January 31 dispatch played key roles in getting the Secretary of State to abandon his seeming sanguinity about the economic implications of partitioning and to offer public assurance (before the New York Chamber of Commerce, no less) that his Department was giving "the most careful consideration of Chinese affairs." Similarly, it is credible to argue that such factors were important catalysts in determining the timing of the administration's initial inquiry to Germany about "what would be the effect on foreign trade of the lease . . . of the territory of Kiao-chou."

It is even more persuasive to argue that such business, press, and diplomatic agitation (augmented by senatorial opinion) helped McKinley change his choice of a diplomatic replacement for Charles Denby. His initial selection (made six days before the German landing in Shantung) was one Charles Page Bryan, a politician-lawyer-editor from Illinois (by way of Colorado) whose past was unmarked by any diplomatic experience. The subsequent partitioning crisis soon rendered the choice ludicrous, but the exigencies of the patronage mill led McKinley to stick by it until mid-January. By that time, however, adverse reaction was monumental. Important elements of the press, led by the *New York Times* and more especially the *Chicago Inter-Ocean,* damned the appointment on the grounds that "The crisis now maturing in China will be calculated to test the skill of the ablest and most experienced diplomatist"—"a man who would be competent to protect our great commercial interests," and Bryan simply was "not fitted by experience temperament or education" to fill the bill. Likewise, there grew "a feeling in the Senate," led by William P. Frye and Henry M. Teller, that the partitioning crisis (toward which we could not be "unconcerned spectators") required "in China one of the ablest and most experienced of public men"; that indeed "The mission to England, France, or Russia is at this time of less importance than is the Chinese mission." Finally, as a consequence of such misgivings (perhaps shared by himself), the President had the older and more experienced Edwin H. Conger, then Minister to Brazil, trade places with "the young Mr. Bryan." McKinley's move not only pleased the business interests and assuaged his critics but also revealed a bit about the relative priorities assigned to Asia and South America by the administration.

These events notwithstanding, it is highly doubtful that external pressures—business or non-business, vested or non-vested—changed the main lines of China policy in any meaningful way. It seems probable that the administration fixed its policy rather firmly in late December 1897 and thereafter held to it somewhat doggedly until the Spanish-American War provided the opportunity for change. Meeting on the day before Christmas, the President and his entire cabinet discussed the Chinese crisis at length and agreed upon the American response to it. Overall they accepted the commitment "to protect carefully all interests and privileges which the United States now enjoys in China." But in terms of actual implementation, it was agreed (as one cabinet

official was quoted) "to keep a watchful eye upon the situation as
it developed," thus postponing positive action until the intentions
of the great powers solidified. Since the meeting took place amidst
rumors of an imminent British proposal for Anglo-American support of the open door, the *New York Times* convincingly interpreted this stance of "watchful waiting" as "put[ting] an end to any
[such] possibility."[21]

What followed thereafter was perfectly consistent with these
views. On the home front Sherman sought to mollify business
anxiety with sugary comments that "our commercial interests
would not suffer" from partitioning; that, "quite the contrary,"
Kiaochou might become another entrepôt like Hong Kong, open
to all. Failing there—as business memorials and press editorials
amply demonstrate—he satisfied himself (and hopefully his listeners) with broad, unspecific declarations of concern about the
situation in China.

Abroad, the American government sought, through pointed
questioning, to divine the intentions of Germany and Russia—the
arch-practitioners of partitioning—"with respect to foreign commerce" and "foreign trade." In so doing, the State Department
placed total stress on the American need for open door trade expansion. Ambassador Andrew D. White, in his conversations with
the German government, was to make clear "the interest which this
Government must necessarily feel in conserving and expanding the
volume of trade which it has built up with China." Ambassador
Ethan A. Hitchcock, in his interview with the Russian Foreign
Minister, was to "[express] the natural interest felt by the United
States in seeing no restriction of the foreign trade of China." In
each instance the replies were, if taken at face value, fairly reassur-
ing. Foreign Minister von Bulow asserted that "the intentions of
the German Empire were entirely in accordance" with the American policy of "holding China open to foreign commerce," and he
promised "that there was no intention to close the port [Kiao-
chou]." Similarly, Russia—while closing Port Arthur on the
grounds that it was "useless as a commercial port" but vital for

"naval and military" purposes—promised not "to occupy Chinese territory, other than the ports named," and vowed not to "interfere with the trade of other nations with China." Indeed, Count Mouraviev said that Russia "would be only too glad to have foreign commerce contribute at Ta-lien-wan." In each instance the Mc-Kinley administration remained suspicious and unconvinced, and more inclined to believe its own diplomats' reports of ulterior motives by the partitioning powers. Denby, for one, warned "that Germany intends in the future to exercise some special influence over Chefoo," while Ambassador John Hay in London went even further in talking of "an understanding between Russia, France and Germany to exclude as far as possible, the trade of England and America from the Far East, and to divide and reduce China to a system of tributary provinces."[22]

But practically the administration had neither the inclination nor the capacity to go beyond diplomatic dialogue in sustaining the open door against suspected subversion. There remained the lingering hope that Great Britain, perhaps aided by Japan, might use its power and influence in the Far East to halt or retard the apparent disintegration of China. But hope was one thing, certitude quite another. John Hay and his staff—good Anglophiles all—were totally convinced that the British were "clear and energetic on the China policy" and would support the "open door" by war if necessary. Denby, however, dismissed British "support for treaty rights" as little more than "grandiloquent declaration as to what she would do," and offered the contrary prediction that she would ultimately join the partitioning and convert the entire Yangtze Valley into her own sphere. McKinley, torn by such conflicting reports, rigorously followed daily press accounts of the China policy debates in the House of Commons—and waited.

In fact, British attitudes on the Chinese crisis were enormously ambivalent. The inclination of some "Home Office" officials to accept the inevitable and join partitioning was offset in part by the still vigorous support of the open door by those with special business interests throughout China. As a consequence, British policy vacillated wildly between these two approaches. Generally, the first steps reflected the division-of-spheres thinking. For one thing, England sought to protect and expand her own interests by pressuring China for the third indemnity loan award, a railroad concession from Burma to the Yangtze, the opening of three new treaty ports, the right of steam navigation on inland waters, and a non-alienation pledge for the Yangtze Valley. At the same time, she sought a general rapprochement with Russia on the basis of "a partition of preponderance" in all areas of Anglo-Russian competition—China and Turkey especially, but Persia and Africa as well. But Russia was apparently not interested. Her insistence that any agreement be limited to China made it clear that the British would give more than they received. Moreover, in China itself Russia worked hard and successfully to block a direct British government loan to China for the third indemnity payment. In the end the British got only an indirect and partial share as the Chinese gave the award to the same private, Anglo-German corporation that had financed the second loan. And worse, both Russia and France used even that as an excuse for additional concessions for themselves.[23]

Rebuffed by the Russians, the British government, led by Colonial Secretary Joseph Chamberlain, reversed policies in midstream and returned to the traditional "open door" policy; but only (and there was the catch) if the United States or Germany, or both would "stand with us in our China policy." Forewarned of the move, Henry White, the American Chargé d'Affaires in London, informed the State Department to expect "overtures" for cooperative American support for equal trading rights—though he wrongly assumed the request would be limited to German encroachments in the Yangtze Valley. In fact, the "overture" (which arrived on March 8) went much further and asked "whether the United States would be prepared to join with Great Britain in opposing" either "preferential treatment" to foreign lessees or "the actual cessions of portions of the Chinese littoral."

The British inquiry was necessarily futile. For one thing, the

American government was already committed to postponing action of any sort until faced with an overt effort at trade discrimination. Since, as the American reply noted, "there has been no occupation up to this time which proposes . . . to close the Chinese trade to the civilized world or to obtain exclusive commercial privileges," there seemed no pressing reason to give the British a blank check to be filled out and cashed at some future time and at their discretion. Moreover, even if the administration had been so inclined, it lacked the capacity to give the British any substantive help. Already on a collision course with Spain over the Cuban revolution, and totally without a power base of its own in the western Pacific, the United States could offer "Brother Jonathan" only the soothing words that "the President has not been unmindful of the situation in China" and "is in sympathy with the policy which shall maintain open trade" there.[24] Finally, even had America had the capacity for dynamic action in Asia, it was unlikely (as it had been in 1895 and would be in 1900) to use it in conjunction with the British, save perhaps informally and for limited ends. For McKinley, as for Cleveland, the open door was a means of avoiding conflict, not creating it; a means of acquiring the economic fruits of empire without *extensive* political-military responsibilities and burdens. Accepting the British proposal would have cut across the whole grain of this orientation and involved America potentially in a dangerous polarization of power camps in the Far East. Better, thought McKinley, to maintain American freedom of action in the face of an uncertain future; better, so he told the British, to retain "traditional policy respecting foreign alliances and as far as practicable avoiding interference or connection with European complications."[25]

Rejected by the Americans (and the Germans as well), England sought to put herself in a military-political position to defend the open door with force, if such seemed desirable, or effectively take part in partitioning, if such proved necessary. Thus she demanded and received a lease of the coast city of Wei-Hai-Wei—not for exclusive commercial privileges but as a military counterpoise to

Russian power in the Gulf of Pechihli. Subsequently, and partly in response to French moves, Britain received an extension at Hong Kong (again for military rather than commercial purposes), a railroad concession from Nanking to Shanghai, and a non-alienation pledge for Yunnan and Kwangtung provinces. None of these moves, though, fully validated Denby's conclusion that England had been "driven by the logic of events to seize her share of the spoils of this empire."[26] They made that course an easier one to fulfill in the future if Great Britain determined upon it, but for the moment she avoided the German and Russian mode of exercising potentially exclusive control over important treaty ports, such as Chefoo and Newchwang.

Whatever the intent of British moves, they did raise (as Denby lamented) the distinct possibility of "a complete partition of China" —certainly a death-dealing development to "[American] interests." For one thing, they gave France an excuse (if one was needed) to exact from China a ninety-nine-year lease of Kuang-chow-wan Bay, a non-alienation pledge for Hainan Island and the four border provinces near Tongking, a concession for a Tongking-Yunnan railroad, and appointment of a Frenchman as head of the Chinese Postal Services. Likewise, England's actions required her to pay a price for German and Japanese acquiescence, since both nations had long-standing interests in Wei-Hai-Wei. (Indeed, Japan still occupied it in 1898 when England obtained the lease.) Germany received a British promise not to contest German rights in Shantung, particularly not to seek railroad concessions from Wei-Hai-Wei across the German sphere. Japan obtained a blanket British promise of support for any Japanese attempt—at any future time and at any place—to secure a similar lease on the Chinese mainland. The quick result was a Chinese non-alienation pledge for Fukien province. At the same time, Japan won yet another prize from Russia, presumably for accepting the Russian sphere in southern Manchuria and for temporarily easing Russian fears of an Anglo-Japanese alliance. That reward, the Rosen-Nissi convention of April 25, 1898, acknowledged Japan's economic preponder-

ance in Korea (Russia promised "not to impede the development
of commercial and industrial relations between Japan and Korea")
and bilaterally recognized the independence of that country—thus
removing her from her past status as a Chinese client-state and
opening her to the exploitation of others. Russia, however, did
secure the mutual right to send military and financial advisers into
Korea—with Japanese consent. It was not all Japan sought, but it
would do for the time being.[27]

These frenzied developments did not, of course, constitute the
"complete partition of China." Territorially, the so-called partitioning efforts of England, France, and Japan were less concrete
and more limited than the earlier moves of Germany and Russia.
Chiefly, with some obvious exceptions, they created optional
spheres (via non-alienation pledges)—to be picked up *when* and
*if* it seemed necessary or desirable. Nevertheless, it was apparent
that one spark could change the fluid situation instantaneously;
that if Germany or Russia made an overt attempt at trade discrimination in their spheres, one of two things would quickly
happen: either there would be a war (which no one wanted and
all feared), or the optional spheres would be converted to real
ones. Under these circumstances, the "Sick Man of Asia" seemed
indeed on his deathbed, and his threatened demise promised a
similar fate for the American hope of an open door frontier in the
Celestial Empire.

Little wonder, then, that the McKinley administration found
itself, by the spring of 1898, viewing the Chinese problem with a
critical attention second only to that of the Cuban issue. Still,
the concern produced only the same watchful waiting that had
characterized American policy since late 1897. Increasingly preoccupied with Cuba, the United States lacked the commercial-
military bases in the Pacific necessary, in the Mahanite thinking
of the day, to implement a more affirmative economic and diplomatic policy—one that would (as Denby stated in early 1898) pre-

serve equal commercial "access" and "the autonomy of China" in the hope of "an immense development of trade."[28] Fortuitously perhaps, the war with Spain was soon to eliminate these obstacles and give the McKinley administration a freer and stronger hand in responding to the crisis in China.

# ⊗ Chapter IV: *A Dose of Insular Imperialism*

> "Territorial expansion, in fact, has been but an incident of the commercial expansion. . . . The recent acquisitions are but outposts of our future trade, and their chief importance consists not in their own resources or capabilities, but in their unquestionable value as gateways for the development of commercial intercourse with . . . the Far East."
>
> —*Frederic Emory,* 1899[1]

American policy in the Pacific, immediately before and during the war with Spain, wrote the final ending to the "Cobdenized" expansionism that had flourished under Grover Cleveland. The new approach was significantly different. To be sure, Cleveland's "free-trade imperialism" and McKinley's "pragmatic expansionism" shared in common a great deal of intellectual real estate. Both accepted the industrial overproduction analysis and the corollary commitment to marketplace expansionism. Both opposed formal, administrative colonialism in heavily populated, major market areas (such as China), regarding it as materially and spiritually too burdensome for the potential rewards involved. Instead, both chose commercial open doors over closed colonies or spheres of influence.

Both accepted (with some reluctance on Cleveland's part) the government's responsibility to act energetically to open new doors and prevent old ones from being closed. Both favored an isthmian canal as America's shortcut to Pacific markets. Both favored a better consular service to aid and advise American businessmen abroad. Both favored an enlarged battleship Navy to keep the main trade routes open. Both favored tariff revision (whether freer trade or reciprocity) to stimulate the export trade.

Yet for all these important points of identity, the McKinley era marked an important change in the tone and tactics of American expansionism—a change characterized by a more non-ideological, pragmatic approach; by more utilitarian, businesslike methods of doing a necessary job efficiently, but at the least possible cost. McKinley's policies were, in other words, essentially those of "pragmatic expansionism."

Specifically, the most obvious and vital difference centered on the question of insular imperialism. Among Democrats of the Cleveland ilk (as with Republicans of the Carl Schurz variety) anti-colonialism was an article of faith. Cleveland's rejection of Hawaiian annexation in 1893 and his later opposition to retention of the Philippines bore witness to that. But to Republicans like Mc-Kinley, weaned on the recent heritage of Seward, Grant, and Blaine, anti-colonialism was relative rather than absolute. One's right hand might affirm it in continental market areas, while one's left hand qualified it with a limited dose of "insular imperialism" in islands and enclaves that were potentially useful as strategic stepping-stones to those very same market areas. Such pragmatic niceties reflected the perceived realities that rapid communications necessitated oceanic cables and cable relay points; that an enlarged Navy demanded operational bases; that market penetration could be facilitated by nearby possessions; that steam technology required coaling stations. (As the *New York Tribune* put it in March 1898, "COAL IS KING"—a fact that "The United States has begun to consider . . ." apparently in relationship to "Chinese waters.")[2] In the Pacific, Seward's purchase of the Aleutians and the occupation of Midway Island, Harrison's attempt to annex Hawaii, and McKinley's revival of that project in 1897 and again in early 1898 all manifested a conscious, rational effort to foster and protect American trade in an "open" Asia through effective control of the Kiska-Honolulu axis (an early nineteenth-century geopolitical idea of Russian origin).

Analyzed against this backdrop, America's insular acquisitions of 1898 were not products of "large policy" imperialism. Hawaii, Wake, Guam, and the Philippines were not taken principally for their own economic worth, or for their fulfillment of Manifest Destiny, or for their venting of the "psychic crisis." They were obtained, instead, largely in an eclectic effort to construct a system of coaling, cable, and naval stations for an integrated trade route which could help realize America's overriding ambition in the Pacific—the penetration and ultimate domination of the fabled China market.

From the very beginning of the Spanish-American War, the McKinley administration intended to retain a foothold in the Philippines as an "American Hong Kong," a commercial entrepôt to the China market and a center of American military power. Formulation of this policy commitment began seven months before hostilities with Spain, when McKinley examined a Navy Department memorandum written by Assistant Secretary Theodore Roosevelt. This multipurpose paper made one especially bold suggestion: in the event of war with Spain, the Asiatic Squadron "should blockade, and if possible take Manila." Historical myth notwithstanding, it was a suggestion that fell on already prepared ground, for the influential Senator from Connecticut, Orville Platt, had earlier taken pains to impress upon the President "that Manila had become one of the most important ports of the Orient and that the importance of that station demanded most careful attention."

Temporarily put in abeyance by a short-lived détente with Spain in late 1897, the proposal was revived and made the basis of

Roosevelt's famous February 25 orders instructing Commodore George Dewey to "start offensive operations in the Philippines" after eliminating the Spanish fleet. The view that this was simply a conspiratorial effort by "large policy" extremists misses two more significant facts: first, Roosevelt's superiors accepted his orders for the Philippine operations even though they unceremoniously countermanded nearly two-thirds of the other miscellaneous orders issued concurrently by the Assistant Secretary; second, the administration had already accepted the substance of Dewey's orders in principle and thereafter permitted the Naval War Board to incorporate the February 25 orders into overall strategy plans for the Pacific. Clearly, while Roosevelt's actions may have been precipitate, they fell within the main lines of the "large policies" of the administration. Of these, Roosevelt, as he privately admitted, was largely "ignorant."[3]

With the outbreak of war the McKinley administration rushed (with almost unseemly haste) to implement its designs upon the likeliest entrepôt, Manila, by determining to send an army of occupation to the Philippine capital. It made this decision on May 2 *before* fully credible news of Dewey's victory at Manila Bay reached Washington and it formally issued the call for Philippine volunteers on May 4, three days *before* an anxious, jittery Secretary of the Navy received authoritative word that the Asiatic Squadron was safe—not immobilized by heavy damages, as he feared. The size of the Army force was to be "not less than twenty thousand men"—quadruple the number recommended by Dewey "to retain [Manila] and thus control the Philippine Islands." It was a move that confirmed Roosevelt in his belief that "the Administration is now fully committed to the large policy." It also persuaded the *San Francisco Chronicle,* on May 4, to splash across its front page the prophetic headline: "WE WILL HOLD THE PHILIPPINES."

On May 11, in one of the most important (and overlooked) decision-making sessions in American history, McKinley and his cabinet gave definite form to their war aims in the Pacific by approving a State Department memorandum calling for Spanish cession to the United States of a suitable "coaling station," presumably Manila. The islands as a whole, however, were to remain with Spain. Acting within the framework of this decision, McKinley on May 19 endowed the commander of the expeditionary force with sufficiently broad powers to effect "the severance of the former political relations of the inhabitants and the establishment of a new political power." Simultaneously, he instructed his Secretary of the Treasury to undertake a study of the islands with an eye "to substitut[ing] new rates and new taxes for those now levied in the Philippines." The stated purpose of both orders, as well as a similar one to Dewey (which he was to "interpret . . . liberally"), was to [give] to the islands, while in the possession of the United States, that order and security which they have long since ceased to enjoy." Shortly thereafter, on June 3, when it became apparent that the great distance between Manila and Honolulu demanded an intermediate coaling and cable station, the President broadened the American position to include "an island in the Ladrones" (Marianas). The choice made was Guam, and the United States Navy promptly seized it.[4]

As of early June, then, the administration envisioned postwar control only of Manila and Guam as way stations to the orient. But dramatic events swiftly undercut this limited resolve and for a critical fortnight set American policy aimlessly adrift. First of all, as the State Department itself noted, the emergence of the Philippine "insurgents" as "an important factor" made it increasingly doubtful that the islands—minus Manila—could be returned to effective Spanish sovereignty. What then—bestow the largess of Philippine independence but with the stipulation of American control in Manila? Certainly it was within American power to impose such a solution upon the insurgents, by force if necessary. Moreover, the revolutionaries might even have accepted it peacefully, especially since they themselves had offered (as far back as November 1897) to turn over "two provinces and the Custom House at Manila" in exchange for an alliance against Spain (though theoretically these would not be permanent cessions but simply collateral pledges against eventual Filipino repayment for American aid). Nevertheless, relinquishing the rest of the islands ran counter to the administration belief that "if we evacuate, anarchy rules"; that (as Dewey later noted) "The natives appear unable to govern."

This presumption that an independent Philippines would be strife-ridden and unstable raised, in turn, the most frightening spectre of all: European intervention, especially by Germany, who considered herself heir-apparent to Spain's insular empire in the Pacific. Actually, the threat was not to American designs on Manila —notwithstanding the Continental feeling that an American foothold in the islands would "complicate the Eastern Question" or the seemingly hostile presence of the German squadron in Manila harbor. Given Germany's diplomatic isolation, Europe's divisiveness, and England's pro-American stance, there was little likelihood of another 1895-type intercession to deprive the victor of his spoils.[5] Germany herself made this clear on several fronts by mid-July. In Berlin one high-ranking German official assured Ambassador White "that Germany does not want large annexations and could not afford to take the Philippine Islands if they were offered her." And in London the German Ambassador told Hay that his government had "no disposition to interfere with, or deprive [the United States] of [her] rights of conquest in any direction." It was on the basis of this and other collaborating evidence that Hay advised the President that he could "now make war or make peace without danger of disturbing the equilibrium of the world."[6]

The real and continuing danger was German intervention against a weak, fledgling republic that might well render the isolated American position in Manila more vulnerable than useful. *This* was no chimera! By mid-June, Andrew White had already confirmed what the State Department feared: that Germany would use the expected "anarchy, confusion and insecurity under a 'Philippine Republic'" as an excuse "to secure a stronghold and centre of influence in that region." Less than a month later, Germany informed White (and Hay as well) that she expected "a few coaling stations" and "a naval base" in the Philippines (not to mention control of the Carolines and "predominant" influence in Samoa). Nor did the passage of time and the solidification of American intentions eliminate such German ambitions. Even after the armistice with Spain, rumors flowed freely that Germany still sought "the Sulu islands" in the southern Philippines—rumors given great credence by Assistant Secretary of State John Bassett Moore. And in late October the State Department continued to receive "trustworthy information" that if the United States failed to take all the Philippines, Germany has "every intention to establish a foothold there."[7]

Rival intervention or nationalistic revolution: either could undermine American plans for Manila. Unable to decide on a course of action, American policy lay momentarily immobilized—at a time when the growing crisis in China itself least afforded the luxury of prolonged indecision. On the one hand, intensified rumors that Russia would close Talienwan to foreign commerce and that she regarded her southern Manchurian leases as "integral portions of Russian territory" weakened the already shaky underpinnings of the open door in that key commercial area. At the same time England's extension of her Hong Kong settlement and her monopolistic approach to Yangtze Valley developments seemed to indicate that nation's growing estrangement from her traditional open door approach, and threatened to leave American policy in China diplomatically isolated.[8] In this deteriorating framework, any sustained impasse over Philippine policy incurred the risk of letting American hopes in China go by default. Against the formidable hosts of Philippine insurgency, German antagonism, and crisis in China, the limited American policy commitment of June 3 (for Manila and Guam) seemed an ineffectual one indeed. Realizing the situation, the McKinley administration in mid-June made a determined effort to break the bind by initiating three dramatic and interrelated moves in Hawaii, China, and the Philippines, designed to increase American influence and leverage in the western Pacific.

On June 11, 1898, the administration once more reactivated the

sagging debate on Hawaiian annexation. First proposed by Mc-
Kinley a year earlier, that venture had floundered amidst diplomatic complications with Japan—complications that produced in
Navy circles much anxiety as well as grand proposals for naval
construction, but which elicited from most administration officials
the calmer conviction that firmness, candor, and patience would
resolve matters satisfactorily. (Even Roosevelt, for all his agitation
about "the Japs . . . feeling decidedly ugly about Hawaii," was
"very sure their feelings will not take any tangible form.") When
American diplomacy did successfully hurdle the Japanese obstacle,
the administration revived the project and placed an annexationist
treaty before the Senate in early 1898. There the partitioning crisis
in China proved to be *nearly* decisive, as sentiment grew (in the
words of Senator Frye) "that the state of affairs in China makes the
annexation of Hawaii to the United States a necessity." Nevertheless, the treaty barely failed of the necessary two-thirds ratification,
apparently killing any prospects of annexation for at least a year.[9]

By early June, however, the Philippine question and the general Far Eastern situation made it both propitious and imperative
that the Hawaiian project be revived in the hope of strengthening America's hand in the Pacific basin (on the long-standing
belief held by Mahan and many Americans that Hawaii was the
key to "commercial and military control of the Pacific").[10] The
ensuing debate on the joint congressional resolution was something of a dress rehearsal for the "great debate" that lay seven
months ahead. It was predicated clearly on the assumption that
passage of the Hawaiian annexation resolution made retention of
the Philippines both possible and likely, while a defeat might
foreshadow a similar fate for any territorial aspirations in the
oriental archipelago. Congressman William Alden Smith made
these and other links explicit with his statement, "If we will take
the Hawaiian Islands, hold on to the Phillipines, and cultivate
good neighborship with the Orient, to which they are the key, the
expansion of our commerce will be augmented a thousandfold."[11]

In the actual debate, administration spokesmen hammered the

same theme: "we must have Hawaii to help us get our share of China." America needed Hawaii not only for its own economic or cultural worth but also for its commercial and military value as a stepping-stone to the China market. The influential Iowa Representative, William P. Hepburn, captured the theme best when he declared: "I can distinguish between a colonial policy and a commercial policy. I can distinguish between the policy that would scatter colonies all over the islands of the sea and the lands of the earth and that policy which would secure to us simply those facilities of commerce that the new commercial methods make absolutely essential."

Other annexationists offered their own variations. Hawaii, they exclaimed, would give the United States "strategic control of the North Pacific"; "a permanent share in the mighty commerce which beats its wings in the waves of the broad Pacific"; "this half-way house to the great markets of the East"; "a harbor which will enable us to protect with our fleet our commerce in the Far East"; and a necessary "crossroads" for "our rapidly increasing commerce with the mighty hordes with whom we shall trade . . . across the Pacific." Even former opponents of annexation found such ideas persuasive. For example, Frederick H. Gillett, Republican Representative from Massachusetts, who earlier regarded Hawaii as "useless and unnecessary," now defined it as "our essential stepping-stone and base." And why? Simply because the triumph at Manila had given the United States the potential capacity to retard the "partitioning . . . in that vast and populous East, which is just entering into the commercial current of the world." Such expressions were mainly Republican (often midwestern), but a few Democrats and one Populist helped to swell the chorus.

Strikingly, even the opposition accepted the annexationists' chief premise that America needed commercial expansion into Asia. As one Democratic opponent on the House Foreign Affairs Committee put it, he favored "as earnestly as any man can the legitimate extension of our commerce"; nor was he "unmindful that the excessive production of our fields and factories must have

an outlet." Some even admitted the modern necessity of com-
mercial-military bases as accoutrements to marketplace expansionism, but they argued that the Pearl Harbor lease of 1886 and
the Kiska holding in the Aleutians already gave "all the advantages, everything required." Most, however, stressed the laissez-
faire, free-trade approach that "commercial expansion" could
best be realized "by competition of quality and price," not by
"annexation of territory"; in the words of the Minority Report
of the House Foreign Affairs Committee: "Political dominion
over the islands is not commercially necessary." But the point did
not carry. On June 15 the House passed the annexation resolution
by an overwhelming vote, 209 to 91. Three weeks later, after
redundant and one-sided discussion (annexationists remained
silent to hurry the process), the Senate affirmed the measure by a
similar ratio.[12] Thus, on July 8, with McKinley's signature, America acquired her halfway house to the Philippines and China.
The acquisition followed by only four days the American occupation of Wake Island, a move intended to meet the technological
necessities of an additional cable base between Hawaii and Guam.

Synchronous with the push on Hawaiian annexation, the administration initiated the first step in an American economic
offensive in China itself by proposing a government commission
to China to recommend measures for trade expansion. Secretary
of State William R. Day's supporting letter to Congress made it
pointedly clear that an industrial production "of large excess over
home consumption" demanded "an enlargement of foreign markets." He also made clear his conviction that "American goods
have reached a point of excellence" which made fulfillment of
that demand quite feasible. Analyzing the world market situation, he concluded that underdeveloped areas offered the best
export outlets and that "nowhere is this consideration of more
interest than in its relation to the Chinese Empire." Aware that "the
partition of commercial facilities" in China threatened America's
"important interests," the Secretary still contended that "the
United States . . . is in a position to invite the most favorable concessions to its industries and trade . . . provided the conditions

are thoroughly understood and proper advantage is taken of the present situation."

Congress failed to appropriate the necessary monies for the China commercial commission—as it would again fail in 1899 and 1900. But the chief reason was most revealing. Most who opposed the measure did so because they considered such one-shot missions to be ineffectual and an inadequate substitute for a thoroughgoing reform of our consular representative in China (and elsewhere as well). Nevertheless, the administration proposal— when coupled with subsequent prodding of Minister Conger to gain more "Precise knowledge . . . of the large and grave questions of commercial intercourse," and with intensive questioning of American consuls as to specific means to expand the China trade—served clear notice of American intent to take "proper advantage . . . of the present situation" in order to play a more active role in China.[13]

Simultaneously, on June 14 the administration capped its trio of dramatic moves by shelving the earlier decision to return the Philippines to Spain, thus opening the disposition of the islands to further examination. Thereafter, despite uneasiness over increased military and administrative burdens, there began a progressive redefinition of the desired area of American sovereignty: from Manila, to Luzon, and finally to the entire group. Significantly, this redefinition involved no real change in the focus of political power; those who influenced and made policy in June 1898 still did so at year's end. What changed was men's minds. As the powerful Mark Hanna put it, from the vantage point of late September, "conservative, far-seeing and thinking men in this country" who initially favored only retention of "a naval base and coaling station" were, "for the most part," the "same men . . . advocating the termination of Spanish rule in the whole group." It was an apt generalization that nicely mirrored the whole transformation of attitudes among the "pragamtic expansionists"—whether in Hanna's own mind, the editorial pages of the *Chicago Inter-Ocean*, or the foreign policy of William McKinley.[14]

For two months after the June 14 shift, American policy re-

116                                    CHINA  MARKET

mained seemingly ambivalent on the vexing problem of what to
retain in the Philippines. Even the armistice agreement of August
appeared to beg the question by reserving the issue of "control,
disposition, and government" for final peace negotiations. But the
ambiguity was more apparent than real. Spain certainly sensed
this and regarded the terms (especially in their original wording)
as clear indication that "the United States intends to take the
Philippine Islands group."[15] McKinley's refusal to entertain a
Spanish proposal to cede only "a station or commercial base"
simply confirmed this view. So did his initial evasiveness and his
final out-of-hand rejection of repeated Spanish efforts to secure (in
the President's words) "inadmissable reservations" to the effect
that peace negotiations would consider only the problem of "administrative reforms," without questioning the "permanent sovereignty of Spain" in the Philippines. Failing at every such corner,
Spain could only wait for the "veiled . . . intentions of the federal
government" to reveal themselves in their anticipated fullness.[16]

McKinley's own cabinet already knew what Spain only feared.
Confronted with a nearly even, three-way split between departmental secretaries (Manila, Luzon, or the whole prize?), the
President—in the calculating but affable manner that was his
trademark—simply maneuvered his subordinates into accepting a
position he had already predetermined. The policy glossed over
internal differences; gave him the flexibility to move in whatever
direction changing circumstances might dictate; and allowed him
the time and opportunity both to test and educate public opinion.
In the process he crushed a move headed by "Judge Day" (and
backed by the Secretaries of the Treasury and the Navy) to limit
American commitment to "a hitching-post," simply by declining to
put the proposal to a vote. (". . . I was afraid it would carry," he
said, only half-facetiously.) In sealing this extremity, he left open
only the question of how far to journey toward the other—Luzon
or the entire group? The beginning of the final peace negotiations in
early October found this question still unresolved. While the American commissioners were instructed to demand only Luzon, they
were also to "accumulate all possible information" on the possible

necessity of controlling the whole archipelago. And since three of the five commissioners already favored the latter possibility publicly, it seemed likely that the information accumulated would lend itself to their interpretation. Whatever, less than a month later, on October 25, McKinley himself finally cut the knot by broadening his instructions to include all the Philippines.[17]

In this evolution of Philippine policy, America's commercial stake in China played the primary role in the thinking of the business and government elite that chiefly shaped and supported McKinley's decisions. It also played a significant, though not paramount, part in the outlook of the military advisers who exercised a more limited but still crucial influence upon the President's policies.

Between June and October, economic and political leaders united vigorously in support of retaining all or a large part of the Philippines. But they de-emphasized the intrinsic worth of the islands and stressed instead their strategic relationship to China—both as a commercial stepping-stone and a political-military lever. Moreover, they increasingly affirmed that Manila alone would not suffice for these purposes, that the United States would have to take Luzon and perhaps the whole group. In part this support for enlarged control reflected the already pervasive fear that native revolution or European penetration might undermine the viability of American power in Manila. But it also indicated a growing belief, born of newly accumulated information, that the economic interdependence of the archipelago made efficient division most difficult. Charles H. Cramp, that reknowned Philadelphia shipbuilder, aptly illustrated the impact of all these factors upon influential Americans when he asserted: "[Manila] is the emporium and the capital of the Philippines . . . and it exists because of that fact. . . . Can anyone suppose that with Manila in our hands and the rest of the Philippine territory under any other Government, that city would be of any value?"[18]

In the business world many associations, journals, and prominent individuals accepted and propagated the analysis that commercial ambitions in China *demanded* American control in the Philippines. Led by the NAM and the American Asiatic Association, special business organizations urged retention of the islands "for the protection and furtherance of the commercial interests of our citizens in the Far East." In a survey of the trade journals of the country, the *Chicago Inter-Ocean* found it "remarkable with what unanimity they have advocated the retention of the Philippines." Even more remarkable was the unanimity of their reasoning: that (in the words of the *Insurance Advocate*) it would encourage "the teeming millions of the Middle Kingdom" to "buy largely from us"; that with "one-third of the human race within easy distance of us, coaling stations on the road, and Manila as the Hong Kong of Uncle Sam's alert and keen merchant trader," the result was preordained. Finally, save for a few prominent dissenters like Andrew Carnegie and Chauncey Depew, McKinley's many personal friends in the corporate world espoused similar viewpoints.[19] Typical in both its analysis and conclusion was the advice of Irving M. Scott, manager of the Union Iron Works, that America needed the Philippines as "a point of observation at or near the centre of activity." Predicting that "the world is ours commercially" if the United States preserved peace and the open door, Scott urged that "the implements must be on hand, the position must be secured, and a vigilant watch kept on every encroachment." He noted that "the first move has been made in China" and concluded that "nothing has so effectually stopped it as the occupation of Manila."

Most of McKinley's close associates in the federal government (many of whom were themselves products of the business community) pressed similar views upon their chief. There were exceptions, of course. Worthington C. Ford, head of the Bureau of Statistics, appeared to feel (like former Minister to China George F. Seward) that "*We do not want the Philippines at any price or under any circumstances.*" A few others like Judge Day held largely to the position (as Carl Schurz summarized it for the

President) that "all desirable commercial facilities" and "all naval stations needed could be secured without the annexation of populous territories," without "dangerous political entanglements and responsibilities." But most thought and counseled otherwise. The redoubtable Mark Hanna, State Department economic expert Frederic Emory, Charles Denby and his successor Edwin Conger, Comptroller of the Currency Charles G. Dawes, Assistant Secretary of the Treasury Frank A. Vanderlip, to name a few, all shared in general the conviction (as Vanderlip stated) that an American-controlled Philippines would be "pickets of the Pacific, standing guard at the entrances to trade with the millions of China and Korea, French Indo-China, the Malay Peninsula, and the islands of Indonesia." By October, McKinley's cabinet—led by his new Secretary of State, John Hay—was nearly as one in voicing that sentiment. Like Hanna two months earlier, they had apparently decided that "we can and will take a large share of the commerce of Asia . . . and it is better to strike for it while the iron is hot." Likewise, the dominant triumvirate on the peace commission —Whitelaw Reid, Cushman K. Davis, and William P. Frye—primarily saw "the great importance of the Philippines with reference to trade in China" and predicted that "if to [Hawaii] we now added the Philippines, it would be possible for American energy to . . . ultimately convert the Pacific Ocean into an American Lake."

Exerting a more narrow influence upon McKinley's Philippine policy was a third group, the military. In general the President's military advisers shared the widespread concern over the strategic relationship of the archipelago to the Asian mainland. Yet, attracted by the siren's call of *imperium* (in which they would play a prominent role), many military spokesmen also promoted retention of the Philippines as the first step toward an expansive territorial imperialism. These hopes were dashed as McKinley refused to heed their advice for a general American advance into Micronesia and the islands of the South China Sea. But military advice could claim one significant result: it resolved the President's

ambivalence (shared by the business and government elite) between taking Luzon or the entire group by convincing him that the
islands were an indivisible entity; that strategically and economically they were interdependent and inseparable. Especially
persuasive were the lengthy and articulate reports of Commander
R. B. Bradford and General Francis V. Greene. Coming in late
September and early October, they were a decisive factor in
broadening McKinley's instructions.[20]

The great repute of these business and government groups,
coupled with their ready access to a like-minded Chief Executive,
gave much weight to their contention (shared in part by the military) that American interests in China necessitated American
sovereignty in the Philippines. But this view gained a powerful
ally in the twin crisis in China itself during the fall of 1898. One
side of the crisis was intensified partitioning of railroad concessions by the European powers. Explicit British modification of
the open door by Acting Foreign Secretary Lord Balfour ("a concession must be given to someone, and when someone has got it,
other people must be excluded . . ."), and the Anglo-German
railroad accord of September delineating exclusive concessions
spheres in the Yangtze and Shantung areas respectively, both confirmed beyond doubt that the open door had no current relevance
to the world of railroad investments. From the McKinley administration's point of view, none of this helped American economic
interests. True, it caused no consternation about the immediate
future of American railroad investments, for the government still
regarded such concessioneering (with some justification) as both
inept and speculative. (For example, the State Department refused to protect the American China Development Company's
newly acquired Hankow-Canton concession against "prejudice
from foreign . . . interference," and it declined to support the company's half-interest option agreement with the British and China
Corporation as "a binding engagement upon the imperial Chinese
Government.")[21] But the carving out of railroad spheres did
further threaten the important American export trade by requiring

American goods to travel from treaty port to market over European railroads. And as noted before, the prospect was not inviting, for these products might well encounter railroad rate discrimination which would render them less competitive.

Meanwhile, America's economic dreams faced another menace from a different quarter in China. In September 1898 a successful *coup d'état* by conservative, anti-foreign elements, headed by the Empress Dowager, managed to crush the pro-Western reform party surrounding the young Chinese Emperor. The new government immediately initiated administrative measures viewed by the United States as inimical to "commercial development" and the "pendulum of progress." Not only did conservative forces fail to control anti-foreign uprisings inspired by their own *putsch*, but Chinese troops and militiamen joined in them. Centered along projected Manchurian railroads, the violent demonstrations offered Russia an excuse for intervention to save her great railroad interests. The mere suggestion of such a prospect was sufficient to conjure up visions of a further fragmented China and a vitiated open door. Indeed, it probably explains the speed with which the McKinley administration met Conger's urgent request for gunboats and Marines. (The reinforcements came—and quickly— from Manila, offering an early illustration of the uses to which the Philippines could be put.)

These developments in China spawned first alarm, then action in Washington. The first move came in September with official renewal of inquiries to Russia and Germany concerning foreign trade policies in their spheres. Germany's replies seemed satisfactory and her action in opening Kiaochou as a "free port" even more so. But Russian refusal to give any "details of the completed lease" and her admission that she had not "as yet fully decided upon the administrative regulation" on foreign trade appeared to be foreboding retreats from earlier positions. State Department concern was translated in October into favorable action upon a textile industry petition concerning the Russian threat in China. Noting that half of America's cotton textile exports to China went to

Russian-dominated areas, the petitioners demanded a "vigorous policy" to prevent "these markets" from being "eventually closed to our trade." Immediately the Department responded by instructing its embassy in St. Petersburg to "use every opportunity to act energetically" against Russian adoption of discriminatory trade policies in Manchuria.[22] Quite obviously, the American government regarded the crises in China as dangerous enough to warrant substantial reaction, and as further argument for control of the Philippines.

There can be no doubt that the Chinese question, illuminated by the opinions of business, government, and the military and by the growing crises in China, had a progressive impact upon the shaping of America's Philippine policy.[23] Nowhere is this more dramatically apparent than in the private, candid, and lengthy exchange between McKinley and his peace commissioners at a White House meeting on September 16. The President, speaking somberly and with none of his frequent evasiveness, explained his reasons for retaining all or part of the islands. Almost all of them were negative, embraced with obvious reluctance. The *only* positive and assertive determinant was his conviction that "our tenure in the Philippines" offered the "commercial opportunity" to maintain the open door, a policy which McKinley defined as "no advantages in the Orient which are not common to all." "Asking only the open door for ourselves," he told his commissioners, "we are ready to accord the open door to others." Explaining further, he made it clear that retention of the Philippines was no first step in an orgy of imperialism and jingoism, but simply a limited though important accoutrement to commercial expansion. "The commercial opportunity . . . associated with this opening," he declared, "depends less on large territorial possessions than upon an adequate commercial basis and upon broad and equal privileges."[24]

This last statement was more than mere rhetoric, and nothing proved it more than the President's policy in Micronesia during the last stages of peace negotiations with Spain. Acting on the advice of the Pacific Cable Company that Wake Island had certain technical drawbacks, the administration instructed its peace commissioners to negotiate for the purchase of "one of the Caroline Islands"—preferably Ualan (Kusaie)—"for cable purposes." Despite strong German protests that "Kusaie lies in the midst of German sphere" and that "Germany regards herself as the only competitor for the acquisition of the Carolines," the United States pressed on with its effort, offering Spain $1 million for the island and "cable-landing rights in other Spanish territory" (an offer which, in turn, provoked an even stronger German denunciation of the American "policy of seeking islands all over the world for coaling stations").

What happened next is most revealing. Declining the American offer, Spain made an even more dramatic counterproposal—the cession of *all* the Carolines and *all* the Marianas in exchange for open door status for Spain in Cuba and Puerto Rico. In so doing, Spain appeared to be playing directly into the hands of the Reid-Frye-Davis group (and some of the American military) who had favored total American control in those islands all along. (Indeed, Reid and Frye implied at one juncture a hope that Spain would break off peace negotiations, giving America an excuse to take the islands.) These three commissioners gave their enthusiastic endorsement to the project and asked for permission to negotiate along the lines of the Spanish proposal (though perhaps with a time limit on the open door for Spain). But McKinley and Hay refused to pay such a price for something they neither needed nor desired. Seeking only individual cable and coaling stations for limited purposes, they were in no way disposed to exercise indiscriminate sovereignty over numerous, widely dispersed islands; to plant the Stars and Stripes on every ocean-bound rock and pebble they could get. Hay rejected the Spanish offer out-of-hand by return cable on December 4, and there the matter died. The whole episode further illustrated that commercial needs, not Manifest Destiny, guided American decision-making in the Pacific

Russian power in the Gulf of Pechihli. Subsequently, and partly remain the chief vehicle of American expansion.[25]

Thus the peace negotiations with Spain, initiated in September within the conscious framework of the Chinese question, concluded three months later on an identical note. Article IV of the treaty made clear the intimacy that bound Philippine and China policy: McKinley would keep his earlier promise to accord the open door in the Philippines, provided the United States received reciprocal treatment elsewhere in the orient. In actuality, this American open door was limited in time and scope, and it later vanished in the midst of emerging American economic aspirations in the Philippines themselves. But for the moment administration spokesmen regarded the proviso as *key* to future American policy in the Far East. Assistant Secretary of State A. A. Adee, that permanent fixture in the Department, stated unequivocally that "the open door paragraph is the most important"; and Whitelaw Reid, the peace commission's most powerful figure, insisted the open door for the Philippines "enables Great Britain and the United States to preserve a common interest and present a common front in the enormous development in the Far East that must attend the awakening of the Chinese Colossus."[26]

The final treaty arrangements on the Philippines were the outgrowth of an evolving set of circumstances dating back to 1895, when the combined impact of the American depression and the Sino-Japanese War offered both the need and the hope that China might become the great absorber of America's industrial surplus. Subsequent developments, culminating in the partitioning of late 1897 and early 1898, critically threatened the hope but in no way dissipated the need. They did, however, dictate the desirability of finding some vigorous means of safeguarding America's present and future commercial stake in the Chinese Empire. Fortunately, the Spanish-American War provided just such an opportunity, and the McKinley administration was quick to exploit it. The result was the effective thrust of American influence into the far Pacific. From Honolulu through Wake and Guam to Manila stretched a chain of potential coaling, cable, and naval stations to serve as America's avenue to Asia. Only the construction of an isthmian canal remained to complete the system.

The grand scheme was not imperial—in the narrow sense of the word. The insular possessions in the Pacific were not pieces of empire, per se, but stepping-stones and levers to be utilized upon a larger and more important stage—China. Paradoxically, American expansion was designed in part to serve an anti-imperial purpose of preventing the colonization of China and thus preserving her for open door market penetration: *the imperialism of anti-imperialism* ("neo-colonialism" in today's parlance). All this McKinley captured in his Presidential Message of December 5, 1898, when he declared that our "vast commerce . . . and the necessity of our staple production for Chinese uses" had made the United States a not "indifferent spectator of the extraordinary" partitioning in China's maritime provinces. Nevertheless, he continued, so long as "no discriminatory treatment of American . . . trade be found to exist . . . the need for our country becoming an actor in the scene" would be "obviated." But, he concluded, the fate of the open door would not be left to chance; it would be, he said, "my aim to subserve our large interests in that quarter by all means appropriate to the constant policy of our government."[27] Quite obviously, the fruits of the Spanish-American War had enormously multiplied the "appropriate . . . means" available to American policy-makers and had completed the setting for America's illusory search after that holy commercial grail—the China market.

# ⊗ Chapter V: *"A Fair Field and No Favor"*

> "We believe that 'a fair field and no favor' is all we require, and with less we cannot be satisfied. . . . We believe our interests in the Pacific Ocean are as great as those of any other power, and destined to infinite development."
> —*John Hay,* 1901

One year after the armistice with Spain, America sent forth into the world the then-famous, now-denigrated Open Door Notes. In and of themselves, they established no new policy lines. Both Cleveland's response to the Sino-Japanese War and McKinley's stance during peace talks with Spain make it abundantly clear that the open door in China was already cardinal American policy long before the 1899 notes appeared.

But the promulgation of the Hay Doctrine did pass the sceptre of open door champion from Great Britain to the United States. For a half-century the British had successfully used an open door policy to create and sustain their economic (and diplomatic) supremacy in the Chinese Empire; the Americans, as "hitchhiking imperialists," gathered the commercial leavings. Now, as Britain's power wavered—and with it her commitment to the open door, the United States made a concerted effort to adapt the nineteenth-century policy to the expansive needs of a twentieth-century industrial America.

This dramatic departure and its timing have long been the source of interpretive controversy. For example, George F. Kennan, in a capsule version of A. Whitney Griswold's work, has viewed the Open Door Notes as a rather haphazard product, sold by an English member of the Chinese Customs Service indirectly to a somewhat disinterested and quickly disillusioned Secretary of State. On the other hand, Charles S. Campbell, Jr., has stressed the midwife role played by special business interests in bringing the policy to life. Yet each analysis, in its own way, has trivialized an event of enormous importance. The first grossly overestimates the influence of a quite peripheral figure, whose ideas were wholly unoriginal (and well known to every journeyman diplomat) and whose efforts in no way affected the timing of the Open Door Notes. The other bases its provocative interpretation upon a too narrow segment of the national community. Both inadequately appreciate that the Open Door Policy accurately reflected the widely shared assumptions and analyses of most social elements in America (including many without special vested interests); that both individual and group pressures were at best minor catalytic factors. Both, by focusing on the particular, miss the really substantive thing about the Open Door Policy—that it represented America's basic response to the methodological question of how to expand. Instead of closed doors, open markets; instead of political dominion, economic hegemony; instead of large-scale colonialism, informal empire. In short, a most interesting hybrid of anti-colonialism and economic imperialism.[1]

On October 19, 1898, President McKinley told a Citizens' Banquet of Chicago that "territorial expansion is not alone and always necessary to national advancement" and the "broadening of trade." Before another year had passed, his State Department was feverishly at work trying to transform this unilateral sentiment into a universally accepted tenet—at least so far as the Chinese Empire was concerned. Behind this belated effort to make the open door a multilateral vehicle were two seemingly contradictory factors: a sense of power and a sense of impotence.

Latter-day critics of the Open Door Policy have managed to evade one central truth—that the policy was one of strength as well as weakness. A less confident nation might easily have joined in the partitioning scramble in China, content to have an assured but fragmentary slice of the market. But America wanted more, much more than that, and was certain of her ability to get it. When Brooks Adams wrote in 1899 that "East Asia is the prize for which all the energetic nations are grasping," few of his readers doubted who would win that prize. When William McKinley told Congress in that same year that "the rule of the survival of the fittest must be . . . inexorable" in the "rivalry" for "mastery in commerce," most of his listeners were doubtless sure who would be the fittest. In each instance, the certitude grew from that sense of American economic supremacy born in the export revival of 1897, nourished by the retooling and refinancing of American industry, and confirmed by the return of full prosperity. Viewed from this vantage, the open door became appropriate means for the most advanced and competitive industrial nation to grab the lion's share of the China market instead of settling for a pittance. No one saw this more clearly or said it more forcefully than the influential *Bankers' Magazine*, when it exclaimed that "without wars and without military aggression that nation will secure the widest and best markets which can offer the cheapest and best goods." "If China was open to trade with all the world . . . the United States and England need not be afraid of any competitors. But Russia, Germany and France . . . are more or less at a disadvantage when they meet either English or American goods. They therefore do not take the philosophical view at all."[2]

The analysis was hardly an isolated one. In the private sector, for example, the Riverside, New York, Republican Club assured Secretary Hay that "the Chinese market . . . rightfully belongs to us and that in free and untrammeled competition we can win it." Old war-horse Joseph C. Wheeler, musing on his belief that "eight thousand miles of ocean could not stay the destinies of mankind," prophesied to President McKinley that the ultimate volume of American exports to China would reach $5.4 billion a year. The International Commercial Congress (an *ad hoc* meeting of Eastern manufacturers and merchants) wrote Far Eastern expert W. W. Rockhill that "no other market in the world [i.e., China] offers such vast and varied opportunities for the further increase of American exports." The NAM's journal, *American Trade*, reported authoritatively that "millions after millions are being invested in Southern mill property, solely in the faith of a continuation of trade . . . in the Chinese empire." Later *The Nation* nicely summarized general sentiments by predicting that "An open door and no favor infallibly means . . . the greater share and gain in the commercial exploitation of China."

Likewise, public officials expressed optimism about America's open door penetration of the China market. Cushman K. Davis, chairman of the Senate Foreign Relations Committee, proclaimed that our position in the orient was now such "that we can commercially [do] what we please" and predicted that the China trade "would put 18 millions of people on the Pacific coast within not many years and give its cities a preponderance like that of Tyron." Charles E. Smith, Secretary of Agriculture and informal adviser on foreign affairs, reported his impression that "the people of the West regard the Pacific as an American lake which should be covered with ships carrying the American flag" and added that "I don't know but they are about right." Administration trade expert Worthington C. Ford noted (with some reservations) that "the commercial future" of the China trade "is wonderful to think of"— a view based on an independent analysis that China could both double its population and living standards, "and this without any revolutionary change." Finally, even the cautious John Hay, in a public letter that coincided with the dispatch of the Open Door Notes, exclaimed that "in the field of trade and commerce we shall be the keen competitors of the richest and greatest powers, and they need no warning to be assured that in that struggle, we shall bring the sweat to their brows."[3]

In view of subsequent developments, such glowing optimism about the future of the China trade appears naive, misguided, and grotesquely overdrawn—much flap about nothing. But the *potential* for trade expansion was real, and it remained so (enough to exercise vast impact upon American policy-makers for the four decades that preceded Pearl Harbor). In 1899 there were signs—however small—that the penetration of the China market was already underway. For one thing, in the relative sense, manufactured products began to account for more than 90 per cent of American exports to China—a fact of some significance to those preoccupied with *industrial* overproduction. (By 1906, 96 per cent of all United States exports to China were finished products, as compared to 27 per cent for Europe.) The absolute volume of manufactured exports also experienced a sharp rise (albeit from a small base), multiplying four times between 1895 and 1899, from $3.2 million to $13.1 million. (Seven years later, despite a Chinese boycott and persistent obstacles from both Russia and Japan, the total had reached nearly $42 million.) Particularly blessed were the iron and steel industry and cotton textile enterprises, both key elements in the American economy. The latter's exports to China, for example, grew from less than $2 million in 1895 to almost $10 million in 1899 (and reached $30 million by the Panic of 1907, accounting for 56.5 per cent of all American cotton textile exports). The figures lent an air of credence to one southern group's assessment that "[the China trade] is everything."[4] All these facts were, to be sure, small straws in the wind and easily written off in retrospect. But in the expansionist psychology of the 1890's they were eagerly seized upon to bolster the widespread expectation that given equal, open door access, the United States could and would win economic dominion in China.

If American commercial ascendancy made the Open Door Policy a fruitful one, American weaknesses made it nearly unavoidable.

Political power was the prime deficiency. The Far East was no

Latin America, where, after 1895, American hegemony was seldom challenged and usually acknowledged. In China the United States faced all the handicaps of the latecomer to a game already in play with a full lineup of great powers. America did have the capacity to play a significant role in Chinese affairs, and its words and acts now carried substantially more weight, thanks to the Spanish-American War. As the American Ambassador to France reported to McKinley: "we did in three months what the great powers of Europe had sought in vain to do for over a hundred years . . ." and "the most experienced statesmen here envy our transcendent achievements and see clearly the future benefits."[5] Still, heightened power and all, the United States was in no position to issue any Olney Corollaries for the Chinese Empire; to make American word fiat; to manipulate with relative impunity and success. Here more subtle methods would be demanded.

The instances are many (and well known) of America's inability to control events in the western Pacific. Significantly, these failures came despite "the President's most serious consideration" of Chinese instability; despite Secretary Hay's "serious attention" to the famous petition of cotton textile spokesmen, exhorting that something be done to keep the door open in northern China; despite Hay's assurances to Paul Dana of the *New York Sun* that "we are keenly alive to the importance of safeguarding our great commercial interests in that Empire."[6] For all this accumulated anxiety, America's newly won status in the Pacific could not prevent Germany's acquisition of Spain's old insular empire in Micronesia.[7] It could not prevent Japan from occupying Marcus Island (a cable point upon which the American Navy had tentative designs) or from establishing an extraterritorial settlement in Amoy (important for its geographic relationship to Manila). It could do little to stop Russia's apparent drift toward trade discrimination in Manchuria. It could do nothing, one way or another, about the rumored impending war between Russia and Japan. Finally, it could not block Italy's far-reaching demands for a sphere of influence in San Mun Bay and Che-Kiang province—demands that ominously had the support of Great Britain; that threatened to set off another whole round of partitioning in China; that led the *New York Times* to conclude that the disintegration of China (and the open door) was "inevitable," and the *Chicago Inter-Ocean* to guess that "the end may be at hand."[8] All the administration did was to watch, wait, and hope—a policy (better, a stance) that offered little hope for the future.

Financial weakness, another marked American liability, was in part an extension of political weakness. Simply put, American commercial expansion could not encompass financial expansion. In the realm of investments (chiefly railroads and mines) no open door existed, and no American syndicate seemed likely to compete on equitable grounds with its European peers. None of this was exactly new, of course; the move toward a "modified" open door (one that concerned only commerce, not investment) had begun in 1895 and, as already noted, accelerated sharply in 1898. But it did not reach its climax until the Anglo-Russian agreement of April 1899. In effect, Great Britain promised not to compete for railroad concessions north of the Great Wall, while Russia made a similar pledge for the Yangtze basin. All that remained between them for open competition was a buffer zone between the Russian and British spheres—and much of this was already covered by the earlier Anglo-German agreement.

This tightly constricted area of activity left American investors with little more than hope of a junior partnership with the British. This would be by no means inconsequential, and in early 1899 there was some optimism along these general lines. On February 1 the American China Development Company and the British and Chinese Corporation agreed on paper to share in each other's future concessions. One day later the *New York Times* reported that yet another British syndicate had agreed to give American capital a one-quarter share of investment in the railroads and mines of Szechwan province. But in fact British support was seldom vigorous, and American financiers fared poorly in competition with their politically and financially subsidized opponents. A prime example was the glaring failure of the American China Development Company to secure the Hankow-Canton concession, despite initially high hopes. The syndicate's inability to meet the rigorous Chinese terms was probably the major reason for the contract loss, but the company, in its frustration, blamed it on inadequate governmental support. In the end the concession "went thataway" while the State Department and the company engaged in futile backbiting as to why.[9] Overall the episode was more souring than cathartic and played no small role in the administration's later attitude toward American investment in China.

A realistic foreign policy is an exact blend of means and ends— it knows what is vital to the national interest, whether that interest can be fulfilled within the framework of national power and ideology, and precisely how. By 1899 the makers of American foreign policy had long since defined marketplace expansion into China as an important element in their variegated effort to stabilize the political economy. But they had to adopt means that would make the best use of American commercial power while minimizing American liabilities: a still inadequate power base and financial frailty.

There were only three viable choices, and the McKinley administration considered them all. One obvious alternative was to accept the disintegration of China as inevitable (even beneficial) and join in the partitioning.[10] In 1899 there were repeated rumors that the United States would take precisely this course. The *New York Times*, during the San Mun Bay crisis, reported that the administration had already determined to have Pechihli province for an American sphere, while at the same time the actions of the American Consul in Amoy seemed designed to convert that port and its environs into an American entrepôt.[11] But the rumors were untrue and the American Consul's efforts repudiated, and both for the same reason: the administration felt that partitioning was an ineffectual vehicle for American trade expansion.[12] For one thing, it would intensify anti-imperialist criticism while adding bureaucratic and military burdens that McKinley wished to avoid (a view shared with his anti-imperialist critics). For another, American sales and arteries of distribution were largely centered in zones controlled by Russia and Germany, and to relocate these in an American sphere would be expensive and time consuming—far better to keep open existing channels if possible. And finally, to re-emphasize an earlier point, a small slice of the pie (which is all partitioning could offer) held little attraction for men who wanted (and thought they could get) the major share of the market.

The second policy possibility was to make common cause with other open door supporters, presumably England and Japan, and use force if necessary to keep trade entrées open.[13] This was the method that Theodore Roosevelt later tried informally, and it did have the merit of reflecting one vital truth—that in the last analysis only force could make the open door work. But this technique also raised basic objections which ultimately made it an impractical choice for the administration. To begin with, no military alliance (especially one with the English) was likely to enhance the political popularity of the McKinley administration. Moreover, such a formal commitment would deprive the United States of complete freedom of action, and the President (far more than his Anglophile Secretary of State) disliked tying American national interests too rigidly to the foreign policies of countries whose own shifting interests might not always coincide with those of the United States. He already had sufficient evidence (and more was to come) of British and Japanese ambivalence toward the Open Door Policy—enough to make them seem somewhat uncertain allies. Finally, any policy predicated upon the *possible* use of force might eventually require its *actual* use, and the use of force in China (save against Chinese themselves) was considered out of the question. A Far Eastern war would be an unpopular war; it might lead to the very consequence one wished to avoid—the fragmentation of China; and it might ignite the general world holocaust that all the great powers feared at the turn of the century. No, this would not do. What the United States wanted was not force but coexistence and economic competition for open markets; an "eat-your-cake-and-have-it-too" policy of peace and market domination. That America could not have both was, again, the certain fallacy of informal marketplace expansionism and the insoluble dilemma that American policy-makers vainly struggled with for the first half of the twentieth century.

There was of course some informal tripartite consultation and cooperation, and some public figures (generally outside the government) did refer to an "open door entente" of Great Britain, Japan, and the United States. But such collusion never aimed at the use of force, and moreover it was generally an on-again-off-again sort of thing, a tactical strategem employed when it was advantageous to American interests and ignored when it was not—which was frequently.

The third policy alternative—and the one embodied in the Open Door Notes—was to gain common agreement among a concert of powers that China would be exempted from imperial competition. This course obviously begged the whole question of force and has been rightly criticized on that ground. But, on the other hand, it was hardly the legalistic-moralistic anachronism that some have made it seem. On the contrary, as we shall see, it tried to make use of two very real and interrelated factors: (1) the *de facto* balance of power that existed between the Russo-French entente and the emerging Anglo-Japanese bloc; and (2) the intense fear of possible world war that preoccupied the foreign offices of Europe. In this framework of balance and fear, the policies of each power were likely to be flexible and even a bit tentative, for rigidity could be disastrous. (Certainly British action was chameleonic, and students of Russian policy in the Far East at the turn of the century find it so baffling and contradictory that there is doubt one existed.) Furthermore, any changes in the status quo were likely to be cautious ones, undertaken on a quid pro quo basis, lest imbalance lead to conflict. Under these circumstances, if a third force dramatically insisted that the status quo (the open door and Chinese sovereignty) be universally accepted, and if that force had the capacity to upset the delicate equilibrium of power (as the United States certainly had in Europe's eyes after 1898), then there was a good chance the powers would acquiesce. The agreement might be more rhetorical than real, but it would (and did) offer useful leverage in exploiting Europe's fears and occasionally manipulating the scale of power.

These were the realities that produced the Open Door Notes. Neither partitioning nor military alliance offered practical means to realize the desired American ends; only the consensus neutralization held any glimmer of hope. That such hope was illusory, that indeed it *had* to be illusory, is worth analyzing later at length. But for the moment it ought to be emphasized that, given America's commitment to economic penetration in China, given the peculiar combination of American strengths and weaknesses, the Open Door Policy was the most *realistic* one at hand.

The choice of a policy was actually less perplexing to the United States than the timing of its implementation. Hay, above all others, was concerned that the effort to secure an open door consensus might fail because it was premature. Part of the Secretary's restraint reflected his nearly paranoid view that "the senseless prejudices in certain sections of the 'Senate and people' compel us to move with great caution in the China matter." But Hay's fears were badly misplaced—as they were frequently. Public opinion could hardly have been more favorably disposed to a vigorous Open Door Policy than it was in 1899.

Chief honors for crystallizing this favorable opinion belong to two Englishmen, Archibald R. Colquhoun and Lord Charles Beresford. Colquhoun's influence went beyond the general public, for he was a frequent correspondent of Hay's, and in his letters he constantly kept before the Secretary of State the ominous and "growing influence of Russia in China," the need to decide "which of the two policies" to "press for"—the "open door" or the "sphere" (implicitly suggesting the former), and the hope "that action will be taken while there is time." But Colquhoun also influenced wider circles of American opinion through his oft-quoted (and presumably oft-read) book, *China in Transformation* (1899), published both in America and England. Within its pages he stressed the Anglo-American community of interests in Asia, the increasing American need for "foreign markets" to absorb its "industrial" surplus, the primacy of the Russian threat, and the need to act quickly and vigorously in defense of the "open door" while the spheres were relatively small and confined to the coastal provinces.[14] Most Americans who read it, praised it—probably reflecting a simple conviction that his thesis made sense.

Far more dramatic was the influence of Lord Beresford, regarded by most Americans as the leading foreign authority on the Chinese question. Like Colquhoun, Beresford had substantial influence upon Hay and probably upon McKinley and Rockhill as well. Also like Colquhoun, he reached an American reading audience through his *North American Review* article, "China and the Powers," and his renowned book, *The Break-Up of China*, in which he also espoused the "open door" policy, warned against the Russian threat to American trade, and urged that "a decision must be arrived at and action of some sort taken very soon." But Beresford's impact upon the American public (and especially upon the business community) took on an added dimension with his trip through the United States in early 1899, following on the heels of his semi-official survey in China itself. His cross-country trek was a triumphant tour de force: a warm visit with his old friend Hay; private talks with the President which left McKinley clearly impressed; conferences with Rockhill and key congressional leaders; private chats with leading American businessmen; and widely heralded speeches on the banquet circuit. His talk before the Chicago Commercial Club led even the anti-British *Inter-Ocean* to exclaim that "his address . . . was a mine of information to businessmen who ought to look at the new possibilities in the East" and to admit that "the Beresford idea" (the open door) "has its advantages" over "the 'sphere of influence' policy." Similarly, his speech to the American Asiatic Association (and guests) in New York excited warm response from his elite audience, prompting ironmaster Abram S. Hewett, the program co-speaker, to assure Beresford that "it is our desire to give the fullest possible expression . . . supporting the policy of the Open Door" and the "preservation of the integrity of the Chinese Empire." Little wonder that Beresford departed firmly convinced of influential support for the open door but still apprehensive about the administration's hesitancy to move immediately to support it.[15]

The magic of the Colquhoun-Beresford interpolation was not in creating a new base for public opinion, because such a base already existed. What it did was to promote added conviction and provide articulation for the Open Door Policy by sanctifying it with British expertise—something a great many key Americans traditionally (if reluctantly) held in awe. In any case, 1899 produced a bumper crop of written and spoken words in behalf of some dramatic effort to gain universal support for the open door in China.

The chief opinion-shaping magazines both sensed and reinforced public demands for trade protection in China. *The Nation,* for example, reported that "powerful influences are now at work to bring about a change" in the administration's China policy, and added its own advice that something, even "a tacit . . . alliance with England," be done to keep "the Orient open to trade of all nations on equal terms." The *Atlantic Monthly* similarly discovered "signs of a healthy and growing interest" in the China question and urged "the utmost vigilance in behalf of our commercial privileges on the continent of Asia." *Harper's Weekly* and the *North American Review* approvingly printed articles by such influential men as John R. Proctor, president of the United States Civil Service Commission, and John Barrett, former Minister to Siam, advocating an enlarged "Monroe Doctrine" to guarantee "the integrity of China" and an "open door" to forestall "our great and growing markets" from being "entirely lost to us." And the editors of business journals such as *Bankers' Magazine* and the *Journal of Commerce and Commercial Bulletin* reflected similar positions, as did the proceedings. writings, and petitions of the NAM, the Philadelphia Commercial Museum, and the American Asiatic Association. (Rather typical was the Southern Cotton Spinners' Association appeal to President McKinley for "preservation of the integrity of the Chinese Empire, and the maintenance of an open-door policy in China with the commerce of all nations.") Even the learned *Annals of the American Academy of Political and Social Science* joined the argument by devoting an entire supplementary issue to American foreign economic policy (chiefly in relationship to Asia). Conceived as a debate to dramatize policy differences, the work was more revealing for the common ground it disclosed. The most stunning examples were the articles by Assistant Secretary of State John Bassett Moore and by arch anti-imperialist Carl Schurz—the first an articulate defense of recent American policy, the other a blistering attack upon it. Yet Moore could insist that the prime "object" of that policy was "to maintain an open door to the world's commerce," while Schurz could agree that the "golden key of industrial progress" lay in "open[ing] to our trade many doors." (Small wonder, one year later, that William Jennings Bryan found imperialism to be a dead issue. The Open Door Notes had already killed it by offering an expansionist method that even "large policy" proponents and anti-imperialists could jointly support.)

Capping this domestic surge of "keep-the-door-open" sentiment were the remarks of Jacob Gould Schurman. Arriving in San Francisco on his return from service on the First Philippine Commission, the renowned educator and articulate anti-imperialist held a dramatic news conference in which he talked little about the Philippines and much about China. The essence of his words were that "the future of China was the one overshadowing question" in the Far East (and that all others, including Philippine affairs, were only important in their relationship to the Chinese problem); that China "should maintain its independent position, but the *doors* should be kept *open*"; that Russia was the chief enemy of American ambitions, and that the United States "should stand with [England and Japan] in preventing the dismemberment of China"—a nearly perfect paraphrase of the Beresford position.[16] Schurman's comments received fair publicity and their impact was important. They were hardly in a league with Senator Proctor's speech on the Cuban Revolution in 1898, but they were welcome frosting on the cake— enough to help ease (temporarily) John Hay's hypertension about the nature of American public opinion.

☙

Hay's fear of precipitous action, his general caution and restraint, also grew out of his hope that a "watchful waiting" posture would eventually offer a more favorable international climate. With a more propitious time in which to act assertively, he might measurably increase the possibility of favorable great-power response to the American position. Thus, throughout the sporadic crises in China in early 1899, the State Department remained relatively silent, apparently hoping for sunnier days. Whether this reflected wishful thinking or a realistic assessment of the balance of power can only be guessed at. Whatever, the wish fortunately proved father to the deed, for by August even Hay could feel with relative assurance that the Far Eastern situation was unlikely to offer another so appropriate time for action.

The more favorable international climate evolved slowly and climaxed suddenly. First, the San Mun Bay crisis passed as quickly as it came, rendering the *Times* obituary on the open door premature. China simply refused the Italian demands; no third power came to the Mediterranean country's support, so Italy backed down —leaving fears of a new round of partitioning to another day. The tension eased, and American relations in the Pacific began to change for the better with three key powers.

Great Britain, despite her acceptance of the "modified" open door concept, made it quite clear that she was willing to have one more go at preserving the commercial open door, provided the United

States used its newly won status to take the lead. Some Americans even saw the British tie-in with American railroad interests as a conscious scheme to keep the United States "on the spot" where "her presence in China might be relied upon to help in keeping the 'open door' to trade for all comers on equal terms." At the same time, there proved to be no Japanese-American friction over the Amoy international settlement, save in the overwrought imagination of the American Consul (who received a State Department reprimand as his reward). On the contrary, relations between the two countries began to take on an amity of tone and an identity of interests that was to prove most useful during the open door negotiations and the Boxer Rebellion. Finally, the hostility that had marked German-American relations in the Pacific in late 1898 rapidly gave way to a very real détente, highlighted by conciliatory talks on the Samoan problem, the establishment of the Chinese Customs Service in Shantung, and the publication of a German White Paper accepting the equal access principle in China.[17] Thus by mid-1899 the State Department believed that England, Japan, and probably Germany could be counted as safely in the open door camp. This fact would, in time, prove most useful in the tricky negotiations that would follow the Open Door Notes. But the immediate utility of Anglo-Japanese-German support was rather limited, for the McKinley administration had no intention of using balance-of-power tactics to coerce the Russo-French entente into line. Instead, maneuver, manipulation, and persuasion were the order of the day, and the ultimate aim was the entente's (especially Russia's) voluntary and peaceful acceptance of the open door principle—even if in words only (for even words can be a useful tool in a diplomat's hands). What Hay still awaited was some small sign that Russia could be maneuvered into such a public commitment. But instead of a mere sign, Russia handed Hay almost the whole loaf—and on a silver platter at that.

This quite unexpected but thoroughly welcome gift came in mid-August in the form of a czarist ukase governing leased territory in China, an imperial decree glowingly characterized by the American Ambassador in St. Petersburg as "the open door in China"—"in so far as Russia is concerned." To be sure, it was not the open door, in so far as America was concerned, for it said nothing about the vital question of railroad rates. Nevertheless, it seemed to say that "Russia has no intention to interfere with in any manner, or to control, Chinese customs duties"; that "no restriction is provided" on "foreign commerce and trade" in the Russian sphere. The *raison d'être* of the Russian declaration remains still obscured; probably it reflected the temporary ascendancy of Count Witte's Far Eastern policy of peaceful, covert penetration, marked by steady but unadvertised ambitions. Whatever the reasons, the Russian move seemed to Charlemagne Tower, the American Ambassador, a guarantee of the "future development of American trade and the certain increase of American mercantile prosperity." To more "doubting Thomases," like the editors of the *New Orleans Picayune,* the "concession [was] undoubtedly made to distract attention from the steady inroads Russia is making upon Chinese territory." Or as the *New York Times* put it: "It is a sop to Cerberus, the watchdog whose three heads may be called England, Japan and the United States."[18] But to Secretary Hay the nature of Russia's long-range intentions (assuming there were some) was immaterial; the real significance was quite immediate. The Russians, either wisely or unwittingly, had offered the United States a psychological wedge; they had opened the door just a crack, and no good Yankee salesman, particularly one so long suffering as Hay, was going to miss a chance to get his foot in.

Buoyed by this happy turn of events, the Secretary discarded his normal restraint to act quickly and decisively, instructing his chief Far Eastern adviser, W. W. Rockhill, to prepare a memorandum on the administration's China policy. Rockhill, with his friend, Alfred E. Hippisley, a long-time English official in the Chinese Customs Service, had in fact badgered Hay for weeks for some dynamic move to insure international commitment to the open door, stressing the Russian threat to American textiles as the most compelling reason. But neither their analysis nor recommendations were new (much reads like passages out of Beresford's book).[19] Hay had been exposed to them before from countless influential sources, and he had long ago adopted them as his own. What had held the Secretary back was not the question of policy but the question of timing. And even here the two "old China hands" exerted no influence; indeed, Rockhill, in despair, had already given up on the private pressure technique and had decided upon published articles as the only avenue of influencing policy.[20] (One is almost forced to conclude that the Russian ukase largely produced the Open Door Notes, and that the chief importance of Rockhill and Hippisley lay in putting out a correspondence so fascinating, so voluminous, and so articulate that historians have been loathe to concede its monumental irrelevancy).

Hay's specific instruction to his assistant called for drafted notes to the great powers, aimed at a relatively "formal engagement" that "the recent extension of spheres of influence, etc., will not result in restricting our commercial freedom in China." An elated Rockhill, certain that the Chinese "question seems now in very good shape," did his superior's bidding with alacrity. Building upon Beresford's *The Break-Up of China* (for the "great weight" it carried with "the American public"), he rested "the policy of the 'open door'" upon the single premise that "the mercantile classes of the United States" regarded it as "essential to the healthy extension of trade in China." Noting that "zones of interest" implicitly threatened this policy, he called upon the great powers to give formal guarantees of equal commercial access to both treaty and non-treaty ports, and assurance of uniform harbor dues and railroad rates in their spheres.[21]

One week later, on September 6, the Rockhill memorandum became the basis for the formal Open Door Notes to England, Germany, and Russia, with later copies sent to Japan, France, and Italy. A precise analysis of the notes sends the reader away with three main impressions—some of them at odds with current historical interpretation.

First, these "first" Open Door Notes, while accepting the sphere of interest as "accomplished fact," did not ignore the relationship between Chinese integrity and the open door. On the contrary, the preamble to the British note emphasized that the open door would help in "maintaining the integrity of China in which the whole western world is alike concerned." All the notes prefaced the phrase "spheres of influence" with the modifying adjective "so-called"—a fact repeatedly brought to the attention of Russian negotiators. And Rockhill's definitive article of May 1900, undoubtedly cleared with Hay, insisted that the Open Door Notes in no way questioned China's "outright sovereignty" in the "sphere of interest." So it seems clear that the State Department saw quite early that the open door was neither a legal or practical possibility unless Chinese independence could be sustained.

Second, and not without contradiction, the notes treated China as a passive object by imposing a policy in which that country had no say, either in formulation or negotiation. In fact the United States neglected even to inform China of its actions until international rumors provoked an official inquiry from the Chinese government. Even then, the essence of the State Department's response was a rather pointed request "that no arrangements will be entered into by the Government of the Emperor which shall be to the disadvantage of American commerce." Clearly, while the United States wanted an independent China, it did not wish one *too* independent —at least not independent enough to close the door on its own. It was a bind that post-1911 Chinese nationalism would do much to sharpen.

Third, the notes only encompassed a "modified" open door— one with a strictly commercial orientation, one that ignored loans, railroad, and mining concessions—on the simple grounds (stated in the Rockhill memorandum) that an open door in "privileges and concessions" was not feasible.[22] The notes tried to neutralize trade advantages inherent in railroad concessions by insisting that railroad rates on all lines, even those operated by foreigners within their spheres, be absolutely non-discriminatory. Thus transportation costs would remain uniform while the market competitiveness of American goods would stand intact.

The open door negotiations themselves have yet to receive their proper attention. Sometimes dismissed as a colossal game of "blindman's buff," they were in fact imaginatively conceived and generally well executed under circumstances that would have taxed the patience, purposefulness, and expertise of the most experienced foreign office.

The original negotiations plan grew out of Rockhill's memorandum. Basically it called for simultaneous negotiations with England, Germany, and Russia, aiming for similar (though not necessarily identical) acceptances in principle of the American position. "The prospect" for approval from each "seem[ed] bright": England because the open door was both traditional and profitable; Germany because her interests were primarily financial rather than commercial, and thus would not be impaired by the American proposals; Russia because the August 23 ukase showed her to be either too conciliatory or too subtle to permit a public rejection of the equal access principle. Interestingly, Rockhill (like Hippisley) saw France's inflexible colonial policy as the major stumbling block to success, and on his advice Hay postponed dispatch of the note to France—apparently hoping that an early Russian acceptance would bring her partner into line.

Rockhill's strategem proved altogether unrealistic. Instead of the anticipated early success, it produced only an icy diplomatic calm. England hesitated out of concern for her recent Hong Kong extension lease; and her consequent insistence that "leased lands" (as opposed to general "spheres of interest") be exempted from the open door would have rendered that doctrine meaningless, since "the holdings of nearly all the great powers are in the form of leases"—or so concluded Joseph Choate, American Ambassador in London. Germany, given her diplomatic isolation in Asia, declined to go out on a limb, preferring to straddle the fence while testing the international winds. Clearly, she would make no move unless it was a safe one. Finally, Russia (despite Rockhill's optimistic predictions) proved utterly reluctant to bind herself to anything so vague, universal, timeless, and implicitly dangerous as the American Open Door Policy. She had had her say in the imperial ukase and saw no need for further declarations on the matter.[23] Moreover, like Germany, she was much interested in seeing how the other powers would respond before making her final policy decisions.

It stands as a credit to Hay's pragmatism and independence that he substantially changed tactics—with great success—when Rockhill's original plan proved abortive. His basic shift was to scuttle the idea of simultaneous negotiations in favor of "falling dominoes": concentrate on each power one at a time; move down the line from the nation most likely to accept the American proposals to the one least likely to comply; use the accumulating acceptances as leverage to pry assent from the more regressive. Within this framework Hay arranged his dominoes somewhat differently than Rockhill might have. First, he inserted Japan (which had been passed over in the September 6 notes) in second position. He did so because the British suggested it; because it fit his own sense of identity with Japan; and because early Japanese acceptance (which he assumed would be forthcoming) would add another useful length to his diplomatic crowbar. Second, Hay brought France (Rockhill's imaginary nemesis) into the negotiations and placed her ahead of Russia—reflecting his own belief that France would prove more amenable than her Eastern ally. His own predilections partly account for this move, for he had long defined Russia as the chief obstacle to the open door, and the notes (in his own mind) had been directed primarily against that nation. But immediate developments also reinforced his preconceptions, for while Russia coldly rebuffed American overtures, France, in informal talks, revealed a most friendly disposition. Indeed, in early November the American Ambassador in Paris, Horace Porter, reported that the French Foreign Minister, fearful that further partitioning might lead to war, saw the American suggestions as a possible basis for stabilization. Porter also added that he found a growing French respect for American power and an increased inclination to lend weight to American policies.

By early November the Secretary of State had evolved a rough

scheme to concentrate first on England and Japan; then pressure
Germany, France, and Russia in succession. (Italy made her way
into the hopper as little more than an afterthought.) The Japanese
proved no obstacle whatsoever. The initial note to Japan leaves the
strong feeling that informal talks had already been held on the
subject, and that Japan had already given "assurances" in regard to
commercial equality.[24] The subsequent lack of real negotiations
on the matter bolsters this impression.

Anglo-American talks, however, still had to get around the sticky
problem of the Hong Kong extension and British insistence on its
"exempt" status. Ultimately Rockhill forged the basic compromise
by suggesting a distinction between leases that carried economic
privileges for the lessee, and those leased "military station[s]" that
brought with them no special "rights as regarding trading with
China." By excluding the latter from the open door proposals, the
British (by stretching a point) might legitimately exempt the Hong
Kong extension. Hay accepted the compromise in principle but
modified it by denying the British the right to make public and
specific mention of their exemption—lest such favored treatment
open the door to endless exemptions by other powers. His qualification proved no great obstacle, for it still permitted exemption by
omission. Realizing this, the British—in their informal reply of
December 1—accepted the open door for Wei-Hai-Wei and all
future acquisitions, "lease or otherwise," while making no mention
of the Hong Kong extension. Ten days later, at Hay's urging, the
British sent a more formal reply—one the American Secretary
thought would "be of great assistance to us in our negotiations with
other powers."

The next "other power" was Germany, a nation sandwiched between the Anglo-Japanese bloc and the Russo-French entente, but
nevertheless in a position to make or break the American efforts. As
Hay viewed it, Germany would remain noncommittal until the
United States could achieve a clear preponderance of power in
behalf of its China policy; then she would feel safe to assent. Because the Secretary felt the Japanese and British responses had

already tipped the balance toward the United States, he decided to step up diplomatic pressure on the fence-straddler in early December. The startlingly quick result was an informal German declaration that "the politics of Germany in China are *de facto* those of the open door, and that Germany proposes to maintain the principle in the future." Nevertheless, she still hesitated to take an unequivocal public stand, lest she "excite controversy" by appearing "to be drawn into a position where she must take sides" between "England on one" hand and "France and Russia on the other." But under further American pressure Germany did agree to accept the American note "if all other powers did so," and gave permission "to have this information communicated to the other Powers."[25] Actually, the qualifying provision was much like one appended to the British acceptance, and its apparent evasiveness no more than a normal diplomatic safeguard, especially since everyone—including Hay— realized that the door could not be kept open (short of overt force) without consensus agreement. Either everyone played by the rules or everyone, in self-defense, did not. In any case, the German "promissory note" was a crucial turning point in the open door negotiations, for it put the entente (especially Russia) in a position where it either had to accept the American position—at least in principle—or else advertise its ulterior ambitions somewhat prematurely to its potential adversaries.

Negotiations with France were frank and amicable, as Hay had come to expect. M. Delcasse, the French Foreign Minister, without benefit of any American prodding, immediately agreed to points one and two dealing with tariff rates in treaty and non-treaty ports. But he regarded the third point on equal railroad rates with some suspicion, fearful that its vagueness "as to industrial privileges" and to what constituted a "sphere" might be a wedge to transform the "modified," commercial open door into a financial one as well; one that might permit" people of all nations to secure vested rights, build railways, and possess and work mines, water powers, etc., in such spheres." For a short while, Delcasse considered offering a substitute open door proposal for clarification, but Germany's quasi-acceptance of the American proposals undercut that alternative. Consequently, the French cabinet agreed to accept the open door "substantially in form presented" by the United States, but with reservations as to point three. Specifically, France limited her pledge of "equal treatment" for "tariffs on railroads" solely to her "leased territory" (which was relatively small), while making no mention of equal railroad rates in her "spheres of interest" (which were relatively large). Further American efforts to include coverage for "spheres" were unproductive, as Delcasse continued to insist that point three, in its full form, might be misconstrued to mean "an industrial parity" that would threaten projected French mines, wells, and railroads in the Chinese interior. Happily, though, he did offer indirect verbal assurance by pointing out that if France adhered to equal railroad rates in her leased territory, she could hardly do otherwise "in territory [she] did not possess or control." This informal commitment was enough to persuade Ambassador Porter that France was "naturally, on the side of preserving the open door," even in the area of "transportation facilities."[26] Hay also chose to regard the French reply as sufficiently satisfactory— a course made easier by the remoteness of French interests in southern China from American ones further north, and by the hope that French affirmation would give him the decisive weapon to bring the reluctant Russians into line.

The postponement of talks with Russia did put the United States in a better negotiating position, but it did not put Russian decision-makers in a better frame of mind. By early December, Russian diffidence had given way to overt hostility as Count Witte managed to convince his governmental colleagues that the Open Door Notes were essentially an anti-Russian vehicle. The argument was a simple one. The key section of the American notes concerned non-discriminatory rates; Russia was the only power in China already engaged in railroad construction, and moreover she possessed the treaty right (in the Li-Lobanov pact) to use differential railroad rates as a means of making an initial profit off her lines. Therefore, the American proposals had Russia as their obvious target. This viewpoint, coupled with Hay's very real Russophobia, transformed the Russo-American bargaining chamber into an arena of mistrust and suspicion.

From the very beginning the railroad rate section lay squarely across the path of diplomatic accord. Neither Rockhill in Washington nor Tower in St. Petersburg obtained anything but firm refusals on that key point. By December 11 it seemed clear to Tower that Russia did not "intend to make the complete declaration that we hope for." In fact, two weeks later he quoted one Russian official as saying, "Well, we have built the railroads, and I think it quite probable that we shall give some preference to our own people." To make matters worse, Tower unearthed a plan to apply Russian tariffs at Dalmy on goods which Russian officials designated as bound ultimately for Russia proper (by implication, making Manchuria a Russian protectorate).[27]

In this unhappy state, Hay felt obliged to play upon Russian isolation by mustering as much bluff and bluster as possible. On December 19 he had Rockhill threaten the Russian Ambassador, Count Cassini, with a presidential message to Congress. McKinley would declare "that his proposals had been accepted by all the Great Powers" except Russia—an event that "would be extremely prejudicial to the friendly relations between the two nations." The probe was not without salutary results, for it apparently persuaded Russia to resume serious negotiations—this time in St. Petersburg, where Hay hoped that Foreign Minister Mouraviev would prove more tractable than Cassini. When no miracles ensued, Hay simply kept pounding away, seeking to convince Russia that America regarded the matter of such vital importance that she would not relent until Russia, like the other nations, took a definite stand. At Hay's urging to "try energetically" again, Tower, in a December 28 interview with Mouraviev, repeated the American position with as much bluntness as diplomatic niceties permitted. One: "American trade, which concerns the welfare of the whole American people, must depend much upon the breadth or narrowness of the policy to be adopted now by the great European Powers." Two:

"A refusal upon the part of Russia to adhere to these propositions would produce the most painful and unfortunate impression in the United States."[28]

Apparently patience had its rewards. American belligerency probably had little effect on Russian foreign policy, but American persistence probably did. Russian Far Eastern policy, under Witte's influence, had vast, ambitious designs, but they were all predicated upon the use of subtle, gradual techniques. Ignoring repeated American inquiries or rejecting them outright would most certainly arouse foreign suspicion and antagonism toward Russia, and given her obvious military-economic shortcomings and her lessened influence in Peking, such a development could be disastrous to her long-term goals.

For whatever reasons, Russia bent a bit. To Tower's great surprise, Mouraviev expressed general sympathy with the open door principle and insisted that Russia objected only to the vagueness of American proposals and hesitated only out of a desire not "to bind herself to something which she does not perfectly understand." Promising "renewed consideration," he closed with the teasing comment that "whatever France does, Russia will do."

The fruits of Russian reconsideration came five days later. Like the French, the Russian reply accepted the first two articles on tariff duties; unlike the French, it said nothing about railroad rates in either leased lands or spheres. It neither accepted nor rejected point three, but its silence was ominous—enough to provoke Rockhill's oft-quoted remark that "it has what we call in America a string attached to it." But prudence (and perhaps a bit of guile) reigned supreme in the State Department, and rightly so. No one knew better than Hay and Rockhill that "none of the European Powers were prepared to . . . get arrayed in hostile camps against each other on this subject." Any negative interpretation of the Russian response would only prompt a mass retreat from their conditional commitments. So Hay chose to regard the Russian answer in a favorable light, stressing its pledges and ignoring its omissions.

He also determined to make the most of the Russian declaration by interpreting it as broadly and as favorably as he could without inciting outright contradiction from St. Petersburg. Seizing on Mouraviev's casual remark on Russian emulation of French policy, Hay proposed to publish the Russian and French replies in joint form. Thus, in "agreement by association" Russia would appear to have accepted at least a modified version of point three. But this ingenious gambit fell before Russia's unexplained reversal—that she "would not be bound by the reply of France, that the Russian Government has acted entirely for itself and not in concert with France." Foiled here, the State Department nevertheless managed to secure one smaller but still valuable concession from Mouraviev (and one often ignored in later accounts): explicit permission to proclaim "the Russian reply as a favorable one." Using this for all it was worth, Hay, on March 20, 1900, sent a published circular note to the powers concerned that all their replies had been "favorable" and would be considered "final and definitive."[29] The descriptive terms were useful ones: they claimed no total and exact acceptance of the American proposals; they simply suggested that each power had had its final say on the matter, and that the United States (and each power involved) regarded each response as "favorable." If the American circular seemed to imply more, so much the better. But on its own explicit terms, it engaged in no amateurish bluff; it invited no contradiction from any power—least of all from Russia.

The domestic adulation heaped upon Hay's Open Door Notes in early 1900 is well known.[30] So is the latter-day scorn of most historical scholars. But both idolators and critics have worshiped and reviled the wrong shrine, because they have approached the notes within a frame of reference quite alien and irrelevant to its formulators. They have made the cardinal error of viewing the Open Door Notes as a grand search for an immediate, impenetrable, permanent panecea to insure the perpetual commercial ascendancy of America in China. Looked at in this unrealistic fashion, the notes became either *everything or nothing*. They either insured that "anything produced in the United States will *permanently* find its way into *all* parts of the Celestial Empire" (italics added), or else they produced only "evasive and noncommittal" responses, empty and vague words, a jumble of legalistic, high-flown phrases—a monument to the American penchant for substituting slogans, scraps of paper and good intentions for the tried and tested behavioral patterns of *realpolitik*.[31]

But the Hay circular was not an end in itself and should not be evaluated as such. It was simply an effort (albeit a dramatic one) to structure a framework within which the more traditional dynamics of diplomacy could operate. Russia's promises might be "as false as dicer's oaths" (as Hay clearly understood), but such public commitments still offered a handy anvil off which American tacticians could play—to force open door opponents to employ more indirect and less effective means for fulfilling their ends, thus limiting their freedom of choice and action; to exploit Europe's fear of world conflagration by offering it a peaceful substitute to the imperial rat race; to convince unbelievers of the earnestness of American intentions and (in the aftermath of the war with Spain) the credibility of American power.[32] All these techniques and others could be and were tried, for the China market, with its vast potential, was worth the effort.

And if the effort failed? Well, that was a bridge American policy-makers hoped they would not have to cross. For the moment, in the early months of 1900, they optimistically believed that the open door would preclude a military solution to the Chinese question. But there remained an unhappy ambiguity—was this a hedged hope that the China market would not necessitate a war, or a firm commitment that it was not worth one? It would be an inheritance of later American administrations to resolve that ambiguity, as best they could, in their own and often differing ways.

# ✇ Chapter VI: *The Dilemmas Unfold*

> ". . . the exercise of such influence over weaker foreign nations as shall prevent them from giving to other countries trading privileges denied to us. This is misnamed the policy of the 'open door.' In truth, it is the policy of forcing doors open and forcibly keeping them open."
> —*John A. Hobson, 1898*[1]

For all its apparent rationality and realism, the Open Door Policy suffered from one fatal flaw. Either out of ignorance or arrogance, it treated China as a passive and somewhat static entity; not an actor but something to be acted upon. In doing so it ignored one of history's few absolutes: the extension of power (however informal) of stronger nations over weaker ones inevitably effects change in the weaker societies—in cultural attitudes (toward their own culture and others), in class and social structure, in political institutions and behavior, in technology and economics, in education and the like. Moreover, such changes—and the traditionalist opposition to them—can and often do cause violent reaction against the intruding, alien powers. This was especially true of a civilization so venerable, egocentric, and non-eclectic as China's, where the nineteenth-century "barbarian" inroads—sometimes peaceful, sometimes not—spawned often tumultuous, violent, and unstabilizing responses. And in the process, the two things most jeopardized—Chinese stability and Chinese independence—were the two most indispensable prerequisites for success of the open door.

On February 24, 1900, the *North China Herald* predicted, "It is morally certain the opening spring will witness a rising such as foreigners in China have never seen before." Two weeks later the prophecy came to pass. Anger over foreign economic exploitation, resentment of Christian missionary activity, anxiety over the appearance of Western technology—all fanned by the death and depredations of drought and famine—combined to ignite open revolt in Shantung province in early March. Led by the secret, xenophobic Boxer organization and encouraged by the Empress Dowager's example, great masses rioted first against Chinese Christians and then against foreigners and foreign property. After a brief respite the Boxer Rebellion spread violently into Chihli province, in which the capital city of Peking and the key port of Tientsin were located. The arrival of additional legation guards (requested by Conger and other Western diplomats) calmed matters slightly in Peking, but the rest of the province erupted in volcanic chaos. The Boxers destroyed railroad stations and bridges, stymied all new railroad construction, and halted rail traffic between Peking and Tientsin. Finally, stimulated by the overt support of governmental conservatives and by the wholesale addition of Chinese Regular Army units, the Boxers turned against the Imperial city itself. By June 4, Conger's dispatches stopped getting through altogether, and by June 15 he discovered the foreign legations "completely besieged within our compounds with the entire city in the possession of a rioting, murdering mob." The foreign powers, acting initially as informal (and often uneasy) allies, responded with a concurrent decision to intervene militarily, though the aims of that intervention (beyond rescuing the legations) were not pre-established.

In the midst of the uprising, the American government's chief concern—save for the obvious one of Conger's safety—was the continuation of open door expansionism. Two things threatened that continuation. First, instability disrupted the routine course of business transactions and made it impossible to sustain, much less expand, the American export trade in northern China. This was especially true of the southern cotton textile industry whose recent increase in exports had been "practically all . . . in the China trade," causing "the South to look to the oriental trade as an important factor in its prosperity." Now, as a result of the rebellion, cotton textile exports to China dropped from $10,273,487 in 1899 (more than the total exported to all the rest of the world) to $5,205,892 in 1900. Consequently, *American Trade* (the NAM's journal) reported that "several" southern firms were "on the verge of suspending operations because of the closing of the Chinese outlet" and warned that "there is ample evidence of the return of the conditions of depression and stagnation which brought the industry to such a critical stage a few years ago."[2]

The more pressing danger, however, was the possibility that one or more of the powers would use the prevailing turmoil as an excuse to further diminish Chinese independence—through overt military occupation or special arrangements foisted upon a China too feeble to resist them. Prime suspect, as always, was Russia— partly because of the McKinley administration's Russophobia; partly because Russia, with its railroad system nearing completion (particularly in Manchuria), had more to lose than any other power by the disturbances in northern China. Actually, Russian policy, under Witte's guidance, was relatively cautious during June, with Russia playing fairly passive roles in the initial engagements around Taku and generally counseling respect for Chinese sovereignty. But Witte's approach did not go unchallenged, and a more militant group, headed by War Minister Kuropatkin, worked mightily to make the Boxer Rebellion "an excuse for seizing Manchuria." Once more they did not labor in vain, for the Russian decision (announced on June 20) to send a four-thousand-man force from Port Arthur to Peking represented a major though incomplete triumph for this viewpoint. At least this was the American (and British) feeling, which put less stock in Russian protestations of guileless innocence and more credence in grandiose rumors that "Russia is mobilizing two hundred thousand troops to be followed by the same number to be sent to China by sea and is chartering all available vessels."[3]

The upshot of these threats to Chinese stability and independence was to pose anew the question of how best to preserve America's present and future interests, raising again—more explicitly than ever—the alternatives of partitioning, consensus neutralization, or alliances and the use of force. Hay, if one can take his words at face value, appeared personally to favor some variation of the last approach. He talked privately of the potential advantages of an Anglo-American alliance and even expressed the hope that "Japan or some other power [would] give Russia a sound thrashing." But as Hay well knew, he lacked "a free hand" to pursue any such tactics, and not simply because political Anglophobia ("all Irishmen are Democrats and some Germans are fools") created "such a mad-dog hatred of England" that the Secretary was forced to "make bricks without straw." Equally as important, Hay's predilections held no attraction for either his President or his fellow cabinet members, including the powerful Elihu Root, the Secretary of War, who (like the "newspapers and politicians" about whom Hay was so paranoid) accused the Secretary of State of "truckling to England."[4] On the contrary, the objections to military alliance remained as compelling in the volatile summer of 1900 as they had been in the calmer days of late 1899. Thus the initial, almost instinctive reaction of the administration was to retain maximum freedom of action, resulting in instructions to Conger and Admiral Kempff to "avoid outside entanglements," make "no alliances," and "act independently in protection of American interests where practicable." Accordingly, American naval forces declined to join the other powers in the protocol demanding Chinese surrender of the Taku forts (first step on the road to Peking) and subsequently refused to take part in the bombardment of Taku or "in taking possession of the Imperial Railway Station" there.[5]

But the problem remained, freedom of action *for what?* So long as the administration used it to sustain its pose of virginal innocence, it afforded America no leverage over the policies of other powers. And in the mounting crisis of late June, amidst growing evidence of Russian aggressiveness, this was a dangerous, double-edged luxury that the United States could not afford. Clearly, more positive uses had to be found; more affirmative choices had to be made. And one was the most obvious, most predictable choice of all: to step up American influence in behalf of consensus neutralization. More specifically, to blunt and bind unilateral acquisitiveness within a concert of powers which would fight and negotiate as a bloc toward common ends.

Within this framework the first and most pressing task was to secure tacit agreement among the powers on their aims in China, both during and after military efforts to rescue their legations and pacify the Boxers. Thus, at the suggestion of John Bassett Moore and with the firm approval of the President, Hay dispatched his famous July 3 circular (the second Open Door Notes) to the powers—though, significantly, only after earlier, informal soundings of English and Japanese opinions. In essence the circular sought to make clear the American position that the anti-Boxer expedition to Peking ought not to involve either a declaration of war or an act of war against the Chinese government itself, and that it should not camouflage covetous designs on Chinese territory. Instead the United States suggested that the powers ought to aim for "safety and peace in China," "Chinese territorial and administrative entity," and "equal and impartial trade with all parts of the Chinese Empire." In short: stability, Chinese independence, and the open door.[6]

The circular asked for no formal replies, chiefly because Hay was skeptical about what they might be. Indeed, he told Moore that "Russia was opposed to it, and probably would reject it"; that France, as "a mere prostitute to Russia" ["Russia's harlot"], would do likewise; and that "Germany would go either way, whichever promised the greatest profit." To Hay's surprise, however, his venture occasioned an outbreak of diplomatic sign language essentially compatible with the American position. For example, Russia (in a note to Great Britain) pledged herself to the "exclusion of everything which might lead to partition of the Empire," perhaps bearing out Moore's contention that Russia would have to accept the American view "since the refusal of it would be equivalent to an avowal of a sinister purpose which at the moment she probably would wish not to exhibit." Similarly, in Germany, Foreign Minister von Bulow told the Foreign Affairs Committee of the *Bundesrat* that the government desired no partition and sought concert of opinion with other interested nations.

Consequently, by July 14 Hay could and did inform Whitelaw Reid confidentially that "the attitude of all the Powers is, on the surface at least, the same as ours." Since the Russo-French entente gave him greatest cause for concern, he expressed his particular delight to Reid over the "frank and cordial . . . cooperation" of France and the unequivocal manner in which Russia had put herself out on a diplomatic limb. The mercurial Secretary, whose expectations often shifted wildly with his state of mind, now clearly felt like crowing a bit, and only fear of creating "some resentment among the Powers as reflecting upon their independence of action" kept him from claiming extensive American credit for the circular's reception. Instead he released a short press statement giving the text of the notes and alluding to the "favorable consideration" given to them. But Reid was not bound by such considerations, and his *New York Tribune* offered extravagant praise for the administration's "distinction of leadership . . . in China," especially in realizing (in best Gladstonian fashion) that "by keeping all the Powers in union together you neutralize and bind up the selfish aims of each."

The administration realized something else as well—that words alone, however helpful, could not cement cooperation; that, as Hay put it, the "talk of the papers about 'our pre-eminent moral position giving us the authority to dictate to the world' is mere flapdoodle." Being good pragmatic realists, administration leaders understood that both the military balance and political conditions had to be *just right* if a concert was not to splinter on the rocks of national rivalries; and these things did not take care of themselves. Accordingly, while the United States (by its own choice) would not join or even give the appearance of joining either the Anglo-Japanese or the Russo-French blocs, it could maneuver between them in a number of ways that might limit centrifugal tendencies. It could, as Hay told Henry Adams, "take refuge in a craven opportunism," doing "what seems possible every day—not caring a hoot for consistency or the Absolute."[7]

This "craven opportunism" (which some commentators today call "realism") took three main forms in the summer of 1900. The first was to encourage the creation of a military balance that would sour any Russian temptation to act unilaterally—yet do so in a way that would minimize Russian antagonism. Thus when Britain suggested that Japan be urged to send a large military complement immediately to northern China, the United States readily agreed, hopeful that the open door stalking-horse would discourage suspected Russian designs in Manchuria. But simultaneously the United States suggested that "the assent of the other powers" was "desirable" to assuage Russian feelings and keep her more cooperatively inclined. Ironically, when the British passed the proposal to Russia they were faced with a rather awkward situation. Accepting the Bristish inquiry in principle, the Russian government nevertheless objected to the implications of "an independent solution of Chinese affairs" and the supposed "mission given by Europe to Japan to send considerable force to China not only to save legations and foreigners but to suppress Boxers insurrection and to establish order at Peking and Tien Tsin." Indeed, Russia wondered aloud if the policies implied did not "infringe upon fundamental principles already accepted by a majority of the Powers as bases of their Chinese policy": to wit, "maintenance of union between the Powers, maintenance of existing 'regime governmental' in China, exclusion of everything which might lead to partition of the Empire and re-establishment by joint efforts of lawful central authority capable of insuring order and security." So akin were the *fundamental principles* to the American position that they forced an anxious British Foreign Office to inquire of Hay's reaction to the Russian note. Unwilling to take sides against England or to hamper the dispatch of Japanese troops, the Secretary of State nevertheless did not wish to miss an opportunity of tying Russia more explicitly to the concert of powers approach. So he simply put off a direct reply on the grounds that he had "no written form" of the Russian note (a technically accurate but misleading statement), while letting the obvious similarity between the Russian principles and the American circular speak for itself. Thus in the end Hay got both the desired Japanese troops and quite unexpected Russian diplomatic support. As he put it himself: "Sufficient unto the day is the blunder thereof. I have been far more lucky than I dreamed I could be thus far."[8]

Second in the American effort to influence developments in China was the administration's decision that United States military units would participate in the allied expeditionary force. It was, in many senses, a most difficult decision to make—partly because of internal opposition, even from McKinley's own cabinet and military advisers (who thought it would weaken other pacification efforts in the Philippines); partly because it contradicted McKinley's and Hay's own *least-cost expansionism* and their conviction that the "ideal policy" was "to do nothing, and yet be around when the water-melon is cut." It was also a decision that dramatized the growing realization that marketplace penetration, if it was to be successful, often compelled the use of force to control and order that marketplace—ironically, even against its local inhabitors, those lucky beneficiaries of open door liberality. However difficult, however ironic, the decision was made—chiefly out of fear that American views would carry little weight, either during pacification or the negotiations to follow, unless American national interests enjoyed some sort of proportionate military representation.

It now became a military question of how much force and what kind. And America rapidly escalated from only a beefed-up naval involvement (the largest American fleet ever assembled on foreign station theretofore), to one army brigade as "necessary to properly represent our government," to "all marines Cavite" (the Manila Bay encampment), to the entire Ninth Infantry "thoroughly equipped and well supplied with everything." By the legations' rescue in August, five thousand United States troops were in China (one-tenth of the allied force), and had it not been for logistical problems, the number would have been twice as large. Most of the troops came from the Philippines, occasioning Hay's remark that "It is to Manila that we owe the ability to send troops and ships to the defense of our ministers, our missionaries, our consuls, and our merchants in China, instead of being compelled to leave our citizens to the casual protection of other powers, as would have been unavoidable had we flung the Philippines away." A "vindication for us in the Philippines business," Reid called it.[9]

The final step to give body to the July 3 circular grew out of Hay's understanding (via Rockhill's prompting) that "The thing to do—the only thing was to localize the storm if possible." If not, if the rebellion spread into central and southern China, then all would be lost. The Chinese Imperial government would surrender all remaining appearance of sovereignty and control, while even such open door powers as England and Japan would be pushed to more militant steps to protect their "optional" spheres. The end result, then, could well be a general war against all of China, climaxed by the final and dreaded partition. Painfully aware of this, the Secretary of State boldly seized upon the suggestion of several provincial Chinese Viceroys in the Yangtze Valley that they would take responsibility for putting "down any attempt at insurrection" and affording "all needed protection to foreigners and missionaries"—provided the powers refrained from any show or use of force. Ignoring the contrary advice of his own Consul General in Shanghai as well as the lukewarm attitude of England and France, Hay initiated a flurry of diplomatic activity aimed at securing a stabilization agreement "with Viceroys about measures to preserve peace." Although no formal bargain was made (in part because the American cabinet opposed Chinese stipulations disallowing anti-foreign acts before they happened), a *de facto* deal did emerge. McKinley ordered United States military forces "not to attack Central and Southern Chinese provinces so long as the local authorities maintain order and protect foreigners." The Viceroys, in turn, reaffirmed their promise to maintain stability and ignored the imperial edict of June 20 that "all viceroys fight foreigners." Presented with this *fait accompli*, the other powers found it prudent to acquiesce in American policy. France approved the arrangement with little comment. England followed suit and quietly scrapped secret plans to seize key Yangtze forts and arsenals. Even Germany, some sabre-rattling notwithstanding, felt obliged by the power realities of life to do the same. Thus by July 8 Hay happily concluded that "All the powers have fallen in with my *modus vivendi* in the Center and South," and two days later, with obvious satisfaction, he wired his "appreciation" to the Viceroys.[10]

The only problem with Hay's adventures in realism was that they labored in an air of unreality. American policy aimed largely for the quick liquidation of military involvement in China and the "re-establish[ment] . . . by joint efforts . . . [of] a central Government which can guarantee tranquility and order." But no other single power in the Far East wholeheartedly shared that aim (or at least not for the same reasons). Consequently, with the rescue of the harried legations in mid-August and the elimination of that goal as a unifying factor, all the latent centrifugal forces began to operate.

Ironically, only Russia and occasionally France embraced an apparently similar policy of encouraging the prompt reconstruction of the Chinese Imperial government. For example, when the

United States recommended that the powers "utilize services of friendly Chinese authorities" to hasten that end, and when it specifically recognized Li Hun Chang's self-proclaimed credentials to negotiate for the Empire, *only* Russia and France gave firm diplomatic support. But there any community ended, for Russia was merely playing the 1895 game all over again, this time for higher stakes—propping up the imperial regime and playing the role of Chinese benefactor, all for a price. Unhappily, the price was Manchuria, or so it appeared in early August after Russia occupied the treaty port of Newchwang, commercial key to much of Manchuria. Of course, Russia responded to protests from England, Japan, and the United States with assurances that the occupation was "military and temporary"; that she "did not propose any territorial acquisition in 'China or Manchuria' "; and that she would not "infringe the rights and privileges which the Russians [as well as the foreigners and Chinese] have enjoyed previously." But the American Consul in Newchwang consistently reported that Russian actions indicated a general intention "to retain this port," a position given additional credence by Russia's own equivocation over eventual withdrawal (adding the ill-defined proviso that "the actions of the other powers be not an obstacle thereto"). Hay, who often talked of Russian "treachery" while glibly commenting that "it is for us to take care that [it] shall not be profitable," now (as if surprised) condemned Russia for "shameless disregard of her solemn assurances" and groused that "we are going to have trouble with Russia in Manchuria."[11]

Actually, the United States was having "trouble" with England and Japan as well. For one thing, they had already joined Germany in thwarting the American plan for prompt negotiations and settlement with China over the issues arising from the Boxer Rebellion. Terming such an effort "premature," English and Japanese representatives at Taku voted for a resolution denying Li Hung Chang permission to come ashore there, thus tacitly supporting the German position that he had "no right to speak for or in the name of China." Far worse were their military actions in Shanghai and

Amoy—actions that threatened the American effort to isolate central and southern China from upheaval; presented Russia an ideal excuse for remaining in Newchwang; and cast grave doubts upon Anglo-Japanese belief in the open door.

In Shanghai the British engaged in a bit of preventive medicine. Fearful that Russian occupation of Newchwang might lead to general partitioning, but still unwilling to concede that eventuality, they sought to safeguard their major interests while still retaining policy flexibility. So, on the one hand, they dispatched troops from India to Shanghai; on the other, they kept the contingent relatively small and avoided overt interference in the municipal government, hoping to make some qualitative distinction between their actions and those of Russia. Nevertheless, the British action did excite the local populace and heighten the chances of rebellion. It did stimulate other powers to take similar steps, and Germany, France, and Japan shortly followed with troop landings of their own. The United States was once more over the barrel of opposing British actions privately but not wishing to do so publicly, leading the "confused" and unhappy Secretary of State to equivocate on the grounds that information was "conflicting and tainted besides with the sensationalism of the newspapers."[12]

Further south at Amoy, Japan took the lead in landing troops. Moreover, she did so in an atmosphere that seemed to signal her abandonment of any lingering commitment to the open door. Only one week earlier the Japanese Minister in Washington had told the State Department that his country's support of the "open door" and "Chinese integrity" was contingent upon similar consensus support by the other powers; that, specifically, "should the Russian operations at Newchwang or the British proceedings at Shanghai assume permanent proportions, Japan would assert her right to do the same as to that part of the Chinese territory fronting Formosa." And on the very day of the Amoy operation the Japanese Foreign Minister Aoki bluntly told Rockhill (then on his way to aid Conger in any post-rebellion negotiations) that the *status quo* could not "be kept"; that Russian moves in Manchuria would force Japan and others to demand "further concessions of territory"; that "the division of China" might be "the unavoidable outcome of the present troubles."

Thus the "Japanese landing" created real American fear that it might "amount to occupation." Nor was that fear allayed by Japanese assurances that their sole purpose was "to protect our Consulate and foreign residents of the place," for American consular reports pictured Amoy as quite orderly and peaceful prior to the landing; that in fact the landing itself was the cause of the very disorder it was supposedly geared to suppress. Fortunately for the United States, Japan had overstepped the implicit bounds established by her British ally-to-be. Still ambivalent, still anxious to avoid an irreparable move toward partitioning, Great Britain quickly stepped in to head off any permanent occupation. In response to a Chinese request she landed her own troops at Amoy, used them as a neutralizing ploy against Japanese forces, and secured a Japanese promise to withdraw as soon as order was restored. One week later, with obvious reluctance, Japan joined England in a cooperative evacuation. But the United States, clearly shaken by the implications of the episode, kept an American warship in port an additional week to keep tabs on the situation.[13]

Amidst this deterioration, Russia gave the nearly fatal jolt to the McKinley administration's nervous system. On August 28 the czarist government dispatched a note to the interested powers which announced, in its final form, the "intention to withdraw Russian Minister and Russian force . . . from Peking," and invited others to follow suit. Its proffered rationale was the preservation of Chinese integrity; continued occupation of the capital city would discredit the Chinese government with its subjects, discourage the Imperial Court from returning from the interior, and forestall the negotiations so necessary for the reconstruction of Chinese stability and authority. True—so far as it went. Left unsaid was where Russian troops would be withdrawn to (Manchuria) and how

Russia would restructure her relations with her obligated Chinese friend (a separate deal for an enlarged and more secure slice of Manchuria). But stated or not, the Russian note was clearly intended as an open invitation for each power to safeguard its own interests by making unilateral arrangements with China—a prospect that held no hope for the future of the open door. Understanding this, A. A. Adee, Acting Secretary during Hay's illness-induced absence, sought to counter the Russian move with a proposal that might gain the advantages of a troop withdrawal while still holding the concert of powers together. In an initial draft reply he suggested that "while enough troops might be withdrawn from Peking to remove the appearance of an occupation of conquest, the legations . . . and an adequate mixed military police guard should remain to keep order and guarantee the imperial authority upon its return to the capital."

At this precise point an incredible event occurred in the highest echelons of the American government. Acting in Hay's absence, and with the President firmly in the lead, the administration consciously and purposefully *gave up on the open door* and decided to *join the partitioning*. Actually, McKinley had been pointing toward this heresy since July, when Hay twice told John Bassett Moore in private conversation that his chief was "inclined to favor the policy of seizing a port in China, and getting a foothold there, as other powers had done . . ."; that while most of the cabinet supported Hay's position in the July 3 circular, "the President seems to take the other view and to want a slice."[14] Now, in late August, the Newchwang-Shanghai-Amoy syndrome finally persuaded McKinley that consensus neutralization was hopelessly dead; that only force could maintain the open door. And since that avenue encountered the unacceptable risk of general war, he concluded that his country and its economy would have to make do with a smaller share of the China market.

Convening his cabinet on August 29 in an arduous, full day's session, McKinley and his advisers carefully debated the available alternatives (including Adee's draft) and then, in line with their conclusions, fashioned a detailed reply to Russia—one which London newspapers termed "the Russo-American surprise." The memorandum made clear that the United States preferred, were it still possible, to continue "the joint occupation of Peking under definite understanding between the powers until the Chinese Government shall have been reestablished": i.e., the concert of powers and the open door. Nevertheless, if Russia insisted on evacuation, the United States would have to face the harsh reality that talk of "harmony of purpose" would be illusory and "continued occupation of Peking would be ineffective to produce the desired results. . . ." Noting that "Any power which determines to withdraw its troops from Peking will necessarily proceed thereafter to protect its interests in China by its own methods," the cabinet concluded "that this would make a general withdrawal expedient." Accordingly, the American government announced to the other members of the concert that it would "give instructions to the commander of the American forces in China to withdraw our troops from Peking after due conference with the other commanders as to the time and manner of withdrawal." Presumably, the United States—by its own definition—would then "proceed thereafter to protect its interests in China by its own methods."

The immediate upshot of the administration's response was to split its supporters at home, both in and out of government. Some, like Senators John T. Morgan and Cushman K. Davis, clearly welcomed the move. Both feared "that a general war, an Armageddon, is imminent"; both favored "get[ting] out of China as quickly as possible" and "withdraw[ing] to Philippines" on the hope that "our missionaries and trade in China will not be bothered" so long as America had a respectable power base in the archipelago. Both conceded, however, that their hope might be misplaced and that "future complications" might force a military "return to China," though they preferred doing so "*de novo* from the Manila base." Neither Senator specifically suggested that scuttling the concert of powers approach meant immediate American participation in partitioning (far from it), but neither did they rule out this possibility as an eventual course. On the other hand, a great many others were not so prepared to ring down the curtain on the open door and fall back upon an open-ended policy of freedom of action. Some, like Whitelaw Reid, were simply confused, "puzzled to know what is to be the end of our sudden acceptance of Russia's proposal to get out of Peking." Others, whether confused or not, were frankly hostile to the administration's decision. For example, Alfred T. Mahan, amidst much personal "consternation" and in an act of acknowledged "rashness," wrote McKinley personally that his decision could "scarcely fail to have a most injurious effect . . ."; that it had unwittingly made America the pawn of her own arch-enemy, Russia; that its clear result would be "to break up the Concert" and all the policies upon which it was based. Similarly, Rockhill (on his way to the hoped-for negotiations with China) announced in a Shanghai press interview that "the concert of powers" had to be maintained at all costs; that "The relief of Peking is merely an incident of the crisis. The really important work remains to be done." Although Rockhill (at State Department prodding) later denied making the statement, he privately conceded to Associated Press newsmen that the denial was only a face-saving device and that the views recorded were indeed his.[15]

Made a bit cautious by the open schism, the administration postponed implementation of the withdrawal decision until the other powers could be heard from on the matter. But time produced no change for the better. Indeed, affairs became even more dangerously polarized, with England, Japan, and Germany opposing the evacuation while Russia, supported by France and clearly encouraged by the American response, clung tenaciously to her August 28 position. Consequently, by September 11 it was clear that "there will be no such agreement" on continued, unified occupation of Peking; that, in the words of Secretary of War Root, "if we remain it will be for a very long period of diplomatic bargaining, in which we will be but a chip floating on the surface of the current of intrigue and aggression of the Powers." Acting on the advice of Root (his chief China policy adviser in Hay's absence), McKinley decided that "sound policy require[d]" immediate action. Not wishing to act behind Hay's back, the President detailed his decision to him in a letter of September 14. Explaining that "We want to avoid being in Peking for a long time" lest "we may be drawn into currents that would be unfortunate," he went on to say that he knew "no other way to get out but to get out." Thus he proposed to "say to the powers that we intend to withdraw to Tien Tsin our Legation and our army, leaving the time of our withdrawal from Tien Tsin to be determined later on."

What was most significant and dramatic about the McKinley-Root position was its half-open, half-hid corollary. The overt part, conveyed to Hay, was that "after Tien Tsin we should take all of our troops to the Philippines, have them put in good camps, keep the force intact and in good condition and be ready for any emergency in China." Unstated (to Hay at least) was what the emergency was likely to be and how the troops would be used in response to it. But Root clearly had some ideas on these matters wholly consistent with McKinley's inclination to get "a slice" of China. As Root saw it, no action whatsoever should be taken until the election of 1900 was past and McKinley and a Republican Congress safely continued in power. At that point, "if China has not indicated a practical disposition to comply with our requirements" (i.e., maintenance of the open door in *all* parts of China), then "Congress should authorize the landing of an adequate force to compel proper action by China."[16]

Hay most certainly must have been stunned by this turn of events. Up to this point he had accepted Root's assurances that there was real hope of continuing joint occupation "under a definite understanding." This being so, he steadfastly denied to friends that there was any truth to the widespread rumors "that I am sulking away from Washington because the President and Root have turned me down." On the contrary, he insisted that "We have all been absolutely as one from the very beginning and are now." His contention of continued friendly relations certainly seems supported by the easy, jocular vein of his cor-

respondence with Root (as, for example, when Root gently
kidded him about swapping "a numbered old English alliance
for a nice new clean Russian article painted yellow"). Now,
however, the President's September 14 letter, though it did not
damage Hay's loyalty to the administration, made it impossible
for Hay to delude himself further that America's China policy
still followed his charted course.

Perhaps personally hurt, and fully convinced of the wrong-
headedness of the turn in policy, Hay made one desperate long-
distance effort to pull the administration up short. He did so in
a letter to Adee (passed on to the President) which the Assistant
Secretary described as "characteristic, hard-hitting and sensible
but somewhat despondent." It was also, as well, a rigorous examination of American alternatives in China and a persuasive
plea for continuation of the consensus neutralization approach.
"The dilemma is clear enough," began Hay's sickbed epistle. "We
want to get out at the earliest possible moment," but "we must
not lose our proper influence in the final arrangement." The latter
was key—how to retain proper influence in what had become a
crumbling and dangerous situation, where there was "not a
single power . . . we can rely on, for our policy of abstention
from plunder and the Open Door"; where even England, if un-
supported, was likely to collect her optional spheres? In answer-
ing his own question, Hay again expressed personal favor for
the alliance/force tactic: "join with England, whose interests
are identical with ours, and makes our ideas prevail." But having
made his point—for the record—he dismissed it as politically
impossible, for "Nothing was clearer than that the whole country
would have risen in uproar if we had formed an alliance with
England." (He might have added—were it politic—that the public need have no fear about such a development, for McKinley
himself had doubts about the identity of Anglo-American interests
and real fears about being drawn into the vortex of a general
great-power war.)[17]

Having relegated one alternative to the wastebin, Hay turned to consider the viability of the McKinley-Root proposition—as Hay interpreted it, disengaging from the concert of powers, then either leaving American interests to the care of others or unilaterally making special arrangements with China. To his mind, the act of disengagement was likely to rule out either subsequent method of protecting America's economic stake in the China market. On the one hand, American withdrawal would make "Germany and England . . . feel resentful," and they would "take no care of our interests, and Russia will sell us out without winking." On the other hand, China—as it did in the San Mun Bay crisis with Italy—would "fall back on her *non possumus,* if we try to make separate terms with her." And in the end, said Hay, "we shall be left out in the cold."

Finally, by process of elimination, Hay concluded that the United States had only one choice (save the *unthinkable* one of dropping the marketplace commitment altogether): remain in Peking with England, Germany, and Japan; get some representative of China to the capital city at once; treat him with all civility; get collective negotiations under way as quickly as possible—and hope. Hope that the bloc's presence and pressure would dissuade China from capitulating to Russian demands for a separate agreement on Manchuria. Hope that the perseverance of the open door camp would give Russia cause for second thoughts; that, having failed to get any takers (save her French ally) for her evacuation proposal, having failed to incite a mad rush for separate deals in unilateral spheres, Russia might hesitate to proceed on a go-it-alone basis. In short, as Hay said, "hold on like grim death to the Open Door," and hope that the Russian move had only been a probing action, and that its failure to produce the desired international response would persuade Russia to shelve it temporarily and return to the collective fold, where once more the concert of powers could hopefully act as a brake on Russian ambitions.[18]

Whether or not Hay's analysis immediately and fully won McKinley over is problematical. But one would guess (in the

light of subsequent behavior) that it gave the President occasion
to doubt the efficacy of his course. Perhaps it caused him to
ponder whether reentering China after either the Armageddon
or a general division of spoils might not be more difficult and
costly than remaining on the scene and trying to head off either
eventuality. Whatever, Hay's counsel fortuitously coincided with
two supporting factors. One was a flood of parallel pleas from
American representatives in China, as Minister Conger, Commissioner Rockhill, and General Chaffee of the American expeditionary force all emphatically advised McKinley not to evacuate
the American legation and American troops. The other was an
Italian compromise proposal (reportedly engineered by Germany)
which offered the United States (and Russia) a graceful way
out of the commitment to evacuate Peking. Based on the premise
that the principles of the July 3 circular could "be better sub-
served by prolonging still for some time, the international occupation of Peking," the Italian note suggested that "those Governments which have accepted in principle the withdrawal of troops
should not hurry the execution of the same, in order to give a
chance for a later understanding among the powers."

Opposed by his own Secretary of State and by his personal
representatives in China, beset by criticism from past supporters
at home, and probably himself ambivalent about the future
direction of his China policy, President McKinley readily seized
upon the Italian suggestion to postpone early fulfillment of the
American pledge to Russia. Thus the response to the Russian
note of August 28 became a flexible (and potentially useful)
position, to be invoked or further ignored as future circumstances
dictated. In like sense, as Hay had hoped, Russia made a *de
facto* return to the great-power communion in Peking, giving the
open door another of its seemingly endless (and uneasy) leases
on life. Thus by September's end a newly optimistic, obviously
self-satisfied Hay could write Adee that while "There is still
plenty of trouble ahead in China . . . it is a comfort to feel that
thus far there have been no mistakes." And the next day, clearly

happy to have the President and American policy tuned back in on his wavelength, the Secretary of State wrote McKinley that "I hope you will not think it impertinent if I congratulate you on your recent China despatches." And in a false bit of modesty, he added: "They make me shy about going back to the Department." Once more, *It began to look as if there was some chance for the Open Door after all.*[19]

# ⚏ Chapter VII: *The Future in Microcosm*

> "I am sick and tired of the whole business and heartily glad to get away from it. I have been able to do something for commercial interests, and in a number of points have been able to carry out the Secretary's views, but have been practically alone in the negotiations. England has her agreement with Germany, Russia has her alliance with France, and the Triple Alliance comes in here, and every other combination you know of is working here just as it is in Europe. I trust it may be a long time before the United States gets into another muddle of this description."
>
> —W. W. Rockhill, 1901[1]

One year after Hay's psychic revitalization, two coincidental events marked the effective and climactic end to chapter one of the still unfinished book on American expansion in the western Pacific. On September 6, 1901, an assassin's bullet struck down President McKinley; eight days later, when it had taken its fatal toll, the young, ebullient Theodore Roosevelt became Chief Executive—a changing of the guard that was eventually to have great impact upon the tone and tactics of open door diplomacy, but not upon its ends. At the same time, on September 7, halfway around the world, W. W. Rockhill, acting for the United States, signed the Boxer Protocol, presumably settling by diplomatic action the many and tangled issues posed by the Boxer Rebellion. In essence the accord signaled an end to the first of endless and increasingly difficult acid tests that the Open Door Policy, by its nature, would have to endure.

In the interval between Hay's revived optimism and these dramatic events lay a multitude of diplomatic stepping-stones: the initial French note of October 4, 1900, around which inter-allied talks first began; the November 26 tentative draft and the December 21 final form of the preliminary agreement among the powers on the general terms for discussions with China; the May 23, 1901, pact on indemnities and its firm acceptance on July 26; the tentative agreement on commercial reform on June 25 and its final explication in the Protocol itself and later, separate commercial treaties. Viewed conventionally and chronologically, the year was a tortuous, twisting, tedious, frustrating one for American diplomacy. Every negotiating point, however major or minor, seemed contested; power alignments shifted in rapid and bewildering fashion, from issue to issue and from time to time; and the trials of conducting complex negotiations on the spot, thousands of miles from Washington and in the midst of an occupational army, led to misunderstood instructions, procedural and substantive disagreements, and ultimately a clear and definite break between Minister Conger on the one hand and Commissioner Rockhill and the Department of State on the other.

In the end, throughout all the confusion and changing expectations, only two things seemed inalterably true about American policy: it sought to maintain the concert of powers and prevent unilateral bargains with China; and it aimed for a final settlement (arrived at as expeditiously as possible) wholly consistent with the open door and Chinese integrity. Assessed superficially, American policy—as witnessed by the Boxer Protocol—fulfilled these ambitions. But in reality the concert of powers was an optical illusion and unilateralism a foregone conclusion. Chinese integrity remained a hollow idol—an open invitation to Western imperialism and a galling affront to Chinese nationalism. Ill omens indeed for the myopic quest to use an "open" Asia to save a "closing" America.[2]

☜☞

The view from the bargaining table unveiled, in miniature, the limited and dualistic nature of America's conception of Chinese independence and entity. In essence the United States defined Chinese integrity in terms of preserving her territory intact, maintaining the external symbols of her sovereignty, and upholding national pride and face—all necessary to give legality and credence to the open door. But the American definition denied to China either the right or capacity to modify or close the open door, or to develop a more balanced, advanced, and sophisticated economy. As a result, the Protocol negotiations found the United States vigorously befriending and protecting China in all things political and territorial, while it sought to limit her internal, economic development so as to expand her value as a market. Translated into specifics, the United States played a moderating role on the issues of punishments and indemnity but took the lead in demanding commercial concessions from China.

Theoretically the United States accepted the proposition—as did the other powers—that those allegedly responsible for the Boxer uprising receive punishments commensurate with their supposed crimes. But in practical terms American policy-makers tried to handle the punishments issue in a manner that would least delay negotiations on other, more substantive issues, and would least denigrate the appearance of Chinese sovereignty. At the same time they hoped that American liberality on the issue might "win friends and influence people" among the Chinese, hopefully for the open door.[3] Russia, ironically, was similarly moderate on the punishments question, but with the hope that it might be a useful ploy for Sino-Russian negotiations over Manchuria's status. Germany, however, took a very harsh, unbending approach—partly because the murder of her Minister to China put German national honor more clearly on the line; partly because of Germany's traditional "spare-the-sword and spoil-the-colony" attitudes.[4]

Compared to indemnities and commercial reform, the punishments question was surely secondary. Nevertheless, on three separate occasions it clearly menaced the aims of American foreign policy. Germany first posed it in the midst of the diplomatic crisis of September 1900, when she insisted that no "diplomatic negotiations with the Chinese Government" could take place until China surrendered to the allies "the first and real perpetrators of the crimes committed in Peking against international law." Presumably the concert—not China—would designate the guilty parties, pass judgment, and mete out punishments. Aware that such a cavalier approach (a war crimes trial for a non-war) would be a disastrous slap at Chinese integrity and run "the risk of indefinite delay" in negotiations as well, the United States sternly and uncategorically objected. In fact, the American government instructed "its Minister in Peking to enter forthwith into conference" with Chinese representatives, without bothering to await the outcome of Germany's "preliminary condition." Confronted with this response and similar ones by Russia and England, Germany realistically decided to compromise. In a significant revision she no longer insisted that the Chinese government actually surrender the Boxer leaders, but only that she provide a list of the accused which the powers might evaluate for completeness. And Germany no longer asked that the sentences be carried out by the allies, but only that they be "controlled" by them. (The United States interpreted "controlled" as meaning only "to keep a check upon.") Overjoyed at Germany's "retreat from their former position," Hay immediately advised "meet[ing] them as far as we can"—and McKinley obliged. Writing Henry White some weeks later, the Secretary of State proclaimed: "The moment we acted the rest of the world paused, and finally came over to our ground; and the German Government, which is generally brutal but seldom silly, recovered its senses, climbed down off its perch and presented another proposition which was exactly in line with our own position."[5]

Exactly three weeks later the first-draft agreement among the negotiators at Peking gave Hay reason to sing another song. Article III, evaluating the Chinese imperial decree on punishments, demanded that two more names be added to the nine already there, and that the sentences be changed from banishment or degradation to death by beheading. Again fearful of slights to Chinese integrity and of delay in negotiations, the State Department insisted that no proper basis had been laid for the *de facto* ultimatum to China—the powers had not produced "indubitable evidence of the guilt" of the accused, and no prior effort had been made to determine precisely what punishments (be it death, banishments, or whatever) the Chinese government "proposes to inflict upon them." And as an obiter dictum it questioned whether the death sentences for all were "justifiable." Nevertheless, the protests made only a minor dent, and the November 26 final draft did little more than tone down the language of the punishments section and reduce the number of implicated from eleven to eight. Fortunately, however, the foreign offices of most countries proved less demanding and vindictive than their diplomatic representatives (many of whom, like Conger, had suffered at the rebellion's hands). Wondrously, only Germany insisted upon "exorbitant demands . . and conditions impossible to execute," and even she (as England predicted) would "not stand out." So with Russia and the United States once more taking the lead, the preliminary agreement of December 21 eliminated all specific names from the list of guilty parties and substituted the phrase "severest punishment" for the earlier "death penalty."[6]

But similar moderation did not always prevail on the question of indemnification for losses of foreign life and property. Nor, in fact, was American policy quite so clear and internally consistent. It did in most respects show an intense concern to keep indemnities somehow consistent with Chinese integrity—and occasionally was successful. It established early (against the vehement objection of American missionary interests) the general principle that Chinese Christians could not use foreign powers as intermediaries in presenting their indemnity claims but would have to deal directly with their own government, thus preserving Chinese sovereignty with her own people.[7] The United States also took the lead in persuading the concert to accept three interrelated ideas about indemnities: one, that compensation be monetary, not territorial (hopefully eliminating additional spheres of interest); two, that the bill of damages be presented to China as "a lump indemnity" (on the assumption that a single, prorated figure would be less than the sum total of separate bills individually negotiated—and more consistent with the principle of common deliberation); and three, that the final sum be within the limits of "Chinese ability to pay" (on the grounds that anything beyond that might force China to enact heavy internal taxation—thus risking new rebellion, or to grant non-pecuniary concessions in lieu of money—thus risking her national integrity).[8]

Translating these principles into practical terms proved considerably more difficult, if possible at all. To begin with, America's assessment of the upper limits of Chinese ability to pay—namely 40 million pounds sterling—proved unpopularly low with all of the other powers. Some of the competing estimates ran as high as twice the American figure, leading a disheartened Rockhill to conclude that some of the powers wanted "to exact the last farthing from this country." As if to confirm his fears, the lump indemnity initially agreed upon totaled 67 million pounds. Nor did subsequent American efforts change the situation. Ignoring British proposals to adopt a compromise amount of 50 million pounds, the United States stubbornly and unsuccessfully tried a variety of tactics to achieve her optimum—ending in a proclamation that she would cut her "reasonable claim to one half if similar reduction will be made by others." In the meantime the exigencies of diplomatic logrolling led England to abandon her compromise course, leaving America without even the half-loaf. Thus the May 23, 1901, indemnity agreement accepted the initial figure (in American currency, $334 million), with the United States claiming (and receiving) the smallest share of any major power—slightly less than 10 per cent of the total.[9]

Compounding the indemnity issue was the controversy over the means of payment—a bitter squabble in which America's support for Chinese integrity sagged considerably under the weight of her commercial ambitions. In essence the American government got caught not only between two diplomatic camps but between two contradictory concerns. On the one hand, England and Japan insisted that the indemnity be paid in 4 per cent Chinese bonds secured by the proceeds from customs dues and the salt gabelle. Moreover, during the period of bond redemption (set at thirty-nine years) China was to accept "such foreign supervision of her finances as may be necessary" to insure full payment. The idea, quite obviously, was to use this approach as a lever to force additional commercial concessions and reform of the Chinese revenue system. Russia and France clearly understood that this tactic would give the chief trading nations (principally Great Britain) "a greater influence than Russia over Chinese affairs." And they pointed out, quite correctly, that the commission charges and other financial extras involved in the Anglo-Japanese scheme would measurably increase China's economic burden. Thus they proposed instead that the indemnity be paid by a loan guaranteed by firm international agreement. In the middle stood the United States, as anxious as England to pry the China market open a bit further but still uneasy about adding to an indemnity figure already too high. For a while America sought to have the best of both worlds, supporting the British plan of payment while proposing that the powers individually accept Chinese bonds at only 3 per cent and without any commissions. But when that compromise met a cold response,

she unreservedly joined England and Japan. So likewise did
Germany—for a price (British abandonment of compromise
efforts to scale down the lump sum). The Russo-French entente,
now diplomatically isolated, grudgingly and unhappily capitulated. In all, the conflict of approaches demonstrated the central
reality (as one American diplomat observed it) that the United
States was "more anxious about her trade than about her bill
of damages."[10]

Indeed, so it was. In fact the Acting American Minister in
Peking might have added that the United States was considerably
more anxious about her trade than she was about Chinese integrity, except as the latter might serve the first. In the commercial
negotiations that dominated the last months of the Boxer Protocol
talks, it was infinitely clear that American concern for Chinese
independence, so often apparent in the punishments and indemnity
questions, did not include any place for China's *economic independence*. Hay insisted that the United States aimed for "conditions no less beneficial to China than to foreign nations"—conditions that would build "up the prosperity of China." But given
practical translation, his carefully chosen conditions proved something less than reciprocal.

In contemporary jargon, the main thrust of America's commercial policy in China at the turn of the century would be
described as "neo-colonial." In negative terms this meant dis-
couragement of any comprehensive industrialization in China on
the simplest and crudest of assumptions that it would diminish
the market share for American surplus manufactures. Rockhill,
for example, felt strongly that "the encouragement of the manufacturing industries of China, and presumably the introduction
therein of foreign machinery, may have far-reaching and highly-
prejudicial economic results." And another of Hay's confidants,
the brilliant Brooks Adams, concluded that "An industrial movement in the villages of the Ho-hang-ho and Yang-tze could only
tend to [America's] embarrassment," and that in some ways, "The
best thing that could happen for her would be for China to remain as she is."[11]

Conversely, America's efforts to colonize China's commerce entailed certain steps to effect further market penetration and perpetuate China's economic dependency. As Hay and his trade adviser, John A. Kasson, saw it, this involved three basic steps: first, explication of a more "strongly worded most favored nation clause" to guard against "special commercial favors to any power on the grounds of reciprocity, territorial occupations or spheres of influence"; second, elimination of inland, interprovincial taxation to facilitate trade expansion in the hinterland (on the assumption, as Hippisley stated it, that "the chief markets are not those bordering on the treaty ports but those in the vast interior"); and third, the conversion of the Chinese tariff from an undifferentiated, *ad valorem* one to specific rates for specific goods— "some higher than now and others lower," in Hay's words.

Of the anticipated changes, the last was easily the most interesting and revealing, if not the most important. Hay had two reasons for wishing to see a more flexible tariff schedule, ranging "from five to fifteen per cent, according to the character of the goods . . ." First and most obvious, the Secretary hoped to see the tariff differential structured in ways that would favor export specialties of the United States. (Witness his efforts, at the behest of flour milling interests, to put flour on the Chinese free list— the only non-raw cereal so enumerated.) More important, he believed that "Lower duties ought to be attached to imports tending to develop Chinese productiveness," so that China might have the exchange wherewithal "to buy what they do not now produce." In other words, Hay (like Worthington C. Ford earlier) fully understood that China would never live up to its market potential until it had experienced some degree of economic diversification and modernization; that until some changes occurred there would be little likelihood of transforming demand and want into effective consumer purchasing. But the key question remained how much and what kind of change to seek, so that China might become a better market without becoming an eventual industrial competitor.

Hay's response was the classic precursor for America's general twentieth-century attitude toward economic development in underdeveloped areas—from the Boxer Rebellion to Harry S. Truman's Point Four program. Chinese modernization was to be encouraged in—and limited to—agricultural diversification and specialized light industry; heavy industrialization and across-the-board consumer manufacturing were to remain *verboten*. Thus Hay (with Rockhill and Kasson) came to feel that "*Agricultural implements* and the *simpler forms of manufacturing machinery* should be specially favored" in the tariff arrangements (italics added).[12] It was an approach more than mildly reminiscent of Europe's eighteenth-century economic policies toward her colonies.

Generally speaking, the United States secured most of her commercial aims, at least on paper. The Boxer Protocol of September 1901 incorporated the principle of tariff conversion to specific duties (and specified the prompt improvement of the water approaches to Shanghai and Tientsin), while permitting China to raise its average tariff duty to 5 per cent. In addition the Protocol called for supplementary commercial negotiations and, at the American suggestion, each trading nation was to bargain separately with China or "avail [itself] of the most favored nation clause." (The suggestion was something of a compromise between the Russian proposal for an international commercial conference and the English plan for a smaller, four-power meeting that would have excluded both Russia and France —and caused, in the American view, "serious trouble.") Ultimately, three nations—interestingly, England, Japan, and America (the last two virtually in tandem)—signed treaties with China, in 1902 and 1903. And all of them secured a more explicit most-favored-nation clause and, as well, an elaborate scheme for the abolition of inland taxation (though the abolition proved more theoretical than real). In return the powers accepted an average 10 per cent tariff duty plus a uniform 7 per cent surtax on imports —modest compensation indeed.[13]

Protocol negotiations did not take place in a vacuum. On the contrary, the ominous and menacing environment in which they functioned demonstrated the insecurity of the open door and the unreality of consensus neutralization. A whole series of developments showed (if it required showing) that a great many nations—including some presumably friendly to the United States —had serious reservations about the viability of the equal access policy, while some possessed both the capacity and the inclination to upset it.

The prime illustration of ambivalence over the open door was the famous Anglo-German agreement of October 16, 1900. England took away almost as much as it gave, and the pact left an Anglophile Secretary of State first elated, then dismayed, and finally resigned. The agreement, which burst wholly unexpected upon the American government, pledged England and Germany to the twin principles of "free and open . . . trade" and the "undiminished . . . territorial conditions of the Chinese Empire," and invited other interested nations to join in that commitment. Hay, jubilant in his initial belief that the pact "confirm[ed] and fortif[ied] my work," deferred to the agreement and scrapped his own plan to include a restatement of the open door/Chinese integrity theme in the preamble of a preliminary Protocol.

Had he a bit more of the diplomat's caution, Hay might well have been more wary of nations bearing unsolicited gifts. Indeed, a more careful scrutiny of the text of the pact quickly revealed several key qualifications that cast serious doubt on its intent. For one thing, the physical scope of the Anglo-German commitment was left ambiguous, for it was limited to "all Chinese territory so far as they can exercise influence." Thus it was unclear whether the accord applied to Manchuria, or to southern China, or indeed to anything besides the Yangtze Valley and Shantung. Moreover, in the substantive Article III of the pact, England and Germany declared that "In case of another power making use of the complications in China in order to obtain . . . territorial advantages," they "reserve to themselves to come to a preliminary understanding as to the eventual steps to be taken for the protection of their own interests in China." Because the contingency involved presumably referred to Russian actions in Manchuria, and because Germany was known to oppose risking war with Russia over that area, Article III raised the real possibility that any "preliminary understanding" might mean an Anglo-German decision to join any partitioning scramble initiated by Russia.[14]

Actually, Hay's diplomatic reports from Berlin and London enabled him to piece together a picture at once less fearful and less hopeful. In essence, as he came to see it, the pact was little more than a German-initiated "scheme . . . intended to guard herself against being discriminated against in the trade of the Yangtze Valley," should future events force England to cash in her option on that area as "her sphere of influence"; that Germany, in any circumstance, would continue to enjoy the open door there. In and of itself the agreement neither accepted nor rejected the possibility of future partitioning; nor did it delineate or eliminate Manchuria as a legitimate area of British interest. These items were left open for British diplomacy to choose from in due course. In short, England continued to hold to the open door as an abstraction, while retaining the flexibility either to act upon or ignore that principle as each new exigency dictated. So the Anglo-German agreement, if it was not the open door's deathblow (as one historian saw it), was neither "the greatest triumph of all" (as Hay first described it).[15] It was just another example that even the staunchest of America's supporters (by Hay's lights) could not *necessarily* be counted upon to support the open door; that under certain circumstances it was *conceivable* she might choose to abandon it.

If British pragmatism was a chink in the consensus neutralization approach, then Russian unilateralism proved to be something of a gaping hole. From the very beginning of the Boxer crisis the United States had feared that Russia might be tempted to exploit the chaos, either to annex Manchuria outright or arrange a separate deal with China establishing a *de facto* Russian protectorate in that area. With decreasing hope of success, American diplomacy had sought to persuade Russia that such moves would be disastrous, that only through collective acceptance of the open door could Russia (and others) have both peace and profits. But to a Russia painfully aware of her own economic backwardness, this line of argument held little attraction. To her the open door staked China off into a giant, one-ring, Darwinian-Roman circus in which the Anglo-American gladiators had all the weapons that went with their more advanced, sophisticated, and industrialized economies. Thus for Russia some form of exclusive control in Manchuria seemed a necessity, and the only question was whether it should be overt or tacit.

Events during the first quarter of 1901 steadily unraveled the answer to that question. In sledgehammer fashion, Russian-initiated blows rained down on the Open Door Policy. The first fell on January 9 when Conger reported that "Russia and China have agreed to negotiate separate treaty at St. Petersburg," posing the prospect that "the concert will soon be broken." Ten days later he recorded his impression that the impending "agreement means, without a doubt, the practical annexation of Manchuria to Russia." Then a fortnight later the American Minister put flesh on the bare bones of intuition by transmitting the first sketchy details of the proposed treaty: (1) Russian control of all customs houses in Manchuria; (2) limitations on and Russian supervision of Chinese police; (3) inclusion of Chinchow in the Russian lease; (4) Russian consent to appointment of Chinese Governor General in Manchuria; (5) a separate indemnity for railroad damages during the Boxer uprising; and (6) transfer of the Inkou-Shanhaikuan railroad from Chinese to Russian control. Finally, the publication of the treaty text on March 4 revealed even further dimensions to the agreement: (1) a virtual Russian monopoly of "mines, railroads and other matters in the Russo-Chinese frontier provinces" (which included Mongolia and Turkistan as well as Manchuria); (2) the Russian right of unilateral military intervention in Manchuria should her interests there be threatened. In short, a sort of Russian Platt Amendment that would have made Manchuria as surely a Russian satellite as Cuba was to be American. As Conger characterized it, "the first step, and a long one, towards the dissolution of the Empire" (and the disemboweling of the open door).[16]

The treaty in question was never ratified, thanks to China's adeptness in playing Russia off against the other powers, and to England's willingness to take Russia almost to the brink of war to block the treaty. (American protests had little impact, despite verbal pyrotechnics about the agreement's "sense of impropriety, inexpediency and even extreme danger.") But Russia's backdown in early April was ephemeral at best, as she now discreetly decided to "quietly await the further march of events." And despite Russian protestations that "her occupation of the territory is merely temporary," the only thing the American government assumed to be temporary was Russian pressure on China. Rockhill, for one, thought it only a matter of time before China capitulated to Russian demands, and that "treaty or no treaty, Russia is in Manchuria to stay"; that China "will only retain nominal control over the Manchurian provinces which seem to be irretrievably lost to her." Conger, in September, advised that with the Protocol talks nearly completed, Sino-Russian negotiations were soon to be resumed"—at a time when the evacuation of allied troops and the dissolution of the concert made it unlikely that China could secure "a more favorable treaty" than the one she had rejected earlier in the year. Even Hay, as early as mid-April, accepted the inevitability of some treaty; and rather than oppose something so foregone, he simply asked of Russia formal assurances that the open door would be respected "in any arrangements which may hereafter be entered into between the Russian and Chinese or other Governments, as to Manchuria and Northern China." But no such assurances were forthcoming.

Thus by late summer Conger was predicting that Russia would "undoubtedly finally acquire sovereign control" in Manchuria and would "seriously hamper, if not destroy, foreign trade." And in like fashion (though with a Brooks Adams–style rhetoric), the new American Consul at Newchwang, Henry B. Miller, concluded, in dispatches that "disturbed [Hay's] sleep," that Russia has "a complete and perfect mastery of this part of China," and that "she will annihilate American trade here . . . , make industrial slaves of the Chinese race and soon become a serious obstacle to the extension of our trade in all the Orient, and eventually a menace to our higher civilization." To all this, Hay could say only that "we shall have to do something, or at least make a show."[17]

In the ambiguous and uneasy circumstances of 1901, the question of what that "something" might be perplexed the McKinley administration no small degree. It was a question that would plague its twentieth-century successors as well, for they too would have to confront ambiguous and uneasy situations (at best) and they too would have to consider and choose from the same set of alternatives available in 1901. In that sense the complications of the Boxer Protocol period constituted almost a microcosm of the future.

One could, of course, continue to plug for collective acceptance of the open door in the hope that circumstances or others nations' foreign policies might undergo a change for the better. In fact this was precisely what the United States would do until 1903, when Russia made it painfully and inalterably obvious that she would have none of it. And later, in the 1920's, when the aftermath of the World War had pitched America to the pinnacle of influence, she would use her moral and economic power at the Washington Conference and thereafter to attempt the creation of a newer and more permanent concert of powers. Ideally, this was what the United States always aimed for, even as late as the Brussels Conference of 1938.[18]

On the other hand, one could accept partitioning as inevitable and take a join-them-if-you-cannot-beat-them attitude, carving out as generous a sphere of influence as possible.[19] The McKinley administration certainly leaned in that direction in the summer of 1900. Moreover, one may argue that the abortive effort in November 1900 "to acquire naval station at Samsa Islet" reflected a similar predilection, although its location in southern China (nearer the Philippines but farther from the main trade zones) and the absence of any financial or commercial strings probably indicated a more limited aim of making American military power more mobile and self-sustaining—conceivably, even in support of the open door.[20]

Or, heresy of heresies, one could abstain from either partitioning or preserving the open door; accept the likelihood of Russian dominance of northeast Asia (Siberia, Manchuria, northern China, and perhaps Korea); and then seek to profit from it by establishing—short of overt alliance—intimate economic and diplomatic relations with that country. In other words, accept both the analysis and the solution advocated by the Wilson-McCook group in 1896–1897. Of course, such a choice would not have been easy or very palatable, and certainly few people (not even Wilson and McCook) had advanced it since the first partitioning crisis prior to the Spanish-American War. But by 1901 it was possible to argue that circumstances had changed; that there no longer existed, as there had in 1898–1900, any real chance of preventing Russian emasculation of the open door; that short of employing force, the thing to do was face the hard facts of life and make the best of them. Indeed, Minister Conger argued precisely that way on the eve of the Protocol signing. Referring to the imminent completion of "her great Trans-Siberian railway" and the opening "up to settlement and development" of Siberia, the American diplomat suggested that Russia's "contingency to the United States, and the possibility of connecting its great railroad system by direct lines of steamers across the Pacific with our own transcontinental routes make friendly policy and trade relations between the two peoples most desirable and important." More emphatically, he felt that "If such relations can be established and maintained without any particular and specific alliance, it will make this trade route, which will practically encircle the globe, one of inexpressible potency and of mutual benefit."[21] Overall it was an approach that found increasing (but still minority) support during Theodore Roosevelt's administrations, went thereafter into marked decline, and largely evaporated after the successful Bolshevik revolution.

Finally, one could accept force as necessary to fulfillment of the open door and act accordingly. If one defined force in economic terms, then American economic power could be drawn upon, as Taft's "dollar diplomacy" would in the China Consortium and Manchurian neutralization scheme. If, on the other hand, one defined force in military terms as well, then one had to face the central reality of popular unwillingness (often shared by public officials) to take on the role of Asian Doorman if that responsibility ran the risk of a major military encounter. In confronting that fact, America often (though not always) sought to resolve it by employing Japanese power instead of its own—using it as a substitute to block Russia, stabilize northern China, and safeguard the open door, all on the assumption that Japan could be trusted or controlled.[22] Cleveland's response to the Sino-Japanese War first foreshadowed this approach, and the McKinley administration moved further in that direction by acquiescing in British plans to use Japanese troops as a counterpoise against Russia during the Boxer Rebellion. And, of course, Theodore Roosevelt carried the tactic to its logical conclusion by making the United States a silent partner in the Anglo-Japanese alliance and by encouraging Japan to move against Russia militarily in 1904. Thereafter, despite frequent friction and alienation, American diplomacy more often than not sought to sustain or reestablish some intimate relationship with Japan, either on bilateral terms or subsumed within some larger concert.

All the avenues available had, of course, certain advantages—most of them obvious. All had rather grave handicaps as well. For example, consensus neutralization presupposed a harmony of in-

terests which did not and could not exist in an era of nationalism
and competitive capitalism; partitioning offered a lesser market and
greater burdens; and cooperation with Russia rested upon the debatable assumption that Russia would welcome it.[23] But of all the
tactics, working through Japan was certainly the most enticing,
for it promised to keep open the whole market while it involved a
minimum of direct American responsibility. But of all the tactics it
also proved to be the most dangerous, for it rested upon the illusion
that American national interests could be fulfilled in some nearly
perfect way through the actions of another nation-state—ignoring
that no two nations are likely to have identical needs and policies,
and this being so, that no single nation would permanently and
willingly sublimate its own interests to those of another.

The Japanese-American relationship proved to be an uneasy one,
as the United States discovered that Japan could not be taken for
granted, nor could she be fully controlled, either through naval
displays and races or through the manipulation of financial strings
within the Japanese economy. Secret dealings with Russia on Manchuria and Korea, differences of interpretation over the series of
Japanese-American executive agreements (1905, 1908, and 1917),
Japanese encroachments upon Shantung during the world war—all
were illustrative. Finally, in 1931, the attempt to use Japan as open
door protector broke down altogether. Compelled by the exigencies
of depression, fearful of the rising tides of Chinese nationalism and
radicalism, and resentful of bearing the brunt of political responsibility while others reaped most of the economic reward, Japan
dissolved the partnership with the United States and struck out on
her own. She was no longer "playing our game," as Theodore Roosevelt had described it in 1905.[24]

In the end, the events of December 7, 1941, laid to rest the central notion of informal empire—that America could reap the material rewards of expansionism without paying its prices or bearing
its burdens. Perhaps, as well, they should have forced America to
confront at last the unasked question of the twentieth century:
could the nation's material needs and ideology be served *only*

through expansion into the "new frontier" of Asia (and elsewhere)? Or could it be, as historian Frederick Jackson Turner noted in his later years,[25] that there were still frontiers (and open doors) at home; that there remained "before us a whole wealth of un-exploited resources in the realm of the spirit"?

# NOTES

## Chapter I: *Exporting the Social Question*

1. The quotations are from John W. Fiske, *American Political Ideas*, New York, 1885, 148–150; Josiah Strong, *Our Country*, New York, 1885, 13–15, 99; and Alfred T. Mahan, "The United States Looking Outward," *Atlantic Monthly*, LXVI (1890), 822.
2. See Fred A. Shannon, *America's Economic Growth*, 1st ed., New York, 1940, 468; Thomas C. Cochran and William Miller, *The Age of Enterprise*, New York, 1951, 181–183, 202; Readings Fels, *American Business Cycles, 1865–1897*, Chapel Hill, 1959, 211, 214. Cochran and Miller conclude that "in the midst of the black depression after 1893, for the first time in such circumstances, America had no new West to look to for hope, no new prairies to gridiron with railroads, no new inland markets to develop for expanding factories"; that "American industry . . . ceased to use up domestic as well as foreign capital, [and] . . . stopped returning the high profits of the old days of mighty expansion." Similarly, economist Alvin H. Hansen argues the "stagnationist" view that "investment opportunities in the aggregate were inadequate after the railroads went into decline." Most contemporary economists, however, dissent from such analyses and insist (almost as an article of faith) that "a comparatively young and underdeveloped country like the United States in the 1890's could hardly have lacked outlets for all domestic savings." (Fels, *Business Cycles*, 214.)
3. Albert K. Steigerwalt, "The National Association of Manufacturers; Organization and Policies, 1895–1914," unpublished doctoral dissertation on microfilm, University of Michigan, 1952, 16.
4. The best single statistical source for wages, prices, profits, and income in the late nineteenth century is National Bureau of Economic Research, *Trends in the American Economy in the Nineteenth Century*, Princeton, 1960. Many of the study's conclusions are tentative and some unconvinc-

ing, primarily because of gaps in hard and soft data and the necessity for frequent extrapolations. See also Bernard Weber and S. J. Handfield-Jones, "Variations in the Rate of Economic Growth in the United States of America, 1869–1939," *Oxford Economic Papers,* New Series, VI (June 1954), 101–136; Clarence D. Long, *Wages and Earnings in the United States, 1860–1890,* Princeton, 1960.

5. Rull Johnson to Walter Q. Gresham, July 24, 1893, Gresham MSS; Memorandum, May 8, 1894, John Bassett Moore MSS; Alexander D. Noyes, *Forty Years of American Finance,* New York, 1909, 219; Urieh H. Crocker, *The Causes of Hard Times,* Boston, 1896, 88–89; *New York Tribune,* May 23, 1894, 6; quoted in James A. Barnes, *John G. Carlisle,* New York, 1921, 321. See also Frank P. Weberg, *The Background of the Panic of 1893,* Washington, D.C., 1929, 21–22.

6. Victor S. Clark, *History of Manufactures in the United States,* II, New York, 1929, 171; W. Jett Lauck, *The Causes of the Panic of 1893,* Boston and New York, 1907, 119; Clark, *History of Manufactures,* II, 169–170; Urieh H. Crocker, *The Depression in Trade and the Wages of Labor,* Boston, 1886, 10.

7. Charles H. Cramp, "American Shipbuilding and Commercial Supremacy," *Forum,* XII (1892), 397. Said Cramp: "Our internal development . . . has reached a point at which capital has reached its zenith of profitable investment, and must look for new fields" (i.e., "the development and retention of external market outlets" to relieve the "plethora of production"). Jerimiah W. Jenks, "The Economic Outlook," *The Dial,* X (1890), 253. Jenks, in denying the primacy of the monetary problem, insisted that "the depression is . . . due to small profits" resulting from "a large increase" in industrial output. Spanish American Commercial Union, *Proceedings,* New York, 1889, 10. Speaking to this interested group, Curtis described excess "capacity of production" as "a problem as serious as that of slavery," and saw the only alternatives as "mak[ing] less or sell[ing] more" (viewing the first choice as "impossible" and the second as "imperative"). Significantly, he added that President Harrison "knows where the trouble lies," and he predicted therefore that "the expansion of American commerce on longitudinal lines is to be the feature of the administration."

8. David A. Wells, "The Economic Disturbances Since 1873," *Popular Science Magazine,* XXXI (1887), 303–304, 580; *Political Science Quarterly,* V (1890), 84–103; Wells, "Economic Disturbances Since 1873," 783; *ibid.,* XXXII (1888), 583; ibid., XXXIII (1888), 14.

9. Crocker, *Causes of Hard Times,* 31; H. L. Wilson, "Face to Face with the Trusts," *Fortnightly Review,* LXXVI (1901), 82; Augustus O. Bacon, *Discrimination in Prices Between Domestic and Foreign Commerce of Our Protected Goods,* Washington, D.C., 1904, 4–5.

10. For a cross section of such views, see Gresham to General F. M. Force, August 30, 1893, Letterbook, Gresham MSS; *ibid.,* Gresham to F. P. Schmitt, August 16, 1893; Carnegie to Cleveland, April 22, 1893, Cleveland MSS; *ibid.,* Jacob Schiff to Cleveland, August 20, 1893; *Bankers'*

*Magazine*, XLVIII (1893), 6; *Commercial and Financial Chronicle*, LVII (1893), 43; *Philadelphia Press*, August 11, 1893, 4; *New York Times*, August 9, 1893, 4; *Chicago Tribune*, August 7, 1893, 4.

11. *Iron Age*, LII (1893), 206; *American Wool and Cotton Reporter*, VII (1893), 873, 905; *New York Tribune*, May 28, 1894, 6.

12. Otto C. Lightner, *The History of Business Depressions*, New York, 1922, 186; Frank S. Philbrick, "The Mercantile Conditions of the Crisis of 1893," *University of Nebraska Studies*, II (1902), 300; Lightner, *History of Business Depressions*, 186; Alexander D. Noyes, *The Market Place*, Boston, 1938, 107–108.

13. See Walter LaFeber, *The New Empire*, Ithaca, 1963, 157–158.

14. William A. Scott, *Money and Banking*, New York, 1910, 97; Edward C. Kirkland, *A History of American Economic Life*, New York, 1951, 525; Paul Leroy-Beaulieu, "Conditions for American Commercial and Financial Supremacy," *Forum*, XX (1895), 393.

15. Barnes, *Carlisle*, 301; see again LaFeber, *New Empire*, 158–159. Noyes, *Forty Years of American Finance*, 270; Michael G. Mulhall, "Thirty Years of American Trade," *North American Review*, CLXV (1897), 572–581; Frederic Emory, "Our Commercial Expansion," *Munsey's Magazine*, XXII (1899), 540–541; Alexander D. Noyes, "The Recent Economic History of the United States," *Quarterly Journal of Economics*, XIX (1904), 183; Lowthiar Bell, "The Iron and Steel Trade," *Fortnightly Review*, XLVII (1887), 88.

16. See Ernest R. May, *Imperial Democracy*, New York, 1961. Professor May rightly emphasizes that America's own perception of its status as a world power proceeded from Europe's prior acknowledgment of that fact. Nevertheless, he often errs by not carefully examining Europe's definition of power (American style)—which was considerably more material (i.e., economic) than metaphysical.

17. Noyes, "Recent Economic History," 182; *New Orleans Times-Picayune*, November 25, 1897, 4; *The Memoirs of Count Witte*, London, 1929, 410; Mulhall, "Thirty Years of American Trade," 577; Henry Adams to W. W. Rockhill, undated, Rockhill MSS.

18. Charles R. Flint, "Our Export Trade," *Forum, XXIII* (1897), 290–291. Flint's views largely mirrored those expressed earlier by the articulate Ulysses D. Eddy, a fellow director in Flint, Eddy and Company, a large export house dealing principally in cotton textiles to China. See Ulysses D. Eddy, "Our Chance for Commercial Supremacy," *Forum*, XI (1891), 420, 427.

19. May, *Imperial Democracy*, 9. For example, *Bankers' Magazine* spoke often of "the tendency . . . to increase the agencies of production too rapidly, thus outstripping the sources of consumption" (XLIX [1894], 83); and *Bradstreet's* blamed the depression not on "any lack of confidence" in the monetary standard but upon "the absence of profitable employment for . . . money" (XXII [1894], 322–323). American Bankers Association, *Proceedings*, 1898, 8–9; *Iron Age*, LXII (1898), 14; *ibid.*, LX (1897), 18; *American Wool and Cotton Reporter*, XI (1897),

46–47. In 1893 the *Reporter* had explicitly denied "the narrowness of the home market" or the need for "a foreign outlet." *Ibid.*, VII (1893), 186.

20. National Association of Manufacturers, *Proceedings*, II (1897), 16. See NAM *Proceedings* II and III (1897–1898) for resolutions favoring such activities and programs. See National Archives, Record Group 46, 55–56a, j34; Philadelphia Commercial Museum, *The World's Commerce and the United States Share of It*, Philadelphia, 1899, back cover, 2; *Congressional Record*, 55th Cong., 3rd Sess. 314, 358.

21. James D. Richardson, ed., *Messages and Papers of the Presidents, 1789–1897*, XII, Washington, D.C., 1899, 5984; *Speeches and Addresses of William McKinley, from March 1, 1897 to May 30, 1900*, New York, 1900, 54; *American Trade*, IV (1901), 177; Gresham to Judge E. Dyer, May 2, 1894, Letterbook, Gresham MSS; Frederic Emory, "Our Commercial Expansion," 544; Richard Olney, "Growth of Our Foreign Policy," *Atlantic Monthly*, LXXXV (1900), 299; *House Document* 536, v. 64, 55th Cong., 2nd Sess.

22. *Chicago Inter-Ocean*, January 7, 1898, 6; *New Orleans Times-Picayune*, January 2, 1898, 4; *New York Tribune*, January 3, 1898, 6. For similar examples in other papers, see *New York Times*, January 1, 1894, 4; *Philadelphia Press*, December 17, 1897, 6; and *Chicago Tribune*, November 29, 1897, 6.

23. LaFeber, *New Empire*, 159–172; *ibid.*, 162, 167; Hilary A. Herbert, "Reciprocity and the Farmer," *North American Review*, CLIV (April 1892), 414; LaFeber, *New Empire*, 165, 167; *Congressional Record*, Appendix, 53rd Cong., 2nd Sess., 195; Isaac Deutscher, *Russia in Transition*, New York, 1957, 165; LaFeber, *New Empire*, 164, 171.

24. Ulysses D. Eddy summed up the general stratagem of reciprocity in 1891 in this fashion: "In the beginning of the campaign for the world's trade, we first throw our outworks around neutral markets in the shape of reciprocity treaties." See Eddy, "Our Chance for Commercial Supremacy," 419.

25. David Arganian, "McKinley and Commercial Reciprocity," unpublished master's thesis, University of Wisconsin, 1958, 27; Richardson, *Messages of the Presidents*, XIII, 6239.

26. William A. Williams, *The Tragedy of American Diplomacy*, Cleveland, 1959, 132; Arganian, "McKinley and Reciprocity," 27; Erastus Wiman, *An Economic Revolution*, New York, 1893, 19; Richardson, *Messages of the Presidents*, XIII, 6239; *Congressional Record*, 55th Cong., 1st Sess., 53, 71; Arganian, "McKinley and Reciprocity," 31–32; NAM *Proceedings*, II, 20–22.

27. *Congressional Record*, 55th Cong., 1st Sess., 242–243, 363, 121–122. For other statements in support of reciprocity, see 133–135, 242, 246, 337. *Ibid.*, 340–341, 199, 209, 230, 526, 533, 220–221, 216–217, 274, 492.

28. *Ibid.*, 125–126, 147–148, 480, 210–211, 224, 205, 482, 551, 182, 147–149, 205, 268–269.

29. *Ibid.*, 245, 555, 1227–1229, 2506, 1227, 1223, 2152.

30. *Ibid.*, 1416; see also 1238, 1527, 1596, 1672, 1972, 2228. *Ibid.*, 2015, 2234, 2231.

31. Voting with Cannon in favor of his amendment on farm export bounties were three Populists, three Democrats (including one former Populist), and three Silver Republicans. With the exception of two southern Senators, all came from Plains or Rocky Mountain states (North and South Dakota, Nebraska, Idaho, Utah, Kansas, Montana, and Nevada). How much of Cannon's analysis they accepted remains problematical, though William M. Stewart of Nevada and Richard P. Pettigrew of South Dakota seemed to be in substantial accord. For the vote on Cannon's amendment, see *ibid.*, 1634.

32. *Ibid.*, 1615, 1630, 1615.

33. *Ibid.*, 2703–2705.

34. Charles A. Beard and G. H. E. Smith, *The Open Door at Home*, New York, 1934, vii; Elihu Root to Theodore Roosevelt, December 13, 1900, Root MSS; Brooks Adams, "The New Struggle for Life Among Nations," *Fortnightly Review*, LXII (1899), 275.

## Chapter II: *The Frustration of Laissez Faire*

1. David J. Dallin, *The Rise of Russia in Asia*, New Haven, 1949, 36; Walter Q. Gresham to Charles Denby, August 8, 1894, Letterbook, Gresham MSS; Philip Joseph, *Foreign Diplomacy in China, 1894–1901*, London, 1928, 67; James D. Richardson, ed., *Messages and Papers of the Presidents*, XII, New York, 1897, 5957; *New York Times*, August 9, 1894, 5. Not all the press shared this indifference. The *Chicago Inter-Ocean*, for example, stated unequivocally that "no great nations can now go to war without affecting our trade and our interests, which extend to the uttermost parts of the earth." See *Chicago Inter-Ocean*, July 29, 1894, 4.

2. Gresham to Albert S. Willis, September 28, 1894, Letterbook, Gresham MSS; see Joseph, *Foreign Diplomacy in China*, 142; Richardson, *Messages and Papers of the Presidents*, XII, 5957; *New York Times*, December 29, 1894, 5; *ibid.*, May 9, 1895, 5.

3. Grover Cleveland to Gresham, telegram, October 12, 1894, Gresham MSS; Gresham to Cleveland, telegram, October 12, 1894, Gresham MSS; Joseph, *Foreign Diplomacy in China*, 67; Gresham to Denby, December 26, 1894, Letterbook, Gresham MSS.

4. This interesting hypothesis is discussed by the controversial Chinese scholar Sheng Hu in various parts of his *Imperialism and Chinese Politics*, Peking, 1955.

5. National Archives, Record Group 59, *China Despatches* 98, No. 2180, Denby to Gresham, March 26, 1895 (hereafter this source will be cited as NA, RG 59); H. S. Sternburg to Theodore Roosevelt, July 30, 1895, Roosevelt MSS; Gresham to Senator John Morgan, January 10, 1895, Letterbook, Gresham MSS; *New York Times*, April 28, 1895, 1. This repre-

sented quite a reversal from the *Times*'s earlier conviction, in the fall of 1894, that Gresham's diplomacy grew out of "his sympathy with China," which in turn reflected his "hope of establishing very large and profitable commercial relations with China." See *New York Times*, November 14, 1894, 5.

6. NA, RG 59, *Notes from the Japanese Legation* 5, S. Kurino to Gresham, November 10, 1894; *ibid.*, November 17, 1894. For a summary of these maneuvers see NA, RG 59, *China Despatches* 98, No. 2208, Denby to Gresham, May 2, 1895.

7. Rumors of Foster's conflict of interests appeared in the American press in December 1894. Despite Foster's insistence that he had "no connection with the alleged Chinese silver loan negotiations," Secretary of State Gresham firmly believed that "Foster's trip will not injure him financially." See *New York Times*, December 29, 1894, 5; *ibid.*, December 30, 1894, 5; Gresham to Denby, December 26, 1894, Letterbook, Gresham MSS.

8. Gresham Memorandum, December 31, 1894, Gresham MSS; Gresham to Denby, April 12, 1895, Letterbook, Gresham MSS; NA, RG 59, *China Despatches* 98, No. 2203, Denby to Gresham, April 25, 1895; Joseph, *Foreign Diplomacy in China*, 142.

9. NA, RG 59, *China Despatches* 98, No. 2205, Denby to Gresham, April 27, 1895; Pierre Leroy-Beaulieu, *The Awakening of the East*, New York, 1900, 244; NA, RG 59, *China Despatches* 98, No. 2217, Denby to Gresham, May 8, 1895.

10. Joseph, *Foreign Diplomacy in China*, 102–103; John W. Foster to Denby, September 26, 1894, James H. Wilson MSS.

11. NA, RG 59, *Consular Reports*, T. R. Jernigan to Gresham, May 10, 1895. See also Thomas R. Jernigan, "A Hindrance to Our Foreign Trade," *North American Review*, CLXIII (1896), 444–447. NA, RG 59, *China Despatches* 98, Personal Correspondence, Denby to Gresham, May 10, 1895; Frederic Emory to Thomas Bayard, May 28, 1895, Bayard MSS; *Chicago Inter-Ocean*, April 22, 1895, 6; *ibid.*, April 29, 1895, 6; *ibid.*, April 10, 1895, 6; *Commercial and Financial Chronicle*, LX (August 3, 1895), 181; *ibid.*, August 18, 1894, 257.

12. See Brooks Adams, *American Economic Supremacy*, London, 1900.

13. I expressed this analytical line earlier in "Commentaries–2," *Studies on the Left*, III (November 1962), 28–33. Enormously valuable insight into Cleveland's "anti-imperial expansionism" can be gained indirectly and comparatively from conceptually similar studies of earlier British policies. Especially useful and exciting is the pioneering article by J. Gallanger and R. Robinson, "The Imperialism of Free Trade," *Economic History Review*, VI, No. 1 (1953), 1–15. So is Bernard Semmel, "The Philosophic Radicals and Colonialism," *Journal of Economic History*, XXI (December 1961), 513–525. Contemporary accounts that both influence and reinforce my interpretation include Walter LaFeber, *The New Empire*, and William A. Williams, *The Contours of American History*. Also useful, though overdrawn, is John Rollins, "The Anti-Imperialists and

Twentieth-Century American Foreign Policy," *Studies on the Left*, III (November 1962), 9–24.

14. NA, RG 59, *China Instructions* 5, Edwin Uhl (Acting Secretary) to Denby, June 3, 1895.

15. NA, RG 59, *China Despatches* 100, No. 2302, August 8, 1895, Denby to Olney; A. A. Adee to the Secretary of the Navy, August 10, 1895, Richard Olney MSS; *Chicago Inter-Ocean*, September 14, 1895, 12; *New York Times*, August 31, 1895, 4; *New York Times*, August 11, 1895, 4; *New York Tribune*, September 23, 1895, 6. Dr. A. B. Leonard, corresponding secretary of the Methodist Board of Foreign Missions, complained during this period that he could not discover who was running this Department of State, since neither Secretary Olney nor First Assistant Secretary Uhl were in the nation's capital. See *New York Times*, August 10, 1895, 5.

16. For a summary of these events, see Adee to Olney, August 29, 1895, Olney MSS. Adee to Denby, telegram, September 4, 1895, Olney MSS.; Adee to Olney, September 9, 1895, Olney MSS; Denby to Olney, telegram, September 8, 1895, Olney MSS; Adee to Olney, September 9, 1895, Olney MSS.

17. For example, see Richardson, *Messages and Papers of the Presidents*, XII, 6058; Jernigan to Olney, personal, December 27, 1895, Olney MSS. NA, RG 59, *China Instructions* 5, No. 1168, Olney to Denby, October 2, 1895; NA RG 59, *China Despatches* 98, No. 2172, Denby to Gresham, March 22, 1895; *ibid.*, 100, No. 2431, Denby to Olney, November 14, 1895.

18. A modest exception was the government's verbal support of Standard Oil of New York against the preferential tax treatment accorded Russian kerosene exports to China. See *ibid.*, 98, No. 2235, Denby to Gresham, May 17, 1895; *ibid.*, No. 2240, May 21, 1895. More typical of the administration's limited conception of its role was the indirect cooperation given to the Southern States International Exposition—an affair run by southern cotton textile companies interested in the China market. See J. W. Avery to Olney, November 8, 1895, Olney MSS.

19. NA, RG 59, *China Despatches* 98, Personal Correspondence, Denby to Gresham, May 10, 1895; John W. Foster to Denby, September 26, 1894, Wilson MSS; Gresham to Bayard, December 24, 1894, Letterbook, Gresham MSS.

20. NA, RG 59, *China Despatches* 98, No. 2225, Denby to Gresham, May 12, 1895; *ibid.*, No. 2249, Denby to Uhl, May 30, 1895; NA, RG 59, *China Instructions* 5, telegram, Olney to Denby, June 22, 1895. Despite Olney's position, both Denby and his son, Charles Jr., continued to argue —explicitly and implicitly—for liberalization of the 1887 instructions. See Denby to Olney, November 25, 1895, Olney MSS; NA, RG 59, *China Despatches* 100, Denby Jr. to Olney, May 25, 1896. *Ibid.*, 100, No. 2502, Denby to Olney, March 16, 1896. One can also speculate that part of the syndicate's failure grew out of its unwillingness or inability to offer terms as generous as its European competitors. If this is so, it reinforces

my opinion that American capital (as opposed to American goods) was not yet competitive in Asia, and this helps to explain the periodical indifference of both Democratic and Republican administrations to an investment open door (as opposed to a commercial open door). The circumstances surrounding the later Hankow-Peking railroad concession add—as will be seen—to this overall impression.

21. *Ibid.*, 98, No. 2264, Denby to Uhl, June 13, 1895; *ibid.*, 99, No. 2282, Denby to Olney, July 8, 1895. American diplomatic correspondence contains a good deal of information on the indemnity loan rivalries as well as corollary Anglo-French machinations in southeast Asia. See, for example, NA, RG 59, *China Despatches* 99, No. 2282, Denby to Olney, July 8, 1895; *ibid.*, 98, No. 2274, Denby to Olney, June 24, 1895. See also Joseph, *Foreign Diplomacy in China*, 133, 150–153.

22. Efforts by various overseas representatives to illuminate such facts of life apparently failed to register real impact with the Department. See, for example, Jernigan to Olney, December 27, 1895, Olney MSS. For a short but useful self-appraisal of Witte's policies, see Sergei Witte, *The Memoirs of Count Witte*, Garden City, 1921, 80–82. Pauline Tompkins, *American-Russian Relations in the Far East*, New York, 1949, 18–19; Joseph, *Foreign Diplomacy in China*, 154–155, 162; NA, RG 59, *China Instructions* 5, No. 1263, Olney to Denby, April 27, 1895; NA, RG 59, *China Despatches* 101, Denby Jr. to Olney, June 11, 1896.

23. *Ibid.*, 100, No. 2510, Denby to Olney, April 6, 1896; *ibid.*, 101, No. 2534, Denby Jr. to Olney, May 25, 1896; *New York Times*, February 24, 1896, 1. Not only did Li presumably influence railroad concessions, but it was also believed that he had some say in ship construction and munitions contracts. Indeed, before his visit to America he indicated to a press interviewer a willingness to look favorably upon American interests in these fields—provided "he could negotiate a loan with American bankers." *New York Times*, June 21, 1896, 17.

24. In like fashion, the "English Foreign Office [had] no confidence in the prospective value of [Li's] visit"—pointing out that the Viceroy's tour through Europe and America was strictly informal; that he was without the necessary credentials to negotiate officially. *New York Times*, June 28, 1896, 17. See Cleveland to Olney, July 4, 1896, Olney MSS; Olney to Cleveland, July 7, 1896, Cleveland MSS.

25. McCook to Olney, July 10, 1896, Olney MSS; William McAdoo to Olney, telegram, August 25, 1896, Olney MSS; Cleveland to Olney, August 19, 1896, Olney MSS; Daniel S. Lamont to Olney, telegram, August 19, 1896, Olney MSS; W. W. Rockhill to Olney, August 4, 1896, Olney MSS. The following additional letters and telegrams in the Olney Papers also shed light on the pressures encountered and accommodated by the administration: Olney to McCook, August 1, 1896; Lamont to Olney, August 7, 1896; Olney to Rockhill, August 11, 1896; Olney to McCook, August 11, 1896; McCook to Olney, August 12, 1896; McCook to Olney, telegram, August 12, 1896; Lamont to Olney, telegram, August 17, 1896; McCook to Olney, August 17, 1896.

26. *New York Times*, August 30, 1896, 1; *ibid.*, September 1, 1896, 1; *ibid.*, September 2, 1896, 4; *ibid.*, September 1, 1896, 1; *ibid.*, September 2, 1896, 1; *ibid.*, September 4, 1896, 8; *ibid.*, September 8, 1896, 4; NA, RG 59, *China Despatches* 101, No. 2603, Denby to Olney, September 29, 1896. Evidently there was some modest but immediate effort by American businesses to convert dream into reality, as the Carnegie Company and other manufacturing concerns began sending their sales representatives to the Chinese Imperial Court. See *ibid.*, No. 2625, October 30, 1896.

27. National Association of Manufacturers, *Proceedings of the Second Annual Convention 1897*, Philadelphia, 1897, 12.

28. NA, RG 59, *China Instructions* 5, No. 1376, December 13, 1896; NA, RG 59, *China Despatches* 101, No. 2614, Denby to Olney, October 18, 1896; *ibid.*, 102, No. 2670, January 4, 1897; NA, RG 59, *China Instructions* 5, No. 1402, Olney to Denby, February 27, 1897.

29. NA, RG 59, *China Despatches* 102, No. 2632, Denby to Olney, November 5, 1896; *ibid.*, No. 2671, January 10, 1897; *ibid.*, No. 2676, January 29, 1897; *ibid.*, No. 2632, November 5, 1896; *ibid.*, No. 2676, January 29, 1897.

## Chapter III: *In the Eye of the Storm*

1. NA, RG 59, *China Despatches* 103, No. 2773, Denby to John Sherman, July 8, 1897; *New York Times*, October 26, 1895, 4. Even the *Chicago Inter-Ocean*, traditionally pro-Russian and anti-British, reversed its field in the fall of 1896. See *Chicago Inter-Ocean*, October 26, 1895, 12.

2. *Who's Who in America*, III, 1901–1902, New York, 1903, 718; James H. Wilson to Rethick, May 3, 1897, Letterbook, Wilson MSS; Wilson to John J. McCook, October 28, 1896, Letterbook, Wilson MSS; Wilson to Theodore Roosevelt, August 25, 1897, Letterbook, Wilson MSS. "Old China Hands," such as Thomas R. Jernigan, Consul General in Shanghai, and Charles Denby, Minister in Peking, partly shared Wilson's analysis. See Jernigan to Richard Olney, December 27, 1895, Olney MSS; NA, RG 59, Dispatch, Denby to John Sherman, April 2, 1897.

3. McCook to Olney, telegram, October 13, 1896, Olney MSS; McCook to Olney, July 10, 1896, Olney MSS; *New York Times*, October 18, 1896, 8; *ibid.*, October 21, 1896, 12; *ibid.*, October 19, 1896, 2.

4. Wilson to McCook, October 27, 1896, Letterbook, Wilson MSS; *ibid.*, October 28, 1896; Wilson to Denby Jr., November 29, 1896, Letterbook, Wilson MSS; Wilson to McCook, October 28, 1896, Letterbook, Wilson MSS; *ibid.*, November 18, 1896; McCook to Wilson, November 17, 1896, Wilson MSS; *ibid.*, November 11, 1896; November 28, 1896; November 30, 1896; Wilson to Denby Jr., November 29, 1896, Letterbook, Wilson MSS.

5. Wilson to Samuel Thomas, March 28, 1897; to Jacob Schiff, May 15, 1897; to McCook, April 29, 1897; to McCook, July 16, 1897, Letterbook, Wilson MSS. William P. Frye to Wilson, March 20, 1897; Roosevelt to Wilson, April 26, 1897; John W. Foster to Abram S. Hewitt, May 15, 1897, Wilson MSS; Wilson to John Hay, November 1, 1896, Letterbook, Wilson MSS; Theodore Roosevelt to Frank Lowell, April 30, 1897, Letterbook, Roosevelt MSS; Alba B. Johnson to Theodore C. Search, June 1, 1897, W. W. Rockhill MSS; William McKinley to Whitelaw Reid, February 18, 1897, McKinley MSS; Wilson to Rockhill, June 8, 1897, Rockhill MSS; Wilson to McCook, May 23, 1897, Letterbook, Wilson MSS; Wilson to Rockhill, June 8, 1897, Rockhill MSS; Johnson to Search, June 1, 1897, Rockhill MSS; Memorandum of John Hay–John Bassett Moore conversation, July 23, 1900, Moore MSS.

6. James H. Wilson, "America's Interests in China," *North American Review*, CLXVI (February 1898), 138.

7. NA, RG 59, *China Despatches* 102, No. 2735, Denby to John Sherman, April 15, 1897; *ibid.*, No. 2789, Denby to Sherman, August 5, 1897; *ibid.*, No. 2823, November 12, 1897; *ibid.*, No. 3845, December 16, 1897.

8. *Ibid.*, No. 2803, September 15, 1897; *ibid.*, No. 2821, November 5, 1897; *ibid.*, No. 2832, November 30, 1897; *ibid.*, No. 2792, August 24, 1897; *ibid.*, No. 2821, November 5, 1897; NA, RG 59, *Notes to Chinese Legation* 1, No. 5, Sherman to Wu Ting-Fang, June 29, 1897.

9. NA, RG 59, *China Despatches* 102, No. 2752, Denby to Sherman, May 24, 1897; *ibid.*, No. 2761, June 10, 1897; see Joseph, *Foreign Diplomacy in China*, 179–180. At least one person, Horace N. Allen, American missionary-diplomat in Korea, blamed the loss of the contract on Denby's lack of cooperation with the American company. Allen to Rockhill, January 30, 1898, Rockhill MSS.

10. NA, RG 59, *China Despatches* 102, No. 2752, Denby to Sherman, May 24, 1897; *New York Times*, May 19, 1897, 7; NA, RG 59, *China Despatches* 102, No. 2752, Denby to Sherman, May 24, 1897; *New York Times*, June 3, 1897, 7; *ibid.*, July 9, 1897, 7.

11. NA, RG 59, *China Instructions* 5, No. 1404, Sherman to Denby, March 8, 1897.

12. NA, RG 59, *China Despatches* 103, No. 2824, Denby to Sherman, November 18, 1897; *ibid.*, No. 2836, December 6, 1897; *ibid.*, No. 2828, November 23, 1897; *ibid.*, No. 2826, November 19, 1897; *ibid.*, cipher telegram, January 6, 1898.

13. *Ibid.*, No. 2846, December 18, 1897. The general inclination of both American and British diplomats was to regard impending Russian encroachments as much more threatening than German actions in Shantung. See *ibid.*, No. 2848, December 27, 1897.

14. *The Memoirs of Count Witte*, London, 1921, 99–102; NA, RG 59, *China Despatches* 103, No. 2882, Denby to Sherman, March 8, 1898; *ibid.*, No. 2897, March 29, 1898.

15. This was especially true of cotton goods. Two-thirds of all cotton drills, five-sixths of all cotton jeans, and nine-tenths of all cotton sheetings

went to northern China. *United States Consular Reports* 57, April 20, 1898, 582. *Ibid.*, 578; *ibid.*, 56, December 14, 1897, 345; *New York Times*, February 7, 1898, 6.

16. Charles S. Campbell, Jr., *Special Business Interests and the Open Door Policy*, Baltimore, 1957, 31; Clarence Cary, "China and Chinese Railway Concessions," *Forum*, XXIV (January 1898), 600–601, 605; Cary, "China's Complications and American Trade," *Forum*, XXV (November 1898), 38–39; Campbell, *Special Business Interests*, 34.

17. *New York Times*, February 3, 1898, 6; *ibid.*, February 4, 1898, 12; *ibid.*, February 6, 1898, 18; Campbell, *Special Business Interests*, 35. Since we have no voting records on Chamber of Commerce petitions, it is impossible to know how many votes reflected existing economic interests in China and how many reflected the more general position, held even by those without special interests, that the long-term health of the economy required substantial trade access to the China market.

18. *Loc. cit.*; NA, RG 59, *Miscellaneous Letters*, Frederick Fraley to William McKinley, February 25, 1898; Campbell, *Special Business Interests*, 35; *New York Times*, February 5, 1898, 6; NA, RG 59, *Miscellaneous Letters*, Committee of American Merchants in Shanghai to New York Chamber of Commerce, March 16, 1898. The members of the American group in Shanghai included Henry Gibbs of Standard Oil of New York; Frazer and Company, whose head was a prominent member of the Committee on American Interests in China; Thomas R. Jernigan, former Consul General in Shanghai; Fearon Daniel and Company, the leading cotton goods importer; and the two leading general import houses, the American Trading Company and the China and Japan Trading Company.

19. Campbell, *Special Business Interests*, 45–46; *Commercial and Financial Chronicle*, LXVI (April 2, 1898), 642. See also *ibid.*, February 12, 1898, 312, and *North China Herald*, February 14, 1898, 221–222.

20. *New York Times*, December 11, 1898; December 27, 1897, 7; February 14, 1898, 6; and March 15, 1898, 6. *New York Tribune*, February 4, 1898, 6; *Chicago Inter-Ocean*, January 5, 1898, 6; *New Orleans Times-Picayune*, December 24, 1897, 4; NA, RG 59, *China Despatches* 103, No. 2842, Denby to Sherman, December 11, 1897; *ibid.*, No. 2858, January 31, 1898; Charles Denby, Jr., "America's Opportunity in Asia," *North American Review*, CLXV (January 1898), 33, 38–39.

21. *New York Times*, January 21, 1898, 6; Campbell, *Special Business Interests*, 37; *New York Times*, November 12, 1897, 5; *ibid.*, January 5, 1898, 6; *Chicago Inter-Ocean*, December 22, 1897, 6. See also *ibid.*, December 23, 1897, 6, and December 28, 1897, 6. Charles G. Dawes, *A Journal of the McKinley Years*, Chicago, 1950, 139; *Chicago Inter-Ocean*, December 19, 1897, 7, and December 31, 1897, 6; Dawes, *Journal of McKinley Years*, 139; LaFeber, *New Empire*, 359; *New York Times*, December 25, 1897, 7.

22. Campbell, *Special Business Interests*, 37; *New York Times*, January 16, 1898, 7; Sherman to Andrew D. White, February 11, 1898, Rockhill MSS; NA, RG 59, *Russia Instructions* 51, Sherman to Hitchcock, telegram, March 17, 1898; NA, RG 59, *German Despatches* 65, No. 318,

White to Sherman, February 28, 1898; NA, RG 59, *Russia Instructions* 51, telegram, Hitchcock to Sherman, March 19, 1898. Note, for example, the Department's instructions to Andrew White to "continue to keep [us] advised on the subject" of German intentions in Shantung. NA, RG 59, *German Instructions* 20, No. 410, Sherman to White, February 28, 1898. NA, RG 59, *China Despatches* 103, No. 2885, Denby to Sherman, March 10, 1898; NA, RG 59, *England Despatches* 191, No. 325, Hay to Sherman, March 25, 1898.

23. *Ibid.*, 190, No. 213, Hay to Sherman, January 11, 1898; *ibid.*, No. 222, Henry White to Sherman, January 19, 1898; William Osborne to McKinley, March 22, 1898, McKinley MSS; NA, RG 59, *China Despatches* 103, No. 3889, Denby to Sherman, March 19, 1898; *ibid.*, No. 2897, March 29, 1898; *ibid.*, No. 2901, April 1, 1898; NA, RG 59, *England Despatches* 190, No. 290, White to Sherman, March 5, 1898 (notations by Adee and Day). Examples of support for the Open Door Policy among British merchants in China abound on the pages of the *North China Herald,* an English-language daily in Shanghai. NA, RG 59, *China Despatches,* 103, No. 2855, Denby to Sherman, January 17, 1898; *ibid.,* No. 2881, March 7, 1898. See Joseph, *Foreign Diplomacy in China,* 226, 244–248, 249, 259, 264–265; R. S. McCordock, *British Far Eastern Policy, 1894–1900,* New York, 1931, 230–240; Dallin, *The Rise of Russia in Asia,* 58; Gregory Bienstock, *The Struggle for the Pacific,* New York, 1937, 132; NA, RG 59, *China Despatches* 103, No. 3867, Denby to Sherman, February 14, 1898.

24. A. Whitney Griswold, *The Far Eastern Policy of the United States,* New York, 1938, 43–44; NA, RG 59, *England Despatches* 190, No. 275, H. White to Sherman, February 23, 1898; Enclosure, March 8, 1898, John Hay MSS; March 17, 1898, Hay MSS. McKinley's original draft of the note used the term "trade interests." The final form inserted a conjunction to make it read "trade" and "interests." See undated Memorandum, McKinley MSS.

25. March 17, 1898, Hay MSS.

26. Joseph, *Foreign Diplomacy in China,* 292–293, 287–290, 308–309; NA, RG 59, *China Despatches* 104, No. 2907, Denby to Sherman, April 5, 1898.

27. *Ibid.,* No. 2912, April 15, 1898. See also McCordock, *British Far Eastern Policy,* 240–263. NA, RG 59, *China Despatches* 104, No. 2892, Denby to Sherman, March 21, 1898; *ibid.,* No. 2917, April 20, 1898; Joseph, *Foreign Diplomacy in China,* 307; NA, RG 59, *German Despatches* 65, No. 405, Andrew White to Day, April 30, 1898; Joseph, *Foreign Diplomacy in China,* 308–309, 298, 309–310, 270; NA, RG 59, *Notes from Japanese Legation* 6, No. 63, Hoshi to Day, May 10, 1898; Bienstock, *Struggle for Pacific,* 143; Tompkins, *American-Russian Relations in the Far East,* 19.

28. NA, RG 59, *China Despatches* 104, No. 2902, Denby to Sherman, April 3, 1898.

## Chapter IV: *A Dose of Insular Imperialism*

1. Frederic Emory, "Our Commercial Expansion," *Munsey's Magazine*, XXII (1899), 544. Emory, as noted earlier, was chief of the State Department's Bureau of Foreign Commerce.
2. *New York Tribune*, March 22, 1898, 6.
3. Theodore Roosevelt to Henry Cabot Lodge, September 21, 1897, Letterbook, Roosevelt MSS; NA, RG 59, *Consular Despatch*, enclosed clipping, O. F. Williams to William R. Day; George Dewey, *Autobiography of George Dewey*, New York, 1913, 179; Margaret Long, ed., *The Journal of John D. Long*, Ridge, N.H., 1956, 217; Margaret Leech, *In the Days of McKinley*, New York, 1959, 162, 195; Roosevelt to B. F. Tracy, April 18, 1898, Letterbook, Roosevelt MSS.
4. Russel A. Alger, *The Spanish-American War*, New York, 1901, 326; Leech, *Days of McKinley*, 210; George Dewey to John D. Long, May 13, 1898, McKinley MSS; Henry C. Lodge, ed., *Selections from the Correspondence of Theodore Roosevelt and Henry Cabot Lodge, 1884–1918*, New York, 1925, I, 299; *San Francisco Chronicle*, May 4, 1898, 1; State Department memorandum, May 9, 1898, John Bassett Moore MSS; John Bassett Moore memorandum, undated, Moore MSS; McKinley to the Secretary of War, May 19, 1898, McKinley MSS; McKinley to the Secretary of the Treasury, May 19, 1898, McKinley MSS; Charles H. Allen, Assistant Secretary of the Navy, to John Bassett Moore, undated, Moore MSS; State Department draft letter to Secretaries of the Treasury, War, and Navy, May 18, 1898, Moore MSS; NA, RG 59, *England Instructions* 32, strictly confidential, telegram, Day to John Hay, June 3, 1898; Leech, *Days of McKinley*, 212, 261.
5. NA, RG 59, *England Instructions* 32, strictly confidential, telegram, Day to Hay, June 14, 1898; NA, RG 59, *Consular Despatch* 19, Rounseville Wildman to Day, No. 19, November 8, 1897; *ibid.*, O. F. Williams to Day, September 5, 1898; Hay to Day, telegram, October 15, 1898, Moore MSS; NA, RG 59, *France Despatches* 115, No. 272, Horace Porter to Sherman, June 10, 1898; Thomas A. Bailey, "Dewey and the Germans at Manila," *American Historical Review*, XLV (1939), 59. For example, Joseph Chamberlain's famous "Birmingham speech" of May 13, 1898, was widely interpreted as a warning to other European powers to avoid any interference in the Spanish-American War. Tyler Dennett, *John Hay: From Poetry to Politics*, New York, 1934, 219. See also relevant portions of Charles S. Campbell, Jr., *Anglo-American Understanding, 1898–1903*, Baltimore, 1957.
6. NA, RG 59, *Germany Despatches* 66, telegram, Andrew White to Day, July 12, 1898; Hay to Day, July 14, 1898, Moore MSS; Walter Millis, *The Martial Spirit*, Boston and New York, 1931, 333. Also Hay to Day, July 14, 1898, Moore MSS.

7. Andrew White to Day, June 18, 1898, Moore MSS; NA, RG 59, *Germany Despatches* 66, telegram, White to Day, July 12, 1898; Hay to Day, July 14, 1898, Moore MSS; Moore to Day, September 3, 1898, Moore MSS; Hay to Day, October 29, 1898, Moore MSS. Complications with Germany must be placed within the context of general American distrust of Germany everywhere in the world by 1898—in Asia, Central and South America, the Caribbean, and Europe itself. For a good summary of this view, see Andrew White to Day, August 10, 1898, Moore MSS.

8. NA, RG 59, *China Despatches* 104, No. 2929, Denby to Sherman, May 15, 1898; *ibid.*, No. 2939, June 6, 1898; Joseph, *Foreign Diplomacy in China*, 337, 357–358. This uncertainty over British policy may have been the motivating factor in Hay's attempt to renew discussion of the earlier proposal for joint support of the Open Door Policy. Though McKinley discouraged the attempt, he did try to encourage the British to hold the line on their China policy by obliquely prophesying that "the outcome of our struggle with Spain" might develop "the need of extending and strengthening our interests in the Asiatic Continent." Day to Hay, July 14, 1898, Hay MSS.

9. Roosevelt to Mahan, May 3, 1897, Letterbook, Roosevelt MSS; *ibid.*, Roosevelt to Long, September 30, 1897. For a good summation of the Japanese views see NA, RG 59, *Notes from Japanese Legation* 6, No. M163, Hoshi to Sherman, July 10, 1897. Roosevelt to Long, June 23, 1897, Letterbook, Roosevelt MSS; *Chicago Inter-Ocean*, January 6, 1898, 6. As late as mid-May 1898 the *New York Times* quoted one Senator that "there is not the slightest probable chance for the House joint resolution to annex the Hawaiian Islands to pass Congress at this session." *New York Times*, May 17, 1898, 2. For a general discussion of the Hawaiian issue in 1897 and early 1898, see LaFeber, *New Empire*, 362–370.

10. Alfred T. Mahan, "Hawaii and Our Future Sea Power," *Forum*, XV (1893), 7. Also Henry Cabot Lodge, "Our Blundering Foreign Policy," *Forum*, XIX (1895), 17. Presumably Japan was given prior notification of the annexationist move, in line with an American promise in early May that "no decisive action would be taken in regard to the Hawaiian matter without duly informing [Japan]." Memorandum of conversation with Japanese Minister, May 6, 1898, Moore MSS.

11. *Congressional Record*, 55th Cong., 2nd Sess., 6006–6007.

12. George F. Hoar, *Autobiography of 70 Years*, New York, 1903, II, 308; *Congressional Record*, 55th Cong., 2nd Sess., 6017; *ibid.*, 5772, 5775, 5879, 5895, 5897, 5916, 5988, 5899, 5782–5783, 5904, 5780, 5924, 5925, 5904, 6016, 6019, 6712. According to the *New York Times*, "The advocates of annexation say they will make no speeches, leaving the opponents to occupy all the time to be consumed in debate." *New York Times*, June 20, 1898, 3.

13. *House Document* 536, 55th Cong., 2nd Sess; NA, RG 59, *China Instructions* 5, No. 22, John Bassett Moore to Edwin H. Conger, August 30,

1898; NA, RG 59, *China Despatches* 105, No. 65, Conger to Hay, October 12, 1898.

14. NA, RG 59, *England Instructions* 32, strictly confidential, telegram, Day to Hay, June 14, 1898; *New York Times*, October 1, 1898, 1. According to John Bassett Moore, even Theodore Roosevelt, a so-called "large-policy" imperialist, went through the same evolution of attitudes as Hanna and other pragmatists. In his uncompleted, unpublished autobiography, Moore recalled a "brief conversation" with Roosevelt, after the latter's resignation as Navy Assistant Secretary, in which Roosevelt "warned me against the acquisition of the Philippines, which lay far beyond what we had considered to be our sphere of government." Moore MSS. The editorial pages of the *Chicago Inter-Ocean* offer a beautiful micro-illustration of the transformation that Hanna described. Ambivalent and cautious in the beginning, by August the paper was ridiculing the idea that America could settle for "that insignificant thing—a coaling station in the East." Indeed, by mid-September it was concerned about McKinley's apparent indecision on the Philippines—until it deciphered that indecision as simply McKinleyite cunning in announcing only for Luzon while letting the realities of circumstance maneuver Spain into giving up the whole lot. See the editorial page (p. 6) of the *Inter-Ocean* for these dates in 1898: May 3, May 30, June 8, June 11, June 27, July 16, July 30, August 8, August 17, September 12, September 17, and October 17.

15. *Spanish Diplomatic Correspondence and Documents, 1896–1900* (translation), Washington, D.C., 1905, 213–214; Day to McKinley, November 18, 1898, McKinley MSS; Memorandum of a McKinley interview with the French Ambassador, July 30, 1898, Moore MSS. The initial American draft of the armistice agreement used the word "possession" instead of "disposition." Spain regarded the choice as indicative of American designs against Spanish sovereignty in the islands. *Spanish Diplomatic Correspondence*, 213–214.

16. Day to McKinley, November 18, 1898, McKinley MSS; *Spanish Diplomatic Correspondence*, 215–216; *Papers Relating to the Foreign Relations of the United States*, 1898, lxiv (hereafter the short title, *Foreign Relations*, will be used); *ibid.*, 823.

17. Charles G. Dawes wrote McKinley that his "postponement of an immediate decision" on the Philippines "makes the right solution certain," because it would give time for further study and reflection—both by the administration and the people. Dawes to McKinley, August 10, 1898, McKinley MSS. Similarly, see Seth Low to McKinley, August 6, 1898, McKinley MSS. Charles S. Olcott, *The Life of William McKinley*, II, Boston and New York, 1916, 61, 63; Moorfield Storey and Marcial P. Lichauco, *The Conquest of the Philippines by the United States*, New York, 1926, 66–67; Leech, *Days of McKinley*, 286; Reid Diaries, September 16, 1898, Reid MSS. As early as June 6, Senator Frye had confessed that "The only fear I have about this war is that peace will be declared before we can get full occupation of the Philippines and Puerto

Rico." Frye to James H. Wilson, Wilson MSS. Whitelaw Reid's public statements before his appointment to the peace commission led the *Inter-Ocean* to conclude that "the appointment indicates that the administration . . . is inclined to hold the Philippines." *Chicago Inter-Ocean,* September 6, 1898, 6. Similarly, Cushman K. Davis said in a Minneapolis speech on September 7 that "This government will secure from the situation in the Orient and in those waters whatever American courage, American honor and American valor have gained." *Chicago Inter-Ocean,* September 9, 1898, 6. For a firsthand account of the commissioners' views, see Reid Diaries, September 16, 1898, Whitelaw Reid MSS. The other two members dissented from the majority view of taking all the islands. Senator George Grey of Delaware opposed any political control but felt himself bound by the President's instructions to seek the island of Luzon. Judge Day, former Secretary of State, favored retention of Luzon only, coupled with a non-alienation pledge and an economic open door for the rest of the islands. Later, in a last-ditch effort to head off absorption of all the islands, he broadened his position to include most of the islands in the northern half of the archipelago. Undated Memorandum, Moore MSS. McKinley to Day, Letterbook, October 25, 1898, McKinley MSS; *Foreign Relations* 1898, 935.

18. See especially Benjamin H. Williams, *Economic Foreign Policy of the United States,* New York, 1926, 325–326. For example, when the Philadelphia Commercial Museum announced the sending of a trade commission to the Philippines on September 20, 1898, the *New York Times* concluded still that "in the view of many persons who have given the subject considerable study, the interests which the United States will retain in the Philippines will be chiefly valuable as a stepping-stone toward the extension of American commerce with the Orient . . ." *New York Times,* September 20, 1898, 2. Charles H. Cramp to Charles Emory Smith, undated, Reid MSS.

19. See especially Campbell, *Special Business Interests,* 16; *Journal of the American Asiatic Association,* I (1898), 1; *Chicago Inter-Ocean,* September 16, 1898, 6. For example, one prominent Chicago financier wrote Hay that almost all business "opinion here favors keeping all the territory won by war and the expansion of trade" following such a policy. W. B. Bliss to Hay, October 31, 1898, Hay MSS. And a West Coast friend wrote him that "We are all expansionists here-away, for we know that the prosperity resulting from the annexation . . . will make itself manifest first on our coast." W. W. Norris to Hay, October 17, 1898, Hay MSS.

20. Irving M. Scott to Charles A. Moore, August 4, 1898, McKinley MSS; "Notes on China," undated, W. C. Ford, Ford MSS; George F. Seward to Hay, November 7, 1898, Hay MSS; Carl Schurz to McKinley, September 22, 1898, McKinley MSS; Campbell, *Special Business Interests,* 16; Memorandum, September 16, 1898, McKinley MSS; Reid Diaries, September 15, 1898, Reid MSS; NA, RG 59, *China Despatches* 104, No. 31, Conger to Day, August 26, 1898; Charles G. Dawes to McKinley, August

10, 1898, McKinley MSS; Storey and Lichauco, *Conquest of the Philippines*, 38; *Foreign Relations 1898*, Hay to Day, telegram, October 28, 1898, 938; Campbell, *Special Business Interests*, 16; Reid Diaries, September 15, 1898, Reid MSS. See especially Leech, *Days of McKinley*, 339–341, and Earl S. Pomeroy, *Pacific Outpost: American Strategy in Guam and Micronesia*, Stanford, 1951, 3–19; Leech, *Days of McKinley*, 327, 330, 334–336, 339–341. Dewey's advice, however, was extraordinarily ambivalent and could be (and was) interpreted as favoring retention of Luzon only or of all the Philippines. In General Wesley Merritt's opinion (as expressed to the peace commission), Dewey "did not wish to express any opinion which would make him unavailable as a candidate for the Presidency." Reid Diaries, October 4, 1898, Reid MSS.

21. Joseph, *Foreign Diplomacy in China*, 346–347, 363–364. Conger, for example, reported that the American China Development Company had bungled a golden contract opportunity because it had no permanent agents on the scene "with authority to act," and because it would only act where contractual terms were so liberal as to insure a quick profit. NA, RG 59, *China Despatches* 105, No. 109, Conger to Hay, December 7, 1898. Campbell, *Special Business Interests*, 39–40.

22. See Lim Boon Keng, *The Chinese Crisis from Within*, London, 1901, 48–67; Meribeth E. Cameron, *The Reform Movement in China, 1898–1912*, Stanford, 1931, 23–55; George Nye Steiger, *China and the Occident: Origin and Development of the Boxer Movement*, New Haven, 1927, 87–106. NA, RG 59, *China Despatches* 105, No. 49, Conger to Day, September 24, 1898; *ibid.*, No. 71, Conger to Hay, October 14, 1898; *ibid.*, telegram, Hay to Conger, October 10, 1898; *ibid.*, telegram, Conger to Hay, November 5, 1898; *ibid.*, telegram, Hay to Conger, October 10, 1898; *ibid.*, No. 36, Conger to Day, September 6, 1898; NA, RG 59, *Russia Despatches* 53, No. 158, Hitchcock to Day, September 29, 1898; Campbell, *Special Business Interests*, 47–48.

23. This is not meant to deny that McKinley's tour "around the circuit" and the impact of public opinion did not also play important roles in the President's final decision. But several qualifications should be noted. McKinley's tour of the country cut both ways: it not only sounded out public opinion but also tended to mobilize it. Second, public opinion never acted as more than a veto factor: it could not dictate; it could only permit the President to do—or prevent him from doing—what he wanted to do anyway. Finally, even among those who saw "popular opinion" as the decisive factor in McKinley's decision, the term was defined sometimes rather narrowly: "popular opinion" equals "men conspicuous in public, professional, and business life." *Chicago Inter-Ocean*, October 10, 1898, 6.

24. Reid Diaries, September 16, 1898, Reid MSS; *Foreign Relations 1898*, 907–908.

25. Edmund L. Baylies to Reid, September 9, 1898, Reid MSS; Hay to Day, November 1, 1898, Letterbook, Hay MSS; American Chargé d'Affaires in Berlin to Hay, November 27, 1898, McKinley MSS; *Foreign Relations*

1898, 962; Reid Diaries, December 3, 1898, Reid MSS; *Foreign Relations*
1898, 939; Reid to McKinley, October 28, 1898, Letterbook, Reid MSS;
Reid Diaries, December 3, 1898, Reid MSS; *ibid.*, December 4, 1898.
The two works most specifically concerned with America's relations to
the Carolines, Marianas, Marshalls, and so on, are Pomeroy, *Pacific Outpost*, and David N. Leff, *Uncle Sam's Pacific Islets*, Stanford, 1940. The
latter is useful mainly for its maps. The former, while more scholarly
and ambitious, is somewhat deficient in the 1898–1900 period.

26. Williams, *Foreign Economic Policy*, 325–326; A. A. Adee to Hay, December 13, 1898, Hay MSS; Whitelaw Reid, *Problems of Expansion*, New
York, 1900, 18.

27. *Foreign Relations* 1898, lxxii.

## Chapter V: *"A Fair Field and No Favor"*

1. George F. Kennan, *American Diplomacy, 1900–1950*, Chicago, 1952, 25–
42. See also Griswold, *Far Eastern Policy*, 36–86. Campbell, *Special
Business Interests*, 45–49. Other general works that cover the Open Door
Notes include Dennett, *John Hay*, 284–296, and A. L. P. Dennis, *Ad-
ventures in American Diplomacy, 1896–1906*, New York, 1928, 170–214.
Interesting though sometimes romanticized Chinese-American views of
the open door can be found in Joshua Bau, *The Open Door Doctrine in
Relation to China*, New York, 1923; Tsung-Yu Sze, *China and the Most-
Favored-Nation Clause*, New York, 1925; and Shutaro Tomimas, *The
Open Door Policy and the Territorial Integrity of China*, New York,
1919. Less dated and more realistic (albeit stridently so at times) is
Sheng Hu, *Imperialism and Chinese Politics*.

2. McKinley, *Speeches and Addresses of William McKinley, from March 1,
1897 to May 30, 1900*, 135; Brooks Adams, "The New Struggle for Life
Among Nations," *Fortnightly Review*, LXXI (1899), 280; quoted in
Campbell, *Special Business Interests*, 91; *Bankers' Magazine*, LXI (September 1900), 341.

3. Patrick O'Hare to Hay, February 14, 1900, Hay MSS; Joseph Wheeler
to McKinley, January 14, 1900, McKinley MSS; Rockhill to Hay, October 19, 1899, Hay MSS; *American Trade*, III (1899), 39; *Nation*, LXXII
(May 9, 1901), 369; Davis to Reid, April 20, 1899, Reid MSS; *Chicago
Inter-Ocean*, August 19, 1899, 5; "Notes on China," undated, Worthington C. Ford MSS; Hay to Charles Dick, September 11, 1899, Hay MSS.

4. Department of Commerce and Labor, *Exports of Manufactures from the
United States and Their Distribution by Articles and Countries, 1800–
1906*, Washington, D.C., 1907, 32–33, 59; *Senate Document* 230, 56th
Cong., 1st Sess., 6–7.

5. Horace Porter to McKinley, November 14, 1899, McKinley MSS.

6. NA, RG 59, *Russia Despatches* 54, No. 259, H. D. Pierce to Hay, February 25, 1899 (notation by Adee); NA, RG 59, *China Instructions* 5, No. 126, Hay to Conger, February 2, 1899; William R. Thayer, *The Life and Letters of John Hay*, II, Boston, 1915, 241.

7. See NA, RG 59, *Germany Despatches* 69, No. 1037, Andrew White to Hay, September 29, 1899. Therein, White summarizes the Spanish-German treaty of February 12, 1899, on the Carolines and the Ladrones, as well as the American reaction to it.

8. Charles H. Allen, Acting Secretary of the Navy, to Hay, August 3, 1899, Hay MSS. On the subject of the Amoy settlement see NA, RG 59, *Consular Despatches* 13, No. 38, A. B. Johnson to David J. Hill, January 12, 1899; NA, RG 59, *China Despatches* 106, No. 132, Conger to Hay, January 20, 1899; *ibid.*, telegram, Conger to Hay, March 23, 1899; *ibid.*, No. 169, March 24, 1899; NA, RG 59, *Consular Instructions* 166, telegram, Adee to Johnson, March 9, 1899; NA, RG 59, *China Instructions*, cipher telegram, Hay to Conger, March 24, 1899. NA, RG 59, *Russia Despatches* 54, No. 259, Pierce to Hay, February 25, 1899; NA, RG 59, *China Despatches* 106, No. 219, Conger to Hay, June 16, 1899; *ibid.*, cipher telegram, June 16, 1899; *ibid.*, 107, No. 248, August 10, 1899; *ibid.*, 106, cipher telegram, March 1, 1899; *ibid.*, No. 167, March 16, 1899; *New York Times*, March 4, 1899, 7; *ibid.*, March 13, 1899, 6; *Chicago Inter-Ocean*, March 11, 1899, 6. See also Joseph, *Foreign Diplomacy in China*, 390, and Campbell, *Special Business Interests*, 52.

9. Tomimas, *The Open Door Policy and the Territorial Integrity of China*, 19–20; Joseph, *Foreign Diplomacy in China*, 390. See *New York Times*, April 30, 1899, 18. Joseph, *Foreign Diplomacy in China*, 382–383; *New York Times*, February 2, 1899, 7. See NA, RG 59, *China Despatches* 106, No. 237, Conger to Hay, July 15, 1899; *ibid.*, 107, No. 278, November 25, 1899; NA, RG 59, *China Instructions* 6, telegram, Hay to Conger, July 14, 1899; *ibid.*, No. 191, July 15, 1899; *ibid.*, No. 224, January 19, 1900.

10. The *New York Times*, quoting presumably from Rockhill, noted official administration ambivalence on partitioning: that while it might be undesirable if it led to trade discrimination, on the other hand it might "break down Chinese conservatism and open up vast markets." See *New York Times*, November 5, 1899, 12; *ibid.*, November 9, 1899, 4.

11. *New York Times*, March 4, 1899, 7. On January 12, 1899, the American Consul wrote the State Department his opinion "that the United States should be a preferred nation in Amoy owing to the fact that this is the chief port in China for the Philippines. . . . This is one port we must preserve if we make of our new possessions in the Orient what is now anticipated." And on May 9, 1899, he approached Chinese officials about the possibility of an American concession on the Island of Kulangsu. See NA, RG 59, *Consular Despatches* 13, No. 38, Johnson to Hill, January 12, 1899; *ibid.*, No. 48, May 9, 1899.

12. In late summer the Department informed the American Consul in Amoy that it could not "give unqualified endorsement of your course"; that he

had "misunderstood the Department's" instructions. NA, RG 59, *Consular Instructions* 166, No. 51, Cridler to Johnson, September 5, 1899.

13. Hay rejected this alternative, "for the present," in early 1899 when he wrote Paul Dana that "our best policy is one of vigilant protection of our commercial interests without formal alliances with other Powers interested." Thayer, *Life and Letters of John Hay*, II, 241.

14. Hay to Rockhill, August 7, 1899, Rockhill MSS; A. R. Colquhoun to Hay, January 12, 1899, Hay MSS; A. R. Colquhoun, *China in Transformation*, New York, 1899, ix-x, 155–157, 235, 366–367.

15. Lord Charles Beresford, "China and the Powers," *North American Review*, CLXVIII (May 1899), 530; Lord Charles Beresford, *The Break-Up of China*, New York, 1899, 7, 63, 416, 426, 431–432; *Chicago Inter-Ocean*, February 20, 1899, 6; *Journal of the American Asiatic Association*, I (March 11, 1899), 29; Beresford, *The Break-Up of China*, 429, 432.

16. *Nation*, LXVIII (March 30, 1899), 236; *Atlantic Monthly*, LXXXIV (August 1899), 279–280; John R. Proctor, "Saxon or Slav?—The Eastern Question," *Harpers Weekly*, XLIII (November 25, 1899), 1179; John Barrett, "The Paramount Power of the Pacific," *North American Review*, LXXXIX (July 1899), 168–169; *Bankers' Magazine*, LXI (September 1900), 341; *Journal of Commerce and Commercial Bulletin*, March 21, 1899, 4; Rockhill to Hay, October 19, 1899, Hay MSS; *ibid.*, Everett Frazer to Hay, November 24, 1899; Campbell, *Special Business Interests*, 50; *New York Times*, November 3, 1899, 9; "Foreign Policy of the United States: Political and Commercial," Supplement, *Annals of the American Academy of Political and Social Science*, Philadelphia, 1899, 90–91, 163–164; Griswold, *Far Eastern Policy*, 70.

17. *New York Times*, March 6, 1899, 1; *ibid.*, March 7, 1899, 2; clipping from *The Times* (London), May 28, 1899, Albert J. Beveridge MSS; NA, RG 59, *China Despatches* 107, No. 290, Conger to Hay, December 9, 1899. See also the remarks and citation in note 12, *supra*. See especially NA, RG 59, *Germany Despatches* 68, No. 714, Andrew White to Hay, January 25, 1899; *ibid.*, No. 706, January 21, 1899.

18. NA, RG 59, *Russia Despatches* 54, No. 81, Charlemagne Tower to Hay, August 23, 1899; *New Orleans Times-Picayune*, August 18, 1899, 4; *New York Times*, August 22, 1899, 6.

19. Hay to Rockhill, August 24, 1899, Hay MSS. The meat of the Rockhill-Hippisley arguments and efforts is reflected in the following correspondence: Hippisley to Rockhill, July 25, 1899, Rockhill MSS; Rockhill to Hay, August 3, 1899, Hay MSS; Hippisley to Rockhill, August 16, 1899, Rockhill MSS; Rockhill to Adee, August 19, 1899, Hay MSS. See also Paul A. Varg, *Open Door Diplomat: W. W. Rockhill*, Urbana, Ill., 1952, 26–36.

20. Griswold, *Far Eastern Policy*, 73.

21. Hay to Rockhill, August 24, 1899, Hay MSS; Rockhill to Hippisley, August 29, 1899, Rockhill MSS; Rockhill to Hay, August 28, 1899, Hay MSS.

22. NA, RG 59, *England Instructions* 33, No. 205, Hay to Joseph Choate,

September 6, 1899; Rockhill Memorandum, December 19, 1899, Hay MSS; W. W. Rockhill, "The United States and the Future of China," *Forum*, XXIX (May 1900), 330; Hay to Wu Ting-fu, November 11, 1899, Hay MSS; *ibid.*, Hay to Choate, November 13, 1899; NA, RG 59, *China Instructions* 6, No. 217, Hay to Conger, November 20, 1899; Rockhill to Hay, August 28, 1899, Hay MSS. This view is advanced by several historians, including Tyler Dennett (see citation in Bau, *The Open Door Doctrine*, xix); Parker T. Moon, *Imperialism and World Politics*, New York, 1926, 341; and Earl H. Pritchard, "The Origins of the Most-Favored-Nation and the Open Door Policies," *Far Eastern Quarterly*, I (February 1942), 171.

23. Rockhill to Hay, August 28, 1899, Hay MSS; Choate to Hay, November 1, 1899, Hay MSS; NA, RG 59, *Russia Despatches* 55, No. 104, Tower to Hay, September 20, 1899.

24. Choate to Hay, November 1, 1899, Hay MSS; Hay to Choate, November 13, 1899, Letterbook, Hay MSS; NA, RG 59, *France Despatches* 118, No. 559, Horace Porter to Hay, November 10, 1899; Porter to McKinley, November 14, 1899, McKinley MSS; NA, RG 59, *Japan Instructions* 4, No. 263, Hay to Alfred S. Buck, November 13, 1899.

25. Rockhill Memorandum, undated, Rockhill MSS; Hay to Choate, November 13, 1899, Letterbook, Hay MSS; NA, RG 59, *England Despatches* 198, No. 216, Choate to Hay, December 1, 1899; *ibid.*, telegram, December 11, 1899; Hay to Choate, December 4, Letterbook, Hay MSS; NA, RG 59, *Germany Despatches* 71, telegram, John B. Jackson to Hay, December 4, 1899; NA, RG 59, *England Instructions* 198, telegram, Hay to Choate, December 8, 1899.

26. NA, RG 59, *France Despatches* 118, No. 589, Horace Porter to Hay, December 15, 1899; *ibid.*, No. 579, December 1, 1899; *ibid.*, telegram, December 14, 1899; *ibid.*, telegram, December 18, 1899; *ibid.*, No. 594, December 21, 1899.

27. Andrew Malozemoff, *Russian Far Eastern Policy, 1881–1904*, Berkeley, 1958, 116–117; NA, RG 59, *Russia Despatches* 55, No. 156, Tower to Hay, November 23, 1899; *ibid.*, No. 167, confidential, December 11, 1899; *ibid.*, No. 172, December 26, 1899.

28. Rockhill Memorandum, December 19, 1899, Hay MSS; Hay to Henry White, April 2, 1900, Letterbook, Hay MSS; NA, RG 59, *Russia Despatches* 55, No. 172, Tower to Hay, December 26, 1899; *ibid.*, No. 174, December 28, 1899.

29. *Loc. cit.*; *ibid.*, No. 176, January 2, 1900; Rockhill to Hippisley, January 16, 1900, Rockhill MSS; Tower to Hay, February 9, 1900, Hay MSS; *ibid.*, February 12, 1900. For example, see NA, RG 59, *France Instructions* 24, No. 746, Hay to Porter, March 20, 1900.

30. Even a cursory perusal of the Hay MSS and of major American newspapers quickly persuades one of the almost unqualified approval given the Open Door Notes by Americans of the day.

31. *New York Times*, January 6, 1900, 7; Griswold, *Far Eastern Policy*.

32. Dennett, *John Hay*, 317.

## Chapter VI: *The Dilemmas Unfold*

1. *Nation*, LXVII (1898), 124.
2. Lim Boon Keng, *The Chinese Crisis from Within*, London, 1906, 247. For the most comprehensive and knowledgeable studies of the Boxer Rebellion and related international problems, see Paul H. Clements, *The Boxer Rebellion*, New York, 1915; Meribeth E. Cameron, *The Reform Movement in China, 1898–1912*, New York, 1931; and George Nye Steiger, *China and the Occident*, New Haven, 1927. Among general works containing useful and relevant sections are Dennett, *John Hay*, 297–307; Dennis, *Adventures in American Diplomacy*, 215–258; and McCordock, *British Far Eastern Policy*, 313–333. Conger considered the signal for the outbreak to be the Empress Dowager's arrest of five pro-Western reform leaders. NA, RG 59, *China Despatches* 108, No. 342, Conger to Hay, March 13, 1900; *ibid*, No. 392, June 15, 1900; *American Trade*, III (1900), 156; Frederic Emory, "Our Growth as a World Power," *World's Work*, I (1900), 69; *American Trade*, III (1900), 114; *ibid.*, IV (1901), 148; *ibid.*, III (1900), 156, 172.
3. Admiral Kempff to Secretary of the Navy Long, June 22, 1900, McKinley MSS. For an analysis of Witte's policies see *Memoirs of Count Witte*, 107–118, and William A. Williams, *American-Russian Relations, 1781–1947*, New York, 1952, 36–38. Dallin, *The Rise of Russia in Asia*, 63–64; NA, RG 59, *Notes from Russian Legation* 13, Chargés d'Affaires de Wollant to David J. Hill, June 20, 1900; Montgomery to George Cortelyou to McKinley (enclosure, American Ambassador in France to Hay), July 23, 1900, McKinley MSS.
4. Hay-Moore conversation, memorandum, July 23, 1900, John Bassett Moore MSS; Hay to John W. Foster, June 23, 1900, Hay MSS; Hay-Moore conversation, memorandum, July 1, 1900, Moore MSS. Early rumors in June of differences between Hay and the cabinet led the administration to compose (but never release) a press statement that "All stories of differences in the Administration as to . . . the course to be pursued in this crisis are absolutely false. The President and all the cabinet have been of one mind in everything." Press release, "not used," June 3, 1900, Hay MSS.
5. NA, RG 59, *China Despatches* 108, cipher telegram, Hay to Conger, June 8, 1900; *ibid.*, June 11, 1900; Kempff to Long, June 25, 1900, McKinley MSS; *ibid.*, Assistant Secretary of the Navy Hackett to Kempff, June 18, 1900; Admiral Remey to Bureau of Navigation, June 18, 1900, McKinley MSS; Kempff to Long, June 20, 1900, McKinley MSS; *ibid.*, June 22, 1900.
6. Hay-Moore conversation, memorandum, July 1, 1900, Moore MSS; McKinley to Hay, July 3, 1900, McKinley MSS; Alfred S. Buck to Hay, July

1, 1900, McKinley MSS; Choate to Hay, June 27, 1900, Hay MSS; Dennett, *John Hay*, 302. The intimate bond between Chinese independence and the open door can be seen in the Department's vehement reaction to Andrew White's failure to mention the latter principle in his presentation of the July 3 circular to the German government. NA, RG 59, *Germany Instructions* 21, No. 1076, Hay to White, July 19, 1900.

7. Hay-Moore conversation, Memorandum, July 1, 1900, Moore MSS; Choate to Hay, July 17, 1900, strictly confidential, McKinley MSS; Hay-Moore conversation, Memorandum, July 1, 1900, Moore MSS; Dennett, *John Hay*, 303; Hay to Reid, July 14, 1900, Reid MSS; Dennett, *John Hay*, 304; *New York Tribune*, August 4, 1900, 8; Hay to Adee, September 14, 1900, Hay MSS; Hay to Henry Adams, July 8, 1900, Hay MSS.

8. Dennett, *John Hay*, 301; NA, RG 59, *England Instructions*, telegram, Hay to Choate, June 27, 1900; Choate to Hay, strictly confidential, July 17, 1900, McKinley MSS; NA, RG 59, *Notes from English Legation* 133, Lord Pauncefote to Hay July 25, 1900; Hay to Adams, July 8, 1900, Hay MSS.

9. *Loc. cit.* On administration division of opinion, see unused press release, June 3, 1900, Hay MSS; Remey to Long, telegram, June 6, 1900, McKinley MSS. Acting Secretary of the Navy Hackett to Kempff, June 18, 1900, McKinley MSS; *New York Times*, June 16, 1900, 2; *ibid.*, September 25, 1900, 7; *ibid.*, June 16, 1900, 2; Kempff to Long, June 19, 1900, McKinley MSS; *ibid.*, June 23, 1900; *ibid.*, June 24, 1900; *ibid.*, Remey to Long, June 25, 1900; *ibid.*, Arthur MacArthur to the Adjutant General, June 26, 1900; NA, RG 59, *China Despatches* 108, telegram, Conger to Hay, August 17, 1900. An additional five thousand troops were on their way to China via Nagasaki, Japan, when rescue of the legations led McKinley to reroute them to the Philippines. Adjutant General to General Chaffee, July 19, 1900, McKinley MSS. See Hay to McKinley, enclosure, July 8, 1900, McKinley MSS; Reid to Cushman K. Davis, June 28, 1900, Reid MSS.

10. Hay to Henry Adams, July 8, 1900, Hay MSS; Hay to McKinley, June 21, 1900, McKinley MSS; Hay to McKinley, June 27, 1900, McKinley MSS. For contrary advice see Senior Consul General at Shanghai to Secretary of the Navy, June 24, 1900, McKinley MSS; *ibid.*, Choate to Hay, telegram, June 23, 1900; NA, RG 59, *France Despatches* 118, No. 680, Porter to Hay, June 27, 1900. *New York Times*, July 3, 1900, 7; Hay to Consul General Goodnow, July 1, 1900, McKinley MSS; *ibid.*, Goodnow to Hay, July 3, 1900; *ibid.*, Nanking Viceroy to Goodnow, July 1, 1900; *ibid.*, Woochang Viceroy's Decree, July 1, 1900; *ibid.*, Goodnow to Hay, July 1, 1900; *ibid.*, July 16, 1900; *ibid.*, July 18, 1900; NA, RG 59, *France Despatches* 119, No. 690, Porter to Hay, July 12, 1900; Hay to Adams, July 8, 1900, Hay MSS; Goodnow to Hay, July 17, 1900, McKinley MSS.

11. NA, RG 59, *Notes from English Legation* 133, Pauncefote to Hay, July 21, 1900; Montgomery to Cortelyou to McKinley (enclosure, American Ambassador in Germany to Hay), July 26, 1900; Long to Remey, Au-

gust 17, 1900, McKinley MSS. For Russian and French support see H. D. Pierce to Hay, August 28, 1900, McKinley MSS; NA, RG 59, *France Despatches* 119, telegram, Porter to Hay, August 30, 1900. J. J. F. Bandinel to Goodnow, July 16, 1900, McKinley MSS; *ibid.*, July 27, 1900; Bandinel to Russian Consul in Newchwang, August 5, 1900, McKinley MSS; Vice Admiral E. Alexlieff to Bandinel, August 6, 1900, McKinley MSS; *ibid.*, Bandinel to Hay, August 29, 1900; NA, RG 59, *Russia Despatches* 108, telegram, Adee to Buck, August 29, 1900; NA, RG 59, *France Despatches* 119, telegram, Adee to Porter, August 30, 1900; Hay to Choate, September 8, 1900, Hay MSS; Hay to McKinley, August 20, 1900, McKinley MSS; Hay to Reid, August 31, 1900, Reid MSS.

12. NA, RG 59, *Notes from English Legation*, 133, Pauncefote to Hay, July 21, 1900; NA, RG 59, *Notes from German Legation* 29, memorandum of Adee conversation with German Chargés d'Affaires; John B. Jackson to Hay, August 27, 1900, McKinley MSS; *ibid.*, Long to Remey, August 17, 1900; Goodnow to Hay, September 3, 1900, McKinley MSS; *ibid.*, September 7, 1900; NA, RG 59, *Notes from French Legation* 43, Adee memorandum of conversation with French Ambassador, August 19, 1900.

13. Adee memorandum of conversation with Secretary of Japanese Legation, August 18, 1900, McKinley MSS; Rockhill to Hay, August 26, 1900, Hay MSS; Acting Secretary of the Navy Hackett to Commanding Officer, USS *Castine*, August 27, 1900, McKinley MSS; Adee to McKinley, August 28, 1900, McKinley MSS; *ibid.*, A. B. Johnson to David J. Hill, August 29, 1900; Rockhill to Hay, August 26, 1900, Hay MSS; Hackett to McKinley, September 5, 1900, McKinley MSS; *ibid.*, Secretary of Japanese Legation to Adee, August 30, 1900; *ibid.*, Hackett to McKinley, September 7, 1900.

14. H. D. Pierce to Adee, August 31, 1900, McKinley MSS; Adee to Hay, September 14, 1900, Hay MSS; Hay-Moore conversation, memorandum, July 1, 1900, Moore MSS; *ibid.*, July 23, 1900.

15. *New York Times*, August 31, 1900, 1; NA, RG 59, *Russia Despatches*, telegram, Adee to Buck, August 29, 1900; John T. Morgan to McKinley, September 5, 1900, McKinley MSS; Cushman K. Davis to Reid, August 26, 1900, Reid MSS; Reid to James H. Wilson, September 11, 1900, Reid MSS; Alfred T. Mahan to McKinley, September 2, 1900, McKinley MSS; *New York Times*, September 3, 1900, 2; *ibid.*, September 9, 1900, 20.

16. John B. Jackson to Hay, September 4, 1900, McKinley MSS; NA, RG 59, *England Despatches* 200, telegram, H. White to Hay, September 11, 1900; NA, RG 59, *France Despatches* 119, telegram, Porter to Hay, September 5, 1900; Elihu Root to McKinley, September 11, 1900, McKinley MSS; McKinley to Hay, September 14, 1900, Hay MSS; Root to McKinley, September 11, 1900, McKinley MSS.

17. Hay to Choate, September 8, 1900, Hay MSS; Root to Hay, September 2, 1900, Hay MSS. For all the strains involved, Hay made it clear to McKinley that he supported "whatever policy you adopt." Hay to McKinley, September 19, 1900, McKinley MSS. Adee to McKinley, September 17, 1900, McKinley MSS.

18. *Loc. cit.* Similar viewpoints came from the American Consul, J. J. F. Bandinel, Newchwang, who wrote Hay that "Russia will bluster, but if steadily opposed will retire. Her strength has been greatly over-estimated, and she is unprepared for war." Bandinel to Hay, August 29, 1900, McKinley MSS. Hay to Reid, September 1, 1900, Reid MSS.

19. Adee to Hay, September 14, 1900, Hay MSS; Rockhill to Hay, September 23, 1900, McKinley MSS; Adee to Hay, September 16, 1900, Hay MSS; Iddings to Hay, September 13, 1900, McKinley MSS; Hay to Adee, September 26, 1900, Hay MSS; Hay to McKinley, September 27, 1900, McKinley MSS; Hay to Choate, September 8, 1900, Hay MSS.

## Chapter VII: *The Future in Microcosm*

1. Rockhill to Hippisley, July 6, 1901, Rockhill MSS.
2. For a more detailed account of Boxer Protocol diplomacy, see Thomas J. McCormick, " 'A Fair Field and No Favor': Amercan China Policy During the McKinley Administrations, 1897–1901," unpublished doctoral dissertation, University of Wisconsin, 1960, 312–379. Any similar account here, especially in chronological fashion, would be both anticlimactic and confusing. For that reason I have constructed this section as an epilogue which differs from earlier chapters in being more eclectic in its selection of material and more topical in its organization.
3. As V. B. Holmes of the Sheffield Milling Company of Minneapolis put it in a letter to Hay: *"Keep the Chinese with us. . . . If we can obtain and maintain our friendship with those people, we will be invincible . . ."* Holmes to Hay, November 3, 1900, Hay MSS.
4. The harsh German approach was also reflected in her repetitive use of punitive expeditions into provincial cities and the countryside during the fall and winter of 1900–1901. These often brutal forays were generally denounced by the Americans as "certainly not defensive proposition[s]" that "greatly disturb the whole country" and "cause delay of negotiations." Indeed, the American commander, Major General Adna R. Chaffee—under direct State Department orders—refused "to take part in any movement which . . . has tendency to promote rather than allay hostilities and unquiet in surrounding country." And at one point Chaffee so caustically and undiplomatically denounced German Field Marshal Waldersee for "spoilation" that his government had to give him a friendly reprimand. See McCormick, " 'Fair Field and No Favor,' " 321–323, 330–331.
5. NA, RG 59, *Notes from German Legation* 29, Sternburg to Hay, September 18, 1900; John B. Jackson to Hay, September 21, 1900, McKinley MSS; Hay to Adee, September 21, 1900 McKinley MSS; NA, RG 59, *China Despatches* 109, telegram, David J. Hill to Conger, Sep-

tember 22, 1900; Hay to McKinley, October 2, 1900, McKinley MSS; Hay to McKinley, October 3, 1900, McKinley MSS; Hay to Henry White, October 16, 1900, Hay MSS.

6. NA, RG 59, *China Despatches* 109, telegram, Conger to Hay, October 26, 1900; *ibid.*, Hay to Conger, October 29, 1900; *ibid.*, November 9, 1900; *ibid.*, Conger to Hay, November 26, 1900; Hay to Andrew White, November 28, 1900, Hay MSS; NA, RG 59, *China Despatches* 109, telegram, Conger to Hay, December 4, 1900; *ibid.*, No. 466, December 5, 1900; Hay to McKinley, November 29, 1900, McKinley MSS.

7. NA, RG 59, *China Despatches* 111, No. 532, Conger to Hay, February 13, 1901; *ibid.*, 113, No. 656, Squiers to Hay, June 19, 1901. By 1901 some members of the American government were having extreme doubts about the efficacy of American missionary activity, feeling that it had become a social irritant in China which did more to disrupt the stable climate necessary for trade than to break new paths for it. Certainly the general missionary position of punishments and indemnities was quite at odds with specific American policies.

8. Hay to Conger, December 29, 1900, McKinley MSS.

9. NA, RG 59, *China Despatches* 112, telegram, Rockhill to Hay, April 8, 1901; *ibid.*, No. 58; Rockhill to Hay, April 12, 1901, Hay MSS; NA, RG 59, *China Despatches* 112, telegram, Rockhill to Hay, April 26, 1901; *ibid.*, No. 749, May 1, 1901; *ibid.*, telegram, May 7, 1901; *ibid.*, telegram, May 12, 1901; *ibid.*, telegram, Hay to Rockhill, May 10, 1901; *ibid.*, No. 92, Rockhill to Hay, May 22, 1901; Rockhill to Hay, May 23, 1901, McKinley MSS.

10. NA, RG 59, *China Despatches* 112, No. 79, Rockhill to Hay, May 1, 1901; *ibid.*, 109, No. 455, Conger to Hay, November 20, 1900; *ibid.*, 112, No. 79, Rockhill to Hay, May 1, 1901; *ibid.*, No. 87, May 16, 1901; Hay to Rockhill, May 9, 1901, McKinley MSS; NA, RG 59, *China Despatches* 112, No. 93, Rockhill to Hay, May 23, 1901; Squiers to James H. Wilson, May 30, 1901, Wilson MSS. The issue of means of payment was further complicated by Japan's position that she could not purchase Chinese 4 per cent bonds except through 5 per cent loans on the international money market, and that therefore she should be compensated by the issuance of additional bonds equal to "the difference between the amount of interest [she] would have to pay for a loan, and the rate of interest insured by the bonds." NA, RG 59, *China Despatches*, 112, No. 93, Rockhill to Hay, May 23, 1901. Eventually, England solved the problem by unilaterally guaranteeing the bonds. See McCormick, " 'Fair Field and No Favor,' " 355.

11. Hay to Conger, December 29, 1900, McKinley MSS; NA, RG 59, *China Despatches* 110, personal, Rockhill to Hay, January 19, 1901; Brooks Adams, "Russia's Interest in China," *Atlantic Monthly*, LXXXVI (August 1900), 316–317.

12. Hay to Jules Cambon, April 20, 1901, Hay MSS; John A. Kasson to Hay, March 2, 1901, Hay MSS; Hay to Cambon, April 20, 1901, Hay MSS; Hay to McKinley, August 14, 1901, McKinley MSS; Hay to Cambon, April 20, 1901, Hay MSS. The American conception of political modernization

was more ambiguous. On the one hand, many Americans advised their government that the old Manchu dynasty had to go; that neither the export trade nor Western civilization could "live in China without a radical and sweeping reformation of its government." On the other hand, there was fear that revolution in China might prove an open-ended, uncontrollable phenomenon that could end in closing the market rather than developing it. Caught in such ambivalence, the McKinley administration tended to play it very cautiously—supporting the old imperial regime but seeking to shift "imperial authority" away from the Empress Dowager to "the Emperor, Kwang Hsu"—or, as the *Chicago Inter-Ocean* put it, "the reorganization of the government under the Emperor, supported by the progressives." Others, like missionary Frederick Ohlinger, were less sanguine about this early version of the "third force" idea and dismissed it as "propping up the rotten concern!" See *American Trade*, III (1900), 159; F. R. Forbes to Hay, August 21, 1900, Hay MSS; Goodnow to Hay, July 17, 1900, Hay MSS; Adee to McKinley, September 21, 1900, McKinley MSS; *Chicago Inter-Ocean*, June 19, 1900, 6; F. Ohlinger to Bishop McCabe, enclosure, September 5, 1900, McKinley MSS.

13. Rockhill to Hay, June 11, 1901, McKinley MSS; Hay to Choate, August 5, 1901, Hay MSS; NA, RG 59, *China Despatches* 114, No. 725, Conger to Hay, September 4, 1901; Rockhill to Hay, August 8, 1901, McKinley MSS; Choate to Hay, August 15, 1901, McKinley MSS; Hosea B. Morse, *The International Relations of the Chinese Empire*, III, New York, 1918, 370–372; William M. Malloy, *Treaties, Conventions, International Acts, Protocols, and Agreements Between the United States of America and Other Powers, 1776–1909*, I, Washington, D.C., 1910, 261–290. As earlier, American concern to protect and foster the export trade to China was far more vigorous and clear-cut than its concern for capital investment in China. Indeed, American abandonment of the Hankow-Canton railroad concession appears to have convinced Acting Minister Squiers "that none of our people seem to appreciate the great opportunities for investment at this time" and to confirm Rockhill in his earlier conviction that "the promoters have no earthly intention of attempting to develop [their concessions], and . . . they simply use [them] as an asset on the stock markets of Europe and America for purposes of speculation." On the other hand, finance capitalist Jacob Schiff felt that the Boxer indemnity offered a magnificent chance for American financial inroads, since "to a considerable extent" it would have "to be placed upon the American money markets, the European financial centres not being in a condition to take a large part of such a loan." And even Hay did advise Rockhill that if an international indemnity "loan is agreed upon, try to have American bankers invited to make tenders." Generally, however, the open door remained as it began—a commercial one only. See NA, RG 59, *China Despatches* 113, No. 646, Squiers to Hay, June 6, 1901; *ibid.*, 110, personal, Rockhill to Hay, January 19, 1901; Jacob Schiff to James H. Wilson, February 8, 1901, Hay MSS; NA, RG 59, *China Despatches* 112, No. 87, enclosure, Hay to Rockhill, May 16, 1901.

14. NA, RG 59, *Notes from English Legation* 134, Pauncefote to Hay, Oc-

tober 23, 1900; Hay to Pauncefote, October 26, 1900, McKinley MSS; Dennett, *John Hay*, 320; Adee to McKinley, October 20, 1900, McKinley MSS; Choate to Hay, October 31, 1900, McKinley MSS; Hay to Pauncefote, October 26, 1900, McKinley MSS; John B. Jackson to Hay, October 25, 1900, McKinley MSS.

15. Hay to McKinley, October 26, 1900, McKinley MSS; Choate to Hay, October 31, 1900, McKinley MSS; Dennett, *John Hay*, 320; Griswold, *Far Eastern Policy*, 81–82.

16. NA, RG 59, *China Despatches* 110, No. 499, Conger to Hay, January 12, 1901; Conger to Hay, January 9, 1901, McKinley MSS; NA, RG 59, *China Despatches* 111, No. 520, Conger to Hay, February 6, 1901; *ibid.*, No. 34, Rockhill to Hay, March 4, 1901; *ibid.*, No. 520, Conger to Hay, February 6, 1901.

17. Rockhill to Hay, January 29, 1901, Hay MSS; NA, RG 59, *China Despatches* 111, No. 46, March 22, 1901, Rockhill to Hay; *ibid.*, No. 584, Squiers to Hay, March 21, 1901; NA; RG 59, *England Despatches* 201, telegram, Hay to Choate, March 1, 1901; NA, RG 59, *Notes from Russian Legation* 13, Cassini to Hay, April 5, 1901; NA, RG 59, *Russia Despatches* 58, No. 412, Tower to Hay, April 8, 1901; NA, RG 59, *China Despatches* 112, No. 606, Rockhill to Hay, April 11, 1901; *ibid.*, 111, No. 51, March 28, 1901; Conger to Hay, September 2, 1901, McKinley MSS; NA, RG 59, *China Despatches* 114, No. 729, Conger to Hay, September 7, 1901; Hay to Cassini, April 20, 1901, Hay MSS; NA, RG 59, *China Despatches* 114, No. 729, Conger to Hay, September 7, 1901; *ibid.*, No. 671, Squiers to Hay, June 27, 1901; *ibid.*, No. 687, Conger to Hay, August 3, 1901; Hay to Adee, August 28, 1901, Hay MSS.

18. The American refusal to join England in attempting to block the proposed Sino-Russian treaty on Manchuria was indicative of continued unwillingness on the part of the United States to abandon the concert-of-powers approach. As Rockhill put it: "It is better to keep [Russia] in the concert even if she impedes its action considerably, than to let her regain her absolute liberty of action." See Rockhill to Hay, June 16, 1901, Hay MSS. Also Choate to Hay, March 9, 1901, Hay MSS; *ibid.*, March 13, 1901.

19. General Chaffee recommended this line of action in December 1900, suggesting that the United States take "the Province of Chihli" as a "special sphere of influence." NA, RG 59, *China Despatches* 109, No. 468, Conger to Hay, December 7, 1900.

20. The original Navy suggestion that the United States seize "a port in Northern China" as "a base of supply for our vessels" was coolly received by the State Department. The revised proposal for a port in southern China, offering less chance of friction with Russia and Germany, was regarded with less alarm. But in practical terms the move never left the ground. Japan, with a non-alienation pledge for Fukien province (where Samsa Islet was located), refused "to accede to the proposal," and rather than damage Japanese-American relations, the McKinley administration quickly dropped the matter altogether without ever

posing it to China. See *ibid.*, telegram, Hay to Conger, November 16, 1901. Also Kempff to Long, June 22, 1900, McKinley mss; Adee to Rockhill, December 6, 1901, Rockhill mss; NA, RG 59, *China Despatches* 109, Hay to Conger, telegram, November 19, 1900; *ibid.*, No. 455, Conger to Hay, November 20, 1900; *ibid.*, telegram, November 23, 1900; *ibid.*, December 7, 1900; Takahira to Hay, December 6, 1900, Hay mss; Alfred S. Buck to Hay, December 11, 1900, McKinley mss.

21. NA, RG 59, *China Despatches* 114, No. 729, Conger to Hay, September 7, 1901. Conger's analysis was supported by Ambassador Tower's conversation with Count Witte in St. Petersburg, in which the latter commented at length on Russia's pressing economic needs and inclination to fulfill them through trade-minded America rather than militarist-minded Europe. Said Witte: "Our markets in Europe are open to you, and the much greater markets of the future in Siberia and the Oriental parts of our Empire shall be open to you as well." Tower to Hay, July 3, 1901, McKinley mss.

22. Conger also developed this as a possibility in his brilliant analytical dispatch to Hay on September 7, 1901. See NA, RG 59, *China Despatches* 114, No. 729, Conger to Hay, September 7, 1901.

23. The concept of a natural harmony of interests generally is associated with the foreign policy of the Progressive period, especially that of Woodrow Wilson, but the antecedents for it are clearly present in the 1890's.

24. Quoted from a selection of Edward H. Zabriskie, *American-Russian Rivalry in the Far East: A Study in Diplomacy and Power Politics, 1895–1914*, Philadelphia, 1946, as reproduced in William A. Williams, ed., *The Shaping of American Diplomacy*, Chicago, 1956, 473.

25. Frederick Jackson Turner, *The Frontier in American History*, New York, 1920, 309.

# BIBLIOGRAPHICAL NOTE

## Primary Material

The three principal sources for this book have been the General Records of the Department of State (Record Group 59, on deposit at the National Archives of the United States), the personal papers and manuscripts of relevant figures, and the journals, proceedings, and petitions of various interest groups. Less important but still most useful were the semipopular periodicals of the day, as well as the major urban newspapers.

Diplomatic historians have frequently overused governmental archives to the relative exclusion of other significant kinds of materials. But abused or not, such archival evidence remains the single most essential source for the student of foreign relations. For the 1890's, diplomatic material is categorized and organized first by country, then by type (diplomatic instructions and dispatches; notes to and from foreign legations; consular instructions and dispatches; miscellaneous letters) and by chronology. Of formal diplomatic information culled for this work, the most useful was that dealing directly with China, but of only slightly less utility was that involving Great Britain, Russia, Germany, France, and Japan. Of the consular evidence, the most helpful concerned the Philippine capital of Manila and the Chinese port cities of Amoy, Chefoo, Newchwang, Shanghai, and Tientsin. Particularly prominent in the Miscellaneous Letter files were letters and petitions from leading businessmen and trade association groups. Beyond the usual diplomatic material, the archival records of the Department of Navy are of value to the study of any topic touching upon China. In the period covered by this book, however, most of the relevant naval data may also be found in the William

McKinley Papers at the Library of Congress or in William R. Braisted's informative study, *The United States Navy in the Pacific, 1897–1909* (1958).

Among manuscript collections, the most valuable—both in terms of volume and character of information—were those of upper-echelon decision-makers: Grover Cleveland, Walter Q. Gresham, John M. Hay, William McKinley, Richard Olney, and Elihu Root. Only slightly less significant were the papers and letters of John Bassett Moore, Whitelaw Reid, William Woodville Rockhill (Harvard University, Cambridge, Massachusetts), and James Harrison Wilson. Others that were carefully investigated and were of occasional help include: Nelson Aldrich, Wharton Barker, Thomas F. Bayard, William B. Chandler, Worthington C. Ford, John W. Foster, Lyman G. Gage, Daniel S. Lamont, John T. Morgan, Theodore Roosevelt, and John Sherman. A second Hay collection at Brown University was consulted but yielded little that was relevant for this book. Unless otherwise noted, all these manuscript collections are located in the Library of Congress.

On the whole, one can find adequate material on the business community, though it would be more complete and sophisticated if corporate records and private businessmen's papers were more readily available. Perhaps the most obvious and important sources were the commercial newspapers, such as the *Wall Street Journal* and the New York *Journal of Commerce and Commercial Review*, and business periodicals including such important representatives as *American Trade, Bankers' Magazine and Statistical Review, Bradstreet's: A Journal of Trade, Finance and Public Economy, Commercial and Financial Review, Engineering Magazine, Iron Age, Journal of the American Asiatic Association, Petroleum Gazette, Railroad World*, and the *Wool and Cotton Reporter*. In addition, the convention proceedings and presidential reports of large trade groups are revealing, often in very special ways (for example, membership totals and their makeup, organization growth, internal debate, key vote results). Typical of these might be the National Association of Manufacturers, *Proceedings of the Annual Convention, 1897–1901; Annual Report of the President, 1897–1901; Circular of Information, 1897–1901*; Philadelphia Commercial Museum, *Report of the Annual Meeting of the International Advisory Board*; and Spanish American Commercial Union, *Proceedings*. Finally, a number of individual businessmen and trade groups produced a spate of sometimes fascinating pamphlets, such as Charles R. Flint, *Industrial Combinations* (1900), Edward J. McDermott, *Commercial and Political Problems from a Southern Viewpoint* (1892), Philadelphia Commercial Museum, *Pamphlets* (1896–1901) and *The World's Commerce and the United States Share of It* (1899), and Erastus Wiman, *An Economic Revolution* (1893).

Beyond these, a number of businessmen wrote articles for a larger reading public in semipopular periodicals such as *Atlantic Monthly, Century Magazine, Fortnightly Review, Forum, Harpers New Monthly Magazine, North American Review,* and the *Review of Reviews.* But so did prominent politicians, military men, intellectuals, and academicians. And in a sense, the pages of such magazines were the grounds on which groups carried on a mutual-education dialogue on the needs and problems of expansion. There are more than a hundred such articles relevant to the theme and subject of this book, and the interested reader, in using the standard periodical guides, would do well to key his initial attention upon the pieces produced by such political and diplomatic figures as O. P. Austin, John Barrett, Cushman K. Davis, Charles Denby, Jr., Frederic Emory, Worthington C. Ford, Hilary A. Herbert, Thomas R. Jernigan, Henry Cabot Lodge, Richard Olney, W. W. Rockhill, Carl Schurz, Carroll D. Wright, and John Russell Young; business leaders like Clarence Cary, Charles A. Conant, John H. Converse, Charles H. Cramp, U. D. Eddy, Charles B. Flint, John Ford, John R. Proctor, Theodore C. Search, and James H. Wilson; intellectuals like Brooks Adams, Urieh H. Crocker, A. D. Noyes, Simon N. Patten, and David A. Wells; military spokesmen such as S. B. Luce and Alfred T. Mahan; and foreign commentators like Lord Charles Beresford, Sir Robert Hart, Paul Leroy-Beaulieu, and Michael G. Mulhall.

Finally, of more limited utility (especially commensurate to the amount of labor involved) were prominent big city daily newspapers. Most of those used, whatever their political orientation, were generally conservative and business-allied, though they often differed on such important matters as money and the tariff. I did not use them to re-create something called "public opinion": the sampling itself was too small and biased, but beyond that, the idea of public opinion (as now employed by diplomatic historians) is too vague and amorphous and its impact upon foreign policy too problematical. But the newspapers were sometimes helpful in providing collaboration for factual data taken initially from other sources; in producing specific bits of information that on rare occasions did not make their way into other records; or in giving me some impressionistic sense of how often and in what form the expansionist analysis and recommendations of the decision-makers and influencers were presented to a larger, more diffused public. I sampled a great many newspapers, but those gone through more or less systematically included the *Atlanta Constitution, Chicago Inter-Ocean, Chicago Tribune, New Orleans Times-Picayune, New York Tribune, New York Times, North China News, Philadelphia Press,* and *San Francisco Chronicle.*

## Secondary Material

Save for a few key exceptions, secondary sources have been only marginally useful for me. Most have already received mention in the notes of this book. Nevertheless, it might be helpful to interested readers to call their attention to the basic works of historical literature that are relevant or standard in the discussion of America's expansion and her Far Eastern policies. A more detailed bibliography can be found in Thomas J. McCormick, " 'A Fair Field and No Favor': American China Policy During the McKinley Administrations, 1897–1901," Ph.D. Dissertation (University of Wisconsin, 1960).

The two best general, systematic treatments of American expansionism are Richard W. Van Alstyne, *The Rising American Empire* (1960), and William A. Williams, *The Contours of American History* (1962). Van Alstyne is especially stimulating on the early eighteenth-century conceptualizations of American empire and on the continuity of nineteenth-century expansionism. Williams' provocative and much-discussed study is more theoretical and particularly effective in relating the forms and directions of expansionism to the evolving nature of the internal social order. More sketchy but highly suggestive is Charles Vevier, "American Continentalism: The History of an Idea, 1845–1910," *American Historical Review* (1960), which stresses the intimate relationships between continentalism and commercialism, between foreign and domestic policies, and between pre–Civil War and postwar expansion. Still useful is Albert K. Weinberg, *Manifest Destiny* (1935), in its pioneering, laborious excursion into the rhetoric and popular ideology of expansion. More rewarding, however, is Henry Nash Smith, *Virgin Land* (1959), a brilliant and literate study which offers not only impressionistic insight into the myth/reality dialectic of expansion but an appreciation of the relatedness of the trans-Pacific commercial thrust ("Passage to India") and the landed development of the Western Empire ("The Garden of the World"). More narrow in time focus but with a wealth of valuable material is David M. Pletcher, *The Awkward Years* (1962), which shows the early 1880's as a significant bridge between earlier expansionist urges and their eventual fulfillment in the 1890's. Taking exception to some of these accounts, especially on the nature and continuity of expansion, is Frederick Merk, *Manifest Destiny and Mission in American History* (1963), which focuses on the 1840's but contains an obiter dictum, not wholly persuasive, on the 1890's.

On the more special topic of late nineteenth-century expansion, the general tendency of most of the standard works has been to extract their subject from the context of social structure and social change. Thus, while abstract phenomena like "America's rise to world power" may be placed vaguely within the framework of economic growth and maturation, the more meaningful cause/effect issues of *expansionist dynamics* are divorced from both earlier American history and from the internal reality of the 1890's. Of these standard treatments, the most influential and in many ways still the best is Julius W. Pratt, *The Expansionists of 1898* (1936), though its full implications cannot be really understood without reading that author's subsequent work, *America's Colonial Experiment* (1950). The general body of Professor Pratt's work operates from a political definition of imperialism, emphasizes the role of selected, key intellectuals, and tends to treat the war as a sharp breaking point that accidentally turned American interest to opportunities abroad. Many of these facets are debatable; still, his main thesis that the powerful business community was largely anti-war and anti-colonial is substantially correct, though it must be refined and treated as a pragmatic tendency rather than an absolute fact of life. Moreover, in his handling of the post-1898 period, his work has reflected a persistent awareness of the industrial thirst for outlets and the lure of the China market—a fact for which this author is intellectually indebted.

Three more recent studies share some things in common with Professor Pratt's work, particularly in their tendencies to stress climactic time points (for example, 1898), to be concerned primarily with issues of formal empire and war, and to view American expansionism as the haphazard, accidental by-product of such variables as social pathology, domestic politics, and international externals beyond our control. In *America's Road to Empire* (1965), the most recent of these works, H. Wayne Morgan provides not only a useful survey of events leading to the Spanish-American War but manages to convey the rationality and purposefulness of McKinley's foreign policy and of decision-making in his administration. The author's forte is clearly domestic politics, but he shows a laudable awareness of the importance of strategic and economic reality, even though he tends to sublimate them in a rather unintegrated pluralism. Richard Hofstadter, "Manifest Destiny and the

Philippines," in Daniel Aaron, ed., *America in Crisis* (1952), has a stimulating hypothesis that American imperialism grew out of an internal "psychic crisis," a viewpoint that deserves further investigation, especially on the role of blocked social mobility in making some Americans more aggressive in their expansionist tactics than others. For the moment, however, the concept of "psychic crisis" remains a bit elusive and rests upon the untested a priori assumption that expansionism was an irrational social phenomenon and ought to be treated as such. Finally, Ernest R. May, *Imperial Democracy* (1961), stresses American expansion from the Venezuelan crisis to peace with Spain, with the bulk of his energies involved in a multi-archival analysis of the international diplomacy prior to the Spanish-American War. Like Hofstadter, Professor May believes that "in some irrational way," domestic "influences and anxieties" led to popular pressure for war and expansion. But his main thesis is that international diplomatic issues "had intruded almost of their own accord," and that in the end "the United States had greatness thrust upon it." Beyond its own intrinsic worth, May's book is important perhaps as a sample of what we may expect from its author's neo-Rankean conceptualization of international affairs, and poses the key question of whether this methodological route may broaden diplomatic history or whether it will channel it regressively into a more narrow, conventional mold.

At the same time, other recent studies (this book included) have tried to understand American expansion within the framework of social structure and change, though none quite so systematically or successfully as Bernard Semmel has done for the British in his *Imperialism and Social Reform* (1960). Walter LaFeber, *The New Empire* (1963), shares in common with Pratt a concern for the function of key intellectuals in the expansionist process, though his choices and the treatment given them are sometimes significantly different. But his main interpretation views expansionism as a response—often a conscious, rational one—to the ongoing problems of economic development and distribution created by the industrial revolution. Professor LaFeber is at his impressive best in his handling of Latin American affairs in the 1890's. In a general survey geared more largely to internal issues, Ray Ginger, *The Age of Excess* (1965), has also explored the ties between foreign policy and domestic social-economic reality. Working independently of LaFeber (and of myself), Professor Ginger has come to a keen appreciation of the role of surplus production in promoting consolidation at home and expansion abroad. Two other studies, though giving little treatment to foreign affairs as such, offer stimulating interpretations that readily lend themselves to an understanding of expansionist dynamics. Both Samuel P. Hays, *The Response to Industrialism* (1957), and Gabriel Kelko, *The Triumph of Conservatism* (1963), convincingly explain much of late nineteenth- and early twentieth-century American history in terms of a search for rationality, stability, and predictability in the social order and the political economy. The former work, spanning the years 1885 to 1914, still offers (a decade after its writing) the best single overview and introduction to those readers interested in the domestic reality of an expansionist era.

Still much neglected as a fruitful area for understanding American expansion is the role played by various functional and interest groups. The chief exception is Charles S. Campbell, Jr.'s admirable study of *Special Business Interests and the Open Door Policy* (1951). Still, despite the substantial contributions made by this classic work, there remains an enormous amount of depth research to be done even on the business community: first, to determine differences in attitudes and behavior that might be affected by corporate size, regional location, general functions (industrial-financial-mercantile), international ties, market patterns (either static or changing), and the like; second, to see whether these differences affect the business role in foreign affairs, or whether (as this book states) the crucial element is not function but class—i.e., a near-consensus, fairly sophisticated class-consciousness about the imperative need to rationalize a shaky social order.

Beyond this, many non-business groups beg for additional attention. Nancy L. O'Conor, "The Influence of Populist Legislators upon American Foreign Policy, 1892–1898," M.A. Thesis (University of Oregon, 1958), is useful, but the general subject of agrarians and expansionism deserves the more systematic, comprehensive, sophisticated treatment that William A. Williams' current research will hopefully provide. Likewise, John C. Appell, "The Relationship of American Labor to United States Imperialism, 1895–1905," Ph.D. Dissertation (University of Wisconsin, 1950), should be read, but the recent research of one of my graduate students leads me to believe that the complicated and ambivalent place of labor groups is far from fully understood. Similarly, the role of foreign service personnel has been largely ignored, though it is clear to me that people like Charles Denby, Charles Denby, Jr., John Barrett, and Thomas R. Jernigan exercised an impact upon Far Eastern affairs even beyond the capacity of their positions. The most successful exception is Fred H. Harrington, *God, Mammon and the Japanese* (1944), a brilliant portrayal of Horace Allen's role in Korean affairs specifically and Asian affairs generally; less successful but still worth reading is Paul A. Varg, *Open*

*Door Diplomat: The Life of W. W. Rockhill* (1952). But, in a more comprehensive way (treating collectively rather than individually), no one has done the sort of work that Nathan A. Pelcovits has done for the British in his *Old China Hands and the Foreign Office* (1948). Finally, while missionaries were of doubtful, direct importance in affecting expansionist policy, their changing conceptions of their own role and its ties to Western penetration, as well as the fluctuating attitudes of business groups and policy-makers toward the missionaries' functional (or dys-functional) place in expansion, offer the possibility of real, incidental insight into the expansionist dynamic itself. But again, the subject is far from fully explored, though one finds useful information and some insights in Harrington's study, in the more general work by Professor Varg in *Missionaries, Chinese and Diplomats: The American Protestant Missionary Movement in China, 1890–1952* (1958), and in Marilyn Young, "United States China Policy, 1895–1901," Ph.D. Dissertation (Harvard University, 1963).

On books dealing more specifically with China, the two standard, general studies of American policy overlap in the period of my concern. Tyler Dennett, *Americans in Eastern Asia* (1922), which should be supplemented by his *John Hay* (1934), spans the nineteenth century, while A. Whitney Griswold, *The Far Eastern Policy of the United States* (1938), covers the period from the Open Door Notes to the crisis of the 1930's. The former is still immensely useful, but the latter, as a standard work, is badly in need of replacement. Except for the present book, the only other specific survey of United States China policy in the 1890's is the previously noted dissertation by Dr. Young. In fact, up until now the best way to get at American policies in this period through secondary sources was via the indirect route: either through monographs dealing with *other* countries' policies (for example, Philip Joseph, *Foreign Diplomacy in China, 1894–1900* [1928]; Andrew Malozemoff, *Russian Far Eastern Policy, 1881–1907* [1958]; and R. Stanley McCordock, *British Far Eastern Policy, 1894–1900* [1931]) or through studies of American bilateral relations with other nations involved in China (for example, William Neumann, *America Encounters Japan* (1963); Edward H. Zabriskie, *American-Russian Relations in the Far East, 1895–1914* [1946]; William A. Williams, *American Russian Relations, 1781–1947* [1952]; and C. S. Campbell, Jr., *Anglo-American Understanding, 1898–1903* [1957]). The literature dealing with more limited events—partitioning, the Open Door Notes, the Boxer Rebellion, the Protocol of 1901—has all been cited in the notes. On related areas in the Pacific, the best work on Hawaii—despite the spate of recent, very informative monographs—is still Sylvester K. Stevens, *American Expansion in Hawaii, 1842–1898* (1945), particularly in its awareness of Hawaii's place in the overall scheme of things and in its sense of historical continuity and change. There is no similar, adequate handling of the Philippine subject. Earl S. Pomeroy, *Pacific Outpost: American Strategy in Guam and Micronesia* (1951), is occasionally useful on that topic.

# INDEX